ADVERTISING'S HIDDEN EFFECTS

ADVERTISING'S HIDDEN EFFECTS

Manufacturers' Advertising and Retail Pricing

MARK S. ALBION
Graduate School of Business Administration
Harvard University

Auburn House Publishing Company
Boston, Massachusetts

Copyright © 1983 by Mark S. Albion.

All rights reserved. No part of this publication may be reproduced, translated, or transmitted in any form or by any means without permission in writing from Auburn House Publishing Company.

Library of Congress Cataloging in Publication Data

Albion, Mark S., 1951–
   Advertising's hidden effects.

   Bibliography: p.
   Includes index.
   1. Advertising—Economic aspects. I. Title.
HF5821.A398   381'.1   82-6776
ISBN 0-86569-111-8   AACR2

Printed in the United States of America

To Aaron and Elaine Birnholz
who, over twenty years, have
taught me the meaning of friendship.

FOREWORD

Because of the prominence and cost of advertising, its social and economic effects are a subject that generates much heat—and only occasionally some light—in dialogues among business people, consumer groups, public policy makers, and educators. This book is one of a relatively recent, and still limited, number of publications that endeavor to enrich aspects of that dialogue. A more robust economic theory of retailing and a considerable quantity of real-life data are the tools the author uses to enhance the dialogue. In so doing, he clarifies many of the issues concerning the effects of advertising and provides evidence that has important implications for both marketing managers and policy makers.

Historically, opponents of advertising have argued that it raises prices. Conversely, proponents have asserted that it has benefits and that its tendency to raise prices is overstated. They claim that advertising intensifies competition among retailers on branded merchandise with the result that the lower gross profits retailers earn on branded merchandise helps restrain retail prices for such products.

Albion helps illuminate this controversy in three ways. He reviews and synthesizes the previous literature, emphasizing that competing views have often based their contentions on different definitions of the relevant market price. He clarifies why advertising may reduce retailer margins on branded merchandise. Finally, he uses the extensive evidence he has obtained to ascertain the circumstances under which, and the degree to which, prices are restrained by competition among retailers on advertised merchandise.

This book should be of great interest to several audiences. Critics of advertising will find within it the means to make their criticism more thoughtful, constructive, and precise. Supporters of advertising will find a thorough documentation of a competitive effect of advertising that may benefit consumers. Advertisers themselves, particularly if they are manufacturers of consumer packaged goods, will find that the book deepens their understanding of how, in addition to its direct effects, advertising stimulates sales through its impact on retailers. Retailers should find the book helpful in the formulation of viewpoints for establishing gross margins on advertised merchandise and making more astute merchandising decisions. Also, the book will aid public policy makers in reaching more balanced judgments of the contribution of advertising to the economic system. Finally, the book should be of interest to educators in that it tests theories derived from the industrial organization branch of economics with proprietary data. The result is a harbinger of the progress that can be expected when individuals with interdisciplinary skills become immersed in data from which it had previously been difficult to draw inferences.

This book provides insights into fairly complicated economic phenomena, from which it extracts what is most relevant for improved marketing management and public policy formulation. Its contents make it important reading for all who are interested in the economic consequences of advertising.

WALTER J. SALMON
Stanley Roth, Sr. Professor of Retailing
Harvard Business School

FOREWORD

Advertising has long been a subject of intense fascination to both economists and business practitioners. So highly visible a part of everyday life, advertising has become a focal point in the debate between the Harvard and Chicago schools of economics. Among business practitioners advertising poses an equally important, if different, dilemma. Knowing full well its potential effectiveness, business practitioners nevertheless find it extremely difficult to set advertising spending levels, because the impact of advertising is so hard to measure precisely and to separate from the other elements of company strategy.

At the heart of much of this uncertainty and controversy about advertising is the fact that its effects are not yet fully understood. We have learned, however, that its effects are multifaceted. Advertising informs customers and reduces shopping costs at the same time as it limits the number of goods a customer considers, raises the prices he is willing to pay, and raises barriers to entry by forcing competitors to match incumbents' spending levels.

Research on advertising has tended to focus on one or two of these effects at a time. Moreover, until comparatively recently, research on advertising has been preoccupied with firms and consumers, failing to consider the critical role of the retail distribution channels in between. Research on retailing similarly has tended to overlook the interactive relationship between consumer goods manufacturers and retailers that so greatly influences the ultimate configuration of brands, prices, and margins observed, as well as advertising behavior. My own work on the manufacturer-retailer bargaining relationship in consumer goods was an effort to begin to integrate the role of the retailer into models of advertising and competition in consumer goods industries,[1] but much remains to be understood.

This book is an important addition to the new view of advertising

---

[1] M. E. Porter, *Interbrand Choice, Strategy and Bilateral Market Power* (Harvard University Press, 1976).

that integrates manufacturers and retailers and recognizes advertis-
ings' multiple effects. Albion has taken an intriguing look at the
impact of advertised brands on the retailer and at the way in which
advertising influences retail margins. This examination exposes the
optimizing behavior of the multiproduct retailer firm and uncovers
important product characteristics that interact with advertising to
determine prices and margins of consumer goods. The implications
of the model are investigated statistically in a unique data base of
51 supermarket product categories involving 488 brands.

This book not only exposes a critical effect of advertising that has
been little studied but also advances our understanding of the economics of retailing as well. It should contribute importantly to the
academic debate about advertising and also be of great interest to
business practitioners confronted with the need to determine advertising policy in individual industries and to formulate policy toward their retail channels.

In appealing to both academic and practitioner audiences, this
book illustrates the power of and need for synthesis between the
perspective and models of the economist and those of researchers
in business administration. Answers to most of the important questions about firm behavior require such a synthesis. This book, growing from the joint program in Business and Economics at Harvard
University, foreshadows what I hope will be an important new era
in research about the firm.

MICHAEL E. PORTER
Professor of Business Administration
Harvard Business School

PREFACE

Marketing professionals and industrial organization economists, especially those interested in relations among vertical stages of economic units, are the intended audience for this book. My goal in writing it was to advance research in business administration by recognizing the structural context within which individual firms make major decisions and to capture the richness and complexity of organizational decision making within this microeconomic framework. In this way perhaps the intersection of fruitful research in economics and administration will be enlarged.

This book has benefited from the assistance and advice of a number of people. John Lintner, former chairman of the joint program in Business and Economics at Harvard University, provided the rich intellectual environment for all of my research. Walter Salmon was involved in every phase of this study, and is responsible for making this research more rigorous and managerially relevant. Michael Porter was instrumental in the development of the theoretical model. David Hartmann assisted in the research design and statistical methodology. And Paul Farris, my colleague in research for the past four years, was invaluable in organizing the fundamental questions and necessary methodology for this study. In addition, he is co-author of Chapter 2 and the first half of Chapter 3, which are revised versions of chapters in our book, *The Advertising Controversy* (Boston, Mass.: Auburn House, 1981) and our article in *Journal of Marketing*, 44 (Summer 1980).

I am also indebted to others whose support made this book possible. Financial support was provided by the Association of National Advertisers, the American Association of Advertising Agencies' Educational Foundation, and the Division of Research at the Harvard Business School. The funding was in large part due to my association with the Marketing Science Institute. Alden G. Clayton, Managing Director, Stephen A. Greyser, former Executive Director, and Raymond E. Corey, Executive Director, made MSI a fertile environment for my research over the past four years. Jim Curley was indispensable in compiling the data base and dealing with computer problems. The majority of the data was available only because of the kindness of the management of a certain retail chain. Clark Fitzgerald facilitated the writing by providing office space for the task.

To the late William Wyatt Barber, Jr., former headmaster of St. Mark's School in Southborough, Massachusetts, I acknowledge a great debt for the educational opportunities he made possible. My heartfelt appreciation to my mother and her mother, my brother John, and Jeanette Hughson. They have been my support and encouragement throughout the years. Most of all, I am thankful to my wife Johanna. She makes me laugh when things look bleak, is joyful when things go well, and is always the light of my life.

MARK S. ALBION

CONTENTS

LIST OF FIGURES

LIST OF TABLES

Chapter 1

THE HIDDEN EFFECTS

The most important question any advertiser must deal with is, "How will advertising affect my profits?" Since the turn of the century, manufacturing marketing managers have commonly replied with a budgeting decision that considers only advertising's immediate potential for affecting sales. Although it is universally recognized that successful advertising will sell more of the firm's product to the trade by increasing consumer demand, the fact that in most businesses it is the retailer, not the manufacturer, who sells the manufacturer's product to consumers has been ignored in the traditional budgeting methods used by most manufacturing firms. Further, the more subtle effect of advertising expenditures on the marketing—in particular, the *pricing*—of the manufacturer's product by the *retailer* has been overlooked. The result: *Advertising's contribution to long-term profit goals has been underestimated.*

One of the most controversial, vigorously debated public policy issues in advertising is the consumer's central concern: "Does advertising make the things I buy more expensive?" Two schools of thought have dominated the research and writing in this area. The first maintains that advertising leads to higher prices; it is often called the "market power" school and is associated most frequently with Harvard University. The second contends that advertising leads to lower prices; this is commonly called the "information" or "market competition" school and is associated primarily with the University of Chicago. The mounds of evidence gathered by both sides total a volume comparable to the collection of legal briefs in the IBM "Methuselah" antitrust case. But in this war of ideas, ideology has replaced theory, dogma dominates dialogue, and the business community, government regulators, economists, marketing researchers, and consumer advocates have been engaged in constructing a new Tower of Babel. Businesspeople—with a shorter time horizon, perhaps, than academics or biblical scholars—have solved the dilemma out of court.

1

Those looking to raise entry barriers and create a profitable niche for their businesses have consulted with Harvard professors; those seeking legal counsel to explain how entry barriers do not exist and, therefore, prices have not been raised unfairly, summon wisdom from the University of Chicago.

Are we therefore left with no definitive resolution of the advertising-price question? Policymakers can be assured that the question is not easily answered, and conclusions are not easily generalized. However, we can say that the approach taken by most researchers and policymakers has been misdirected, based as it is on an incomplete view of a consumer product market.[1] By neglecting the role of distributors, particularly retailers, in the sale of the manufacturers' brands, policymakers have overlooked the ability of advertising to increase retail price competition (and productivity) on these advertised brands. Consequently *policymakers have overestimated the impact of manufacturers' advertising on retail prices and underestimated the benefits of advertising to the consumer*.

This contention does not, however, ignore the fact that advertising can and does lead to higher factory (wholesale) prices charged by manufacturers to distributors. Furthermore, the retail prices of advertised brands are commonly greater than their unadvertised counterparts. Advertised brands do command a price premium—a surcharge that is paid for by consumers. But a less obvious, though just as important, economic reality must not be cursorily dismissed: Distributors take lower margins on advertised brands than the unadvertised brand competitors. The difference between the manufacturers' selling prices of advertised and unadvertised brands *overstates*, therefore, the difference between their retail selling prices.

Table 1.1 provides a hypothetical example to illustrate this assertion. The numbers were selected for simplicity, but the relationships shown remain realistic. What the numbers demonstrate is that the differentials among the factory prices of the three types of brands is greater than the differentials among the retail prices of the three types. For example, the leading advertised brand is sold by the manufacturer at a 20 percent premium over the less advertised brands, but is then resold by the retailers to consumers at only a 10 percent surcharge. Likewise, even though the retailers buy the leading advertised brand at a 37 percent premium over the unadvertised brands, they charge consumers only 20 percent more for the leading advertised brand. This disparity between the factory price and retail price differentials—20 percent vs. 10 percent, 37 percent vs. 20 percent—occurs because of the difference in the gross margin taken by the retailers among the three types of brands. The advertiser, therefore, may command wholesale price premiums that

Table 1.1 Retail Gross Margins of Advertised and Unadvertised Brands

	Leading Advertised Brand	Less Advertised Brands	Unadvertised Brands and Private Labels
Average retail price	$1.00	$0.90	$0.80
Retail gross margin	5%	15%	25%
Factory price (wholesale)	$0.95	$0.765	$0.60

SOURCE: Albion and Farris, 1981, p. 169.

are even greater than the retail price premiums—a point to be developed and discussed in the final chapter.

The retail gross margin of a "product"—the common generic term for the economic unit of analysis, which could be an item, brand, and/or product category—is the difference between the retailer's selling price and buying price for the product as a percentage of the selling price. Thus, for the leading advertised brand, the gross margin is ($1.00 − $0.95)/$1.00 = 5 percent. This represents the true economic price of retailing, that is, the cost to consumers for the services provided by retailers. If we could buy directly from the manufacturer (or wholesaler), we should be able to save 5 percent, or 5¢ per purchase of the leading advertised brand. Warehouse stores and factory and wholesale outlets allege to do just that—that is, to eliminate the cost to consumers of retail outlets. Otherwise, the fact remains: When buying most products, we give the manufacturer a profit margin to produce and the distributor a profit margin to bring that product from the manufacturer's plant to us, the consumers.

The primary concern in this book is what distributors, essentially retailers, charge us for their services—the retail gross margin—and the effect of manufacturers' advertising on this cost to consumers. Commonly, we must also pay manufacturers indirectly (in the price of their products) to cover the costs of advertising, and quite often we are willing to pay this premium for a variety of reasons. However, the main contention of this book is that a subtle, hidden effect of advertising often goes unnoticed: *Manufacturers' advertising saves consumers money by lowering the gross margin charged by retailers on the advertised brand.* This is not to say that the *net* effect of advertising is to reduce consumer cost (reflected in the retail price), this saving must first be balanced against any changes in the manufacturer's factory price. In addition, the effect of brand advertising on the retail gross margins of other brands in the product category and of other product categories must be considered (and will be) before any conclusion about net benefits or costs can be reached. Rather, it is to say that a consumer cost savings may very well occur at the retail level.

A hidden effect of advertising is its ability to reduce the retail gross margin, thereby lowering the final retail price to consumers, *all other things being equal*. Other hidden effects of advertising can be uncovered by looking at the reasons why retailers are willing to take a lower gross margin on the advertised brands than on the less advertised or unadvertised competitors, and what effect this action has on the gross margins of the other brands carried by the retailers in the product category. The purpose of this book is to establish those reasons and their effects both theoretically and empirically.

Importance of the Hidden Effects

Over eighty years ago, Emily Fogg-Meade recognized that manufacturers could use advertising to force middlemen and dealers to cut their profit margins on the advertised brands. Since that time other researchers have acknowledged this economic truth, but have not understood many of its implications. As the major portion of this book will investigate the relationship between manufacturers' advertising and retail pricing behavior, it makes good marketing sense to offer first some reasons why this entire exercise is worthwhile and what it all means. Chapter 10 will complete the body of the book with a much more in-depth look at the important managerial, public policy, and research implications.

First of all, establishing that an inverse relationship between manufacturers' advertising and retail gross margins exists (the more advertising by a manufacturer, the lower the margin taken on the brand by the retailers) has important managerial implications. By neglecting the effect of their advertising on the pricing policies, price competition, and productivity of retailers—effects reflected in the retail gross margin—manufacturers often underestimate advertising's contribution to their own long-term sales and profit goals when setting their advertising budgets. Traditional budgeting methods of manufacturers typically concentrate on incremental sales gains generated by increased advertising outlays; included in this rationale is the effect of advertising on their own factory selling price. It is our contention that *this advertising policy can seriously underestimate the manufacturers' incentive to advertise*.

For example, in recession periods discretionary business expenditures, such as advertising, are often reduced to help buoy profits. What manufacturers may overlook is that their economic family includes the resellers of their products as well. Retailers too may be affected by the recession; they too have seen their profits dip; and they too will have to do something about it. If retailers are not healthy or wealthy, they usually will be wise enough to change some of their discretionary policies, just as the manufacturers have done. The outcome may be hazardous to the long-term health of any manufacturer: As the manufacturer cuts the advertising budget, the retailers enlarge their own profit margins, thereby raising the retail price. The result: *With no change in the manufacturer's selling price, the retail selling price has been raised.*

The retailer's pricing actions must be considered by the manufacturer in any long-term advertising policy. The manufacturer's advertising helps retailers sell the brand. A short-term reduction in advertising expenditures would rarely cause an immediate change in the retail pricing. But when establishing (and maintaining) a consumer brand franchise, sustained by a flow of advertising messages to the public, a cut in the advertising budget—especially if continued for a long enough period of time—may be unwise. The reduction in advertising may have a delayed effect. Reduced sales means slower turnover and lower productivity for the resellers of the brand; a weakened consumer franchise translates into reduced consumer awareness of the brand, less need for the retailers to carry that brand to maintain customer patronage, and reduced pressure on the retailers to price the brand competitively in order to draw store traffic. As a result, the retailers require a larger profit margin on the brand to be as profitable as before. With no change in the manufacturer's factory price, the retailers must raise the retail price of the brand to obtain the larger profit margin. The manufacturer is left with a smaller percentage of the final selling price, for even though the same factory price is received, the brand is sold at a higher retail price, further reducing sales. And rebuilding that consumer franchise after long-term advertising reduction may be, dollar-for-dollar, even more expensive than it was to build it the first time.

Because good business is not built on pessimism and negative actions, the whole process may of course be reversed by an increase in the advertising budget. More important, however, are some questions regarding the process: How long can a manufacturer reduce advertising before these delayed, hidden effects occur? How much of a cut in advertising is required to start this process? Will this occur in every consumer market? Like those of any good economist, my answers, based on the research to follow, are, respectively: it depends, it depends, and probably not. What we will see is that, although an inverse relationship between manufacturers' advertising and retail gross margins exists, its strength and importance varies among different product markets. We will discuss both why the relationship varies and what characteristics of product markets best predict how strong the relationship will be.

A comparison of two food categories illustrates this point. In the catsup market, Heinz has factory prices that are well above their less advertised national competitors (Hunt's and Del Monte), and even further above private label brands. However, retailers generally mark up Heinz at about 15 percent or less, Hunt's and Del Monte at around 20 to 25 percent, and private labels by as much as 30 percent. The result is that the retail price of Heinz is much closer to the less advertised competition than the factory price differentials would indicate. The canned condensed soup market provides a good counterexample. Here, retailers generally mark up Campbell's at about 13 to 18 percent, whereas the private label brands carry a lower mark-up of just 11 percent. Casual generalizations, therefore, must be avoided. It should be reiterated, however, that the pricing behavior in the catsup market is more the rule than that in the soup market.

Retail managers are mostly interested in the characteristics of what is to them a not-so-hidden effect of advertising. They know that lower sales means slower turnover, and price accordingly. They are also very aware of the importance of "traffic builders" (also often called "loss leaders") to their long-term sales and profit goals. As consumers often use well-known, highly advertised brands to compare the general pricing policies of various stores, retailers promote, advertise, and compete heavily on these brands, often selling them below cost. However, the retailer hopes that, once in the store, the consumer will not purchase just the promoted products—called "cherry picking," which is disastrous for store profits—but will also buy other products. On these other products the retailer has set much higher profit margins, and will either more than make up for the sales of the loss leaders or go out of business.

What the retailer needs to know is the most effective way to increase profit margins in these low-margin product categories without losing store traffic. To address this concern, we will examine some of the components of the retail pricing process: How much do advertising, sales levels, retail price competition, and daily weather reports affect the gross margins set by the retailer? In addition, the retailer would like to know what characteristics of product categories are related to the level of category gross margins, and the efficacy of manufacturers' advertising in reducing the average gross margins of entire product categories. Some of these category characteristics are under the retailer's discretion, such as the number of different package sizes carried in a product category; others are not, such as the total amount of manufacturers' advertising in a product category. By answering these questions we do not expect to be able to change the weather, but we do hope to improve the retailer's understanding of the pricing process and thus facilitate better merchandising decisions.

A policymaker is the businessperson's public sector counterpart—and all too often, adversary. Whereas business is concerned with building barriers to entry and increasing profits, policymaking is concerned with eliminating entry barriers and what are felt to be monopolistic profits. But policymaking that neglects the effects of manufacturers' actions on the distributors in the market implicitly assumes that the manufacturing and distribution stages are independent of each other. They are not. And since it is the *total* excess profit that is a relevant criterion for consumers' welfare (allocative efficiency), public policy has often neglected crucial factors involved in the pricing process.

Much public policy and existing antitrust statutes have overlooked advertising's ability to increase retail price competition and productivity.[2] Whereas it may be agreed that advertising *increases* the market power and prices of the *manufacturers*, it should also be noted that this very same advertising *reduces* the market power of the *retailers* and the price of their services—the retail gross margin. Important consumer benefits of advertising may very well exist in the hidden effect of advertising on retail pricing.

That advertising saves consumers money by reducing the retailers' mark-up of a brand is, however, only one part of the advertising-price story. Certainly policymakers who concentrate only on the manufacturers in the market will have overestimated the impact of advertising on retail price and underestimated its consumer benefits. Likewise, they cannot neglect the manufacturing stage of the market, where advertising may increase market power and factory prices. The fact that advertised brands typically command a higher relative retail price than their less-advertised competitors is proof enough that these consumer savings at the retail stage are outweighted by a consumer surcharge included in the manufacturers' factory prices.

Have we decided that advertising does raise prices, but that we should just be careful not to overestimate the impact? Not exactly. The missing link evident here is that the critical advertising-price issue is not the effect of manufacturers' advertising on *relative* brand prices, but rather *the effect of advertising on the absolute market price level of a product category*.

For example, we are not so interested in whether Heinz catsup has a higher retail price than the less advertised Del Monte's catsup, not because the question is easily answered (Heinz does have a higher price), but because *it is the wrong question*. What we are interested in is whether advertising has raised or lowered the average retail price per bottle of catsup. This question is not so easily answered. Whereas changes over time or differences among geographical areas in the market-price levels of a product category can be observed, it is difficult to separate the effects of advertising on price from the many other possible factors involved.

Since it is the cost to consumers of a product category that is the critical concern, many researchers have approached the advertising-price issue by examining the effects of advertising on other costs of the firm, industry, and marketing system as a whole. Advertising, it is claimed, lowers the costs of getting a product to a market in many different ways: through scale economies of distribution and production, through communication and marketing efficiencies (for both the firm doing the advertising and the entire industry), and through lower search costs for consumers and improved efficiency at the retail level. As one might expect, this view has been embraced by the business community.

Whether advertising does in fact lead to all or any one of these cost-saving efficiencies is only one set of questions. Whether these efficiencies are greater than the cost of advertising and, if indeed they are, whether these cost-savings are passed on to consumers, are another set of queries. But the biggest problem with this approach to the advertising-price issue is *measurement*. Most of these effects are very difficult to quantify, and although they might exist, the magnitude of the effects are unclear. We have yet to find the necessary ruler, and it will be some time before businesspersons and policymakers or the academic community as a whole agree on any yardstick at all.

Other researchers who argue that advertising can lead to lower absolute market prices base their assertion on the assumption that manufacturers' advertising results in lower retail gross margins.[3] However, it remains questionable whether this inverse relationship connotes an inverse advertising-price relationship. The profit margins of the manufacturers and the retail gross margins of the other brands must be taken into account. Furthermore, as will be detailed in Chapter 10, the ability of advertising to lower retail gross margins is a double-edged sword: *It can also serve as an entry barrier for the advertiser*. Therefore, although this book will provide evidence for proponents of the consumer price benefits of advertising, it would be unwise to extend the implications of these hidden effects too far.

In short, what we will show is that *the cost of bringing a product to consumers is lowered by advertising*. And this reduction in cost, manifest in the reduced retail gross margin, is *measurable*. Moreover, not to leave the job undone, we will demonstrate how to measure this cost reduction and, using our data, measure the extent of this reduction. What we offer is proof that a sometimes hidden cost-saving to consumers of manufacturers' advertising can be quantified and is of sufficient magnitude to be worthy of future consideration.

The hidden effects of advertising have important implications for economic research, in particular the theory of derived demand. Traditional models implicitly assume that all distributors are passive participants in the market and operate as a derived demand of consumers' wants satisfied by manufacturers' products. In other words, under this theory retailers merely stock the products demanded by consumers and produced by manufacturers, but do not themselves influence the buying or selling of the products. This set of assumptions has become increasingly inaccurate with the rise of large retail chain stores. Researchers have interpreted the theory of derived demand to imply, moreover, that margins and profits at the retail and manufacturing stages are positively related.[4]

The research in this book indicates that these models are unrealistic, obscuring too many of the essentials of many product markets. Furthermore, the strict interpretation of the theory of derived demand results in a contention that is erroneous for a market with multiproduct retailers whose products have some degree of demand interdependencies. That is, the consumer who goes to buy bread also may pick up some butter. We will demonstrate the importance of these interdependencies in our economic model of retailing, focusing on the ability of certain products—both individual brands (Heinz catsup) and entire product categories (flour)—to increase the sales of other products at the store by affecting store traffic. This type of interdependency is called a *"one-way" cross-elasticity* since the merchandising of certain products affects the sales of others, but not vice versa. For example, by decreasing the price of meat, a store may sell more steak sauce, but rarely will a reduced price of steak sauce affect the sale of meat, at least not to the same extent. A reduced price of meat, moreover, has a better chance of increasing store traffic and thereby the sale of many products other than steak sauce as well. This type of cross-elasticity is essential to the retailer's pricing and the effect of manufacturers' advertising on retail prices; it is realized through changes in retail gross margins—a critical hidden effect of advertising.

Organization of the Book

The purpose of this book is to establish theoretically and empirically a critical marketing relationship: the effect of manufacturers' advertising on retail pricing policies. More specifically, we examine how advertising affects the retail gross margin of a brand, both directly and indirectly, through its impact on retail price competition and productivity, retail prices, and sales. In so doing we also describe how and why the advertising–gross margin relationship differs over ranges of advertising outlays and among various product categories.

This analysis is carried out by building a descriptive model of the large, multiproduct retailer, in particular the *supermarket retailer*, since the model is tested on a group of supermarket product categories. Accounting for over 20 percent of all retail sales, grocery products have been selected because of their importance to consumers. In fact, recent studies by the Department of Agriculture purporting to show manufacturers' advertising results in higher consumer prices singled out food as a prime example. Moreover, we concentrate on the large retail chain store, because it controls nearly 60 percent of all sales in food retailing. In our view, supermarkets are highly representative of most other chain stores selling other kinds of consumer convenience goods; an analysis of the department store, for example, would be similar for our purposes in most respects. We therefore use the more general term "retailer" in many cases, even though we are more precisely discussing the supermarket retailer.

The book is organized into ten chapters and three appendices. Each chapter has a summary for those who wish to skim through parts of the book. The two chapters following the introductory chapter provide a review of the theoretical and empirical literature on the economic effects of advertising, concentrating on the effect of advertising on price. Chapter 2 contains the two economic views on how advertising works—(1) to persuade and (2) to inform consumers—and the evidence on the relationship between advertising and prices. Also included is a review of the literature concerning the effect of advertising on business costs. This chapter thus serves as the initial background for research in these areas.

Chapter 3 offers the work of Michael Porter and Robert Steiner on the economic effects of the manufacturer's policies. Both recognize explicitly the importance of distributors/retailers. The models they present focus on the role of the manufacturer's advertising and its effects on the interaction between manufacturer and retailer. Developed from the manufacturer's perspective, these models serve as intellectual antecedents to this research, reconciling much of the evidence gathered and synthesizing the two opposing economic views. The chapter concludes with a detailed review of the history of research on the relationship between manufacturers' advertising and distributors' gross margins. It is demonstrated that no comprehensive body of evidence exists on this relationship.

Chapters 4, 5, and 6 provide the descriptive theoretical model of the retailer. The purpose of the model is to allow us to examine the relationship between manufacturers' advertising and retail pricing. To examine this relationship properly, the model focuses on the question of why retail brand gross margins differ among product categories. This question has two parts: First, why do product category gross margins differ, and second, why do brand gross margins differ within a product category? For example, why do candy bars have a higher retail gross margin than canned tuna? And why does Bumble Bee have a lower gross margin than private label canned tuna?

Chapter 4 describes the retailer's economic environment—revenues, costs, and competition. Within this framework we then derive the model formulation required to assess why brand gross margins differ among product categories. Two sets of relationships are suggested: One explains variations in the magnitude of product category gross margins; the other explains the divergence of the level of brand gross margins from the average level of their respective product category gross margins. Chapter 5 focuses on this first set of relationships. A model of shelf space allocation among product categories is used under two competitive conditions: perfect competition and monopolistic competition. The assumption of monopolistic competition among retailers is considered to be more realistic, and based on this assumption, the key concept of the entire theoretical model is introduced: *the one-way cross-elasticity of a product*. This concept acknowledges the ability of certain products, commonly called "traffic-builders," to affect the sales of other products at the store by increasing store traffic—even though the other products may not have that same ability—thus making the interdependence (cross-elasticity) only one-way. The aspect of consumer behavior underlying this one-way cross-elasticity is that of product *salience*: the degree to which consumers notice and care about the terms of sale of a product. It is argued that this concept of one-way cross-elasticities is essential to an explanation of the level of product category and brand gross margins, and that the factors related to the level of product category gross margins affect the strength and significance of the advertising–gross margin relationship among brands as well.

Chapter 6 analyzes the second set of relationships—factors affecting deviations of the level of brand gross margins from the average level of their respective product category gross margins. Central to the entire discussion is the effect of manufacturers' advertising on brand gross margins. Three reasons why the advertising should lead to lower retail gross margins are presented, using the key notion of the salience of a brand to consumers. It is held that consumers are more likely to use highly advertised brands as a benchmark to compare store pricing policies, thereby influencing the retailer's pricing of these (and therefore possibly other) brands.

Chapters 7, 8, and 9 test the model on a group of 51 fast-moving, highly salient supermarket product categories; included are 488 brands and over 3,500 individual supermarket items. Data from 1978 are used; 1977 data are used for comparative purposes only, since they are not as complete as the 1978 data. Multiple-regression analysis is the primary statistical technique employed, and cross-tabulation results and graphs serve to present an overview of the data. The regressions allow us to isolate the advertising–gross margin relationship and other important relationships, independent of other potential influences. Both simultaneous and single-equation estimations are considered, as are linear and nonlinear specifications of variables, depending on the specification suggested by the theoretical model.

Chapter 7 deals with the empirical determinants of the level of gross margins among product categories. For example, what factors might cause frozen foods to have higher gross margins, on average, than cake mixes? Chapter 8 addresses the issue of the level of brand gross margins within a product category: For example, what factors cause Skippy peanut butter to have a lower gross margin than Planter's? We demonstrate the importance of the effect of advertising on retail brand gross margins, and discuss how the responsiveness of these gross margins to manufacturers' advertising varies not only over the range of advertising outlays, but also according to certain characteristics of the product category. Furthermore, we isolate and measure the relative importance of the two essential factors that explain why advertising reduces the gross margin charged by the retailer to consumers: (1) by increasing retail productivity through increased sales; and (2) by intensifying retail price competition through increased brand salience to consumers. The empirical analysis is completed in Chapter 9 with a look at particular product categories and groups of categories, such as ready-to-eat cereals, laundry detergents, and pet foods.

Finally, Chapter 10 contains a review of the first nine chapters, together with an overview of the findings. Implications of the findings for managers, policymakers, and researchers are included, with some avenues for future research outlined. An illustration of how to quantify the potential consumer savings attributable to the effect of advertising on retail gross margins appears in the public policy section. More precise quantification for specific product categories, it is proposed, may be accomplished in the future with a detailed time-series data set (such as 1970–1980) for the particular categories under consideration. Three appendices are also included for reference purposes. Appendix

1 provides a mathematical proof of the effect of one-way cross-elasticities on the retailer's profit-maximizing gross margin in equilibrium; Appendix 2 provides a detailed description of the data base. In addition, the representativeness of the data base is shown. Appendix 3 lists the brands used in the study.

Endnotes

1. Not included in this assertion is the research done by Michael Porter and Robert Steiner. Their work (and to a lesser extent that of Brian Harris and W. Duncan Reekie) is discussed and summarized in Chapter 3. Also, previous research by Paul Farris with this author has not overlooked the role of distributors in the market.
2. An exception is the recent cereal antitrust case. See B. F. Harris, "The Cereal 'Shared Monopoly' Case: Some Possible Effects of the FTC's Restructuring Proposals on Cereal Retail Prices," in N. Beckwith and associates (eds.), *1979 Educators' Conference Proceedings* (Chicago: American Marketing Association, 1979b), pp. 631–635. For a more detailed description of his research, see other citation under Harris in the bibliography.
3. To my knowledge, Louis Stern was the first researcher to make this connection explicit. See L. W. Stern, "The New World of Private Brands," *California Management Review*, 8 (Spring 1966), pp. 43–50. Since then, Steiner, Farris, and Albion have done further work in this area. It should also be acknowledged that Steiner maintains, as discussed in Chapter 3, that the best indicator of the level of absolute retail prices for a product category is the percentage of private label sales in the category.
4. See J. M. Ferguson, "Comments on Farris and Albion, 'The Impact of Advertising on the Price of Consumer Products,' " *Journal of Marketing*, 46 (Winter 1982), p. 103.

Chapter 2

ADVERTISING AND PRICES

What are the economic effects of advertising? Does advertising lead to higher or lower prices? Or does the answer depend on the market and time period chosen for analysis? To answer these questions we need to consider first how advertising works and what evidence exists that may be relevant to addressing the advertising-price issue. As Harold Demsetz asserts:[1]

> Advertising is a subject about which the ratio of poetic opinion to systematic analytics approaches infinity. Like romance, advertising is an activity to which most people have been exposed and about which little is known.

Though no more averse to romance than any other occupational group, economists and marketers have approached the question using different models, analyzing vastly different types of data and often drawing broader (and improper) inferences from their research than their data allow. The result is as expected: controversy, confusion, and many unkind words at consortiums. Even within one group of researchers—economists—two schools of thought have developed, with advocates from each school raging tirelessly at each other. It seems that the more the subject is studied, the more disparate the views of many of the so-called experts become. And surely, the less willing many are to listen to opposing ideas.

In this chapter we review these two schools of thought and their views of how advertising works—on the one side, to persuade, and on the other, to inform consumers. The traditional doctrine maintains that advertising is a form of *persuasion* that creates product differentiation and allows the firm to exercise market power at the consumer's expense; accordingly, industry concentration, excess profits, and prices rise as price sensitivity is reduced. The more recent approach views advertising as *information*—an inexpensive means for communicating with large numbers of potential buyers—which stimulates competition and diminishes market power; as such, industry concentration, excess profits, and prices fall as price sensitivity is increased.

Following this theoretical overview—what may be called the "thesis" and "antithesis" of explanations of the economic effects of advertising—is a review of the empirical evidence on the relationship between advertising and prices. A discussion of the difficulties inherent in translating studies of price sensivitity into conclusions about price levels is included. Also reviewed is the research on how advertising may affect business costs by generating potential cost savings that can be translated into lower market prices. These findings lead to a more general discussion of why advertising may lead to higher or lower market prices. The chapter concludes with a summary pointing out the need to synthesize the two views in a broader framework that can reconcile what appears to be confliciting evidence. Such a framework is presented in Chapter 3, and extended in the book by means of models that include the distributors in the analysis of product markets.

Two Economic Models of Advertising

Ever since the time of the great economist Alfred Marshall more than sixty years ago, economists have attempted to separate advertising into "good" versus "bad," or information versus persuasion. Marshall himself distinguished between what he called "constructive" and "combative" advertising, defining the former as an attempt to inform people of the opportunity to purchase and the latter as an effort "designed by one manufacturer to draw customers away from another." A number of empirical studies have followed. All in all, the conclusion reached by Lady Margaret Hall is perhaps most apt:[2]

> No one pays to advertise his products in order to establish the eternal verities. All advertising is persuasive in intent. Since we cannot identify the distinction between informative and persuasive advertising by reference to the experience of either of the two persons affected, either the consumer reading the advertisement or the advertiser himself, it seems better to leave the distinction to the realm of ideas where it properly belongs.

In this spirit, two schools of economic thought have evolved, generating mounds of research from a less-than-formidable theoretical background.[3]

Table 2.1 presents the theoretical economics background for the development of two schools of thought on the economic effects of

Table 2.1   Development of Advertising in Economic Theory

- No account of advertising in price theory before 1933
- First considered by Chamberlin in 1933 as merely a "selling cost" of slightly differentiated products
- Normative models related advertising and price elasticity:
    Dorfman and Steiner (1954) → Static Model
    Nerlove and Arrow (1963) → Dynamic Model
      Assumption for both models: Firm sets price level and advertising
        expenditure to maximize profits.
- Conclusions to date:
    Advertising is inversely related to price elasticity for the firm; this is true
      of industry only if firm is monopolist.
    No conclusion or theory of advertising *affecting* price elasticity.

advertising. As is shown in the table, economic price theory did not explicitly include advertising until the seminal work of Edward Chamberlin (1933). Since that time it has been theorized only that there is an optimal level of firm advertising, which is inversely related to price elasticity (Dorfman and Steiner, 1954; Nerlove and Arrow, 1963). No single theoretical formulation has been derived to posit that advertising affects the price elasticity of demand. Indeed, it can be argued, and often has been, that the causal direction is the reverse. A basic rationale for why price insensitivity can cause greater advertising outlays is straightforward: The more profit a manufacturer makes from a sale, the more the manufacturer should be willing to spend to obtain an extra sale. Therefore, if demand for a particular product is inherently price inelastic, whatever the reason, we would expect a higher level of advertising intensity from these firms than from others. Advertising itself need not be responsible for this price inelasticity of demand for a correlation between the two to exist.

Given this lack of any generally accepted theory on advertising's relationship to price sensitivity, two divergent streams of research have appeared. The two principal models that economists use to describe the effects of advertising differ markedly with respect to their assumptions about the way advertising influences the price sensitivity of consumers. Table 2.2 summarizes the main points of the advertising = market power school and the advertising = market competition school. The first model, which may be credited to Kaldor (1949–1950), Bain (1956), and Comanor and Wilson (1974), views advertising as a persuasive communications tool that marketers use to make consumers less sensitive to price and to increase the firm's market power. The second model, which may be credited to Stigler (1961), Telser (1964), Lancaster (1971), and Nelson (1974), regards advertising as informative in nature, and contends that it increases consumers' price sensitivity and stimulates competition among firms in the market. Both general theories are plausible, but both also have shortcomings: Neither one is able to capture all of the potential effects of advertising. As noted more than 40 years ago by Borden (1942), "Advertising is informative in content, persuasive in intent."

Advertising = Market Power

The market power model views advertising as a communications tool capable of changing consumer tastes and establishing brand loyalties among buyers of advertised products. When advertising differentiates the product from competitive offerings, buyers perceive fewer close substitutes and become less price sensitive in their purchase decisions. This view also maintains that firms increase prices to a level not possible without advertising, and that competitors have difficulty entering the industry because of the brand loyalties created by advertising. The predicted results are higher profits for the large advertisers, higher prices for the consumer, and less competition in the market. All these results stem from the theoretical mainstay of this model, product differentiation.

Although there is no single, generally acceptable definition of the phenomenon, the concept of product differentiation occupies a central position in theories of the economic effects of advertising. Most studies focus on situations where advertising is presumably able to increase the *perceived* product differentiation of physically homogeneous products. As a result, highly advertised brands can command a price premium and enjoy high brand loyalty from consumers. For example, branded aspirin (such as Bayer) has been said to be physically identical to private label aspirins that sell for less than half the price. Yet national brands continue to hold more than 95 percent of the market. Products in the pharmaceutical as well as breakfast cereals industries are other common examples used by critics of advertising to argue that advertising results in "artificial" product differentiation, which leads to increased prices.

One of the more obvious problems with this model is that both price insensitivity and brand loyalty could be created by a number of factors, such as higher product quality, better packaging, favorable use experience, and/or market position. Therefore, though they are probably related to each other, price insensitivity and brand loyalty need not be the result of advertising. More important, there is also no theoretical reason why advertising cannot lead to more price competition. If competitors feel that a leading brand has differentiated its product by advertising, they may cut their prices to compete. The reaction need not always be to increase advertising ex-

Table 2.2 Two Schools of Thought on the Role of Advertising in the Economy

	Advertising = Market Power	*Advertising = Market Competition*
Advertising	Advertising affects consumer preferences and tastes, changes product attributes, and differentiates the product from competitive offerings.	Advertising informs consumers about product attributes and does not change the way they value these attributes.
Consumer Buying Behavior	Consumers become brand loyal and less price sensitive, and perceive fewer substitutes for advertised brands.	Consumers become more price sensitive and buy best "value." Only the relationship between price and quality affects elasticity for a given product.
Barriers to Entry	Potential entrants must overcome established brand loyalty and spend relatively more on advertising.	Advertising makes entry possible for new brands because it can communicate product attributes to consumers.
Industry Structure and Market Power	Firms are insulated from market competition and potential rivals; concentration increases, leaving firms with more discretionary power.	Consumers can compare competitive offerings easily and competitive rivalry is increased. Efficient firms remain, and as the inefficient leave, new entrants appear; the effect on concentration is ambiguous.
Market Conduct	Firms can charge higher prices and are not as likely to compete on quality or price dimensions. Innovation may be reduced.	More informed consumers put pressure on firms to lower prices and improve quality. Innovation is facilitated via new entrants.
Market Performance	High prices and excessive profits accrue to advertisers and give them even more incentive to advertise their products. Output is restricted compared to conditions of perfect competition.	Industry prices are decreased. The effect on profits due to increased competition and increased efficiency is ambiguous.

penditures. In fact, Lambin (1976) found that rival brand advertising stimulated active competitive rivalry in a number of European product markets. Firms responded by increasing their own advertising, but also by making price and quality adjustments. As such, the advertising = market power model only captures one side of the potential economic effects of advertising.

Advertising = Market Competition

An alternative model has developed from information theory, beginning with the research of Stigler (1961). This model maintains that advertising, as a form of market competition, provides information to consumers and thereby increases price sensitivity, lowers prices, and reduces monopoly power. Proponents of this model stress that because advertising serves to announce a product's existence and/or major attributes, the consumer's need to search for information about the product is reduced. Work by Lancaster (1966, 1971), based on consumer utility maximization, has been most notable in advancing within a theoretical framework the role of advertising as a characteristic—an attribute—of a product. As summarized best by Ornstein:[4]

> *The essence of this new view is that advertising provides information on brands, prices, and quality, thus increasing buyer knowledge, reducing consumers' search costs, and reducing the total costs to society of transacting business. . . . By increasing information, advertising increases the number of substitutes known to buyers, thereby increasing price elasticity of demand and reducing price-cost margins. Far from being a barrier to entry, advertising facilitates entry by allowing previously unknown products to gain rapid market acceptance. . . . Advertising serves consumers by increasing product variety and by permitting firms to exploit economies of scale in production and distribution—which in turn yield lower consumer prices.*

Focused on the consumer demand side of the market, the key point of this model, as developed primarily by Nelson (1970, 1974a, 1974b, 1975, 1978), is the assumption that the price elasticity of demand depends upon the amount of knowledge consumers have about close brand substitutes, not upon the existence of a certain number of substitutes. Accordingly, the central question is: What is the probability that the consumer will find or know about alternative brand offerings within a product category? In this model, therefore, monopoly power results from consumer ignorance, which can be reduced by advertising. Within this context the result of advertising is to increase price elasticity and lower prices by in-

Table 2.3 Summary of Seven Empirical Studies on Advertising and Price Sensitivity

Study	Independent Variable	Dependent Variable	Relationship Found	Conclusion
Comanor and Wilson (1974)	Industry price elasticity (factory price) of 38 consumer goods industries	Industry advertising-to-sales ratio (two-stage least squares estimation)	Negative	Advertising decreases factory price sensitivity
Lambin (1976)	Brand advertising intensity (various measures) of 18 to 23 brands	Brand price elasticity of demand (factory price); cross section of firms and industries were studied	Negative	Advertising decreases factory price sensitivity (but, firms may not necessarily increase prices)
Wittink (1977)	Share of advertising for a single brand in different sales territories	Sensitivity of market share to relative retail price	Positive	Advertising increases retail price sensitivity
Schultz and Vanhonacker (1978)	Share of a single brand's advertising and promotion expenditures	Same as Wittink	Negative	Advertising and promotion expenditures decreases retail price sensitivity
Eskin (1975)	Manufacturer advertising and retail price for a single brand in different territories and stores	Retail sales per store adjusted for store size	Negative	Advertising increases retail price sensitivity
Eskin and Baron (1977)	Same as Eskin plus three additional cases	Same as Eskin	Negative	In two of the three additional cases, advertising increases retail price sensitivity; no effect found in the third case
Prasad and Ring (1976)	Surrogates for advertising exposures achieved in various media and interactions with relative retail price	Share of panel purchases (market shares)	Negative interaction between relative price and media exposure indices	Negative sign for two of three interactions between relative price and three different media types; inference made that higher retail prices reduce the effectiveness of advertising

creasing the amount of product information available to consumers.[5] Examples commonly given of this process are the toy and eyeglass industries.

A major criticism of this model concerns the validity of presuming that consumers are perfect judges of the merits of competing brands. Critics have also questioned the central assumption, embedded in Lancaster's work, that consumer choice criteria are unaffected by advertising. Indeed, many researchers have suggested that advertising is most important to marketers (and perhaps consumers) when products have "hidden values" (vitamin content in food, for example), and can be a powerful force in influencing product attributes that consumers believe are important. However, this point bears on the unresolved—and probably unresolvable—debate about whether advertising "creates" needs or demonstrates ways of fulfilling existing needs.

Empirical Studies of Advertising and Price Sensitivity

The two schools of thought differ essentially on whether advertising decreases price elasticity (the market power school) or increases prices elasticity (the market competition school). *No differentiation is made in these models between factory price elasticity and retail price elasticity*. As will be discussed later, both elasticities are critical in ascertaining the gross margin of distribution.

Relatively few studies have explicitly examined the effect of advertising on the price elasticity of demand. These studies are summarized in Table 2.3 and described in more detail as follows:

1. Comanor and Wilson (1974) used simultaneous equations for multiple regression analysis with both a short-run and a long-run measure of price elasticity. The long-run measure was significant at the 5 percent level as long as profits were included as an independent variable. It should be noted that the results are sensitive to model specification, and that the measure of price elasticity is with respect to industry-wide *factory* price (from the manufacturer to resellers). The data used were very aggregated (three-digit Standard Industrial Code level).

2. Lambin's (1976) large-scale econometric study included four simple regressions (four different measures of advertising intensity) on a sample of 18 to 23 brands. The results contained one significant (5 percent level) negative correlation, two insignificant negative correlations, and one insignificant positive correlation between advertising intensity and price elasticity, measured at the factory price level.

3. Wittink (1977) employed cross-sectional (25 metropolitan areas) and time-series (26 observations, each four weeks apart) data, keeping the data interval roughly similar to consumers' purchase interval of the brand (two to six weeks), for a heavily advertised national brand belonging to a frequently purchased, branded goods category. A market share model was used, with variables expressed relative to the competition.

4. Schultz and Vanhonaker (1978) analyzed 45 monthly observations on a frequently purchased branded good. Since they are led to conclude that brand-loyal customers are *more* price sensitive, the specification of their model must be questioned, as most research shows brand loyalty and price sensitivity negatively related.

5. The Eskin (1975) and Eskin and Baron (1977) studies are well-controlled statistical examinations of the test marketing of convenience food items to see how advertising and price affect retail sales. Four cities (two with low advertising, two with high) were examined over a six-month period, with 30 stores within each city, and three different price levels within each city. It should be noted that the brands studied were at the beginning of the product life cycle.

6. Prasad and Ring (1976) focused their step-wise regression analysis on data from a 64-week longitudinal study of two consumer panels of 750 families. One panel was exposed to heavier television advertising than the other for a frequently purchased canned food item. Advertising was found to be most effective with low relative retail prices, as high advertising levels by the manufacturer were *not* found to support higher consumer prices for this brand.

In an interpretation of these studies, it should be emphasized that a correlation between advertising and price elasticity is not sufficient to infer causality, and that none of these studies control for advertising's content. Causality is difficult to show, and the literature examining the persuasive and informational content of advertising is somewhat disappointing, as would be expected by the definitional problems alone.

Keeping these caveats in mind, we conclude that each of the two basic views of advertising has some degree of support from the published empirical evidence. Some studies show that advertising decreases price sensitivity, whereas others report that advertising increases price sensitivity. Nonetheless, *the overall pattern is interesting*. With a single exception, the studies reporting that advertising *increases* price sensitivity looked at *retail* prices to consumers. Studies reporting that advertising *decreases* price sensitivity examined manufacturers' *factory* prices.

Once factory prices are distinguished from retail prices, these findings imply an inverse relationship between advertising and the gross distribution margin, which is the sum of the wholesale and retail gross margins. Most retail chains buy directly from the manufacturers, thus making the gross distribution margin and the retail gross margin essentially indistinguishable for our purposes. As the economic price in a product market for the services of distributors, the gross distribution margin is a function of these two price elasticities of demand. The manufacturer faces price sensitivity in dealing with product distributors, and the retailer must consider the price sensitivity of consumers. The greater the price elasticity facing the manufacturer and the less the price elasticity for the retailers selling the manufacturer's product, the greater the gross margin. Therefore the relationship between advertising and these two price elasticities is important in establishing a relationship between advertising and the gross distribution margin. If advertising decreases factory price elasticity and/or increases retail price elasticity, it should lead to a reduced gross margin.

Translating Price Sensitivity to Price Levels

Two separate difficulties are encountered when we try to translate findings on advertising and price sensitivity to conclusions about price level. The first difficulty is that marketers do not behave the way economic theory predicts. Decreased price sensitivity is not necessarily translated into higher prices. The second problem is that simple price comparisons are not meaningful unless the products being compared are the same in all important aspects. For instance, some manufacturers—and some retailers—offer better warranties, higher quality, faster delivery, and so forth. The following four questions must be answered to draw conclusions about price levels:

1. Do manufacturers actually raise prices in response to decreased price elasticity?
2. How should the relative price differentials among manufacturers' brands be adjusted to reflect product quality differences?
3. Because price levels are also related to costs, what are the effects of advertising on production, distribution, and other marketing costs?
4. What effect does advertising have on retail price competition? Whereas studies of retail advertising show its ability to lead to lower retail prices, what effect does manufacturers' advertising have on retail prices?

In addressing the first two questions, we focus on the *relative* price, the price charged for one brand versus the price of another brand in the same category, such as the retail price of Heinz versus Del Monte catsup. For the last two questions, the discussion shifts to the *absolute* market (retail) price, which is the average dollar paid for a bottle of catsup, pound of coffee, and so on. As mentioned in the first chapter, *it is the effect of advertising on the average market price of a product category, not the relative brand prices in a category, that is the essential advertising-price issue*. We need, therefore, to answer the third and fourth questions as well. Whereas there is some literature addressing question 3, we will quantify one of the effects of advertising on market costs—the gross margin—and address question 4 in this book.

Management Behavior

It is not obvious that the increased ability to raise prices always leads to that outcome. Few firms are able to estimate the price elasticity of demand in their markets with any degree of precision. Rarely do they know what the profit-maximizing price is. The kinds of experiments required to measure price sensitivity are expensive and often unreliable. These problems are minor, however, compared with the marketer's uncertainty about market effects. How will competitors react to a price increase? Will they begin to advertise lower prices? Or will they follow suit and increase their prices as well? Will retailers continue to feature the firm's products despite increased prices? In other words, what are the competitive reactions?

Because these questions cannot be answered with certainty and because price changes can be costly and difficult to implement, relatively small changes may not be worth the bother. In some cases environmental factors may also restrict the degree to which brand prices can differ (for example, cigarettes sold through vending machines). Thus it cannot simply be assumed that prices are quickly adjusted to take full advantage of changes in price sensitivity, especially if other goals, such as market share for the firm's entire product line, are more important than short-term profits for a single brand.

Comparing Relative Prices

There is relatively little published evidence on the extent to which advertised goods have higher or lower factory prices than unadvertised goods, perhaps because it is extremely difficult to measure price in any meaningful fashion. In addition to the obvious problems of adjusting for different sizes, package forms, and so on, a number of important assumptions about quality levels must be made.

To calculate quality levels, the particular attributes important to the nature of the product must first be decided. Even if so-called unbiased estimates by groups such as Consumer Research or Consumers' Union are used, choices must be made, often subjectively based. There are substantial disagreements between the relative ratings of these two organizations for the same products, although interestingly enough, both organizations report high average ratings of product quality for most goods. The question remains "quality for whom?" Most markets are not homogeneous, but include different market segments—groups of consumers who differ in what they want from a product. Any single index of quality probably varies substantially in its appropriateness for different market segments.

In addition, it may be difficult to use consumer perceptions of existing products as a basis for measuring product quality without introducing a perceptual bias. McConnell (1968), for example, had 24 consumers evaluate three allegedly different brands of beer (actually, it was the same beer with different identifying numbers). With no actual quality difference among the brands and only price differential as a signal, he found a positive relationship between price and perception of quality. Similarly, if the recent Schlitz beer taste tests can be considered valid (including, most memorably, the televised tests during the Super Bowl in 1981), beer drinkers were choosing Miller over Schlitz not because of taste but for other, less objective and less easily measurable reasons. The "Pepsi challenge" also falls in this difficult-to-evaluate category. Accordingly, quality, the critical intervening variable between advertising and price, can be difficult to measure.

Although it has often been argued that producers of high-quality products have more reason to advertise (more to say) than makers of relatively low-quality products, Schmalensee (1978) points out that there is no underlying theory dictating a strong relationship between product quality and advertising. A survey of eight studies[6] indicates that advertised products tend to be of higher quality, but the studies do not support the proposition that the relationship is strong and significant. The measures of quality used in these studies include government grades for food, indices of consumer-rating services, "objective" criteria, and management judgment.

Empirical Studies. Perhaps because of the problems associated with measuring quality, thus limiting the opportunity to obtain meaningful estimates of relative prices, few studies have related relative prices to advertising. Early research by Borden (1942), and now many others, has shown not surprisingly that advertised brands have higher relative retail prices than unadvertised brands and private label brands. But only four studies, to the best of my knowledge, have examined the relationship and accounted for quality differences.

Two of these studies have examined the relationship between manufacturers' advertising and relative *factory* prices. Buzzell and Farris (1976) report regression analyses of advertising-to-sales ratios in which relative factory prices were included with several other factors. The results indicate that firms with higher relative prices advertise their products more intensively than do businesses with lower relative prices. Measures of product quality were based on managerial judgment of product quality relative to that of a firm's three major competitors, and they did not affect the direction of the advertising–factory price relationship when included in the regressions. Further work by Farris and Reibstein (1979) confirms the general positive relationship between relative price and relative advertising, even when the effect of product quality is removed from the relationship. They also divided their sample of 221 consumer product businesses a number of different ways: low-quality versus high-quality products, durables versus nondurables, low dollar amount of purchase versus high dollar amount, and the like. In each of the business categories, a statistically significant and positive relationship between relative factory price and relative advertising was found.

Two other studies have examined the relationship between manufacturers' advertising and relative *retail* prices. The Leo Burnett Agency (1979) used a Nielsen data base of 25 United Kingdom markets between 1970 and 1978. Of the 75 brands analyzed, the 48 brands priced above the average had a 5 percent higher advertising share above sales share than the 27 brands priced below average, although the higher-priced brands had lower average advertising-to-sales ratios. Leo Burnett explained the results by reporting that although "the association of higher prices and heavier advertising seems contrary to the usual claim that advertising reduces prices, by increasing turnover and producing economies of scale, the association is however compatible with that claim." The reason given is that advertising adds value to the product, and these products are inherently of better quality. As such, the study implied that advertised brands are a better value and, concomitantly, have a lower price per measure of quality.

W. D. Reekie (1979) provides evidence from a sample of 41 fast-moving products, also in the United Kingdom, from 1972 to 1977, along with some data collected by the United Kingdom Board for Prices and Income. He shows that advertised brands have had smaller price increases than unadvertised brands, but the relative retail price of the advertised brands remains higher. He implies that accounting for differences in product quality, advertised brands are a better buy, and that these brands have kept the absolute market-price level of their product categories down in the inflationary 1970s.

In summation, available evidence indicates that highly advertised products tend to have higher prices than less advertised or unadvertised competing products. Whether this situation disappears or even reverses itself if adequate adjustments for product quality are made is a question open to conjecture. In my opinion, the association would be affected more at the *retail* than the *manufacturer* level It is almost inconceivable, however, that advertised products could sell for less than unadvertised competing products. Even if both are of comparable quality, and even if advertised products have lower costs, because of production and distribution economies, consumers would demand lower prices for unadvertised products. It is unlikely that unadvertised brands could compete at parity prices with advertised brands if their sole distinguishing feature is a lack of advertising.

In an case, *relative* prices are less important than the level of *absolute* market prices that would exist without advertising. To confront this question, the influence of advertising on other costs of the firm, industry, and marketing system as a whole needs to be considered.

Advertising and Costs

The firm's advertising may be the source of potential cost savings to its industry in three different ways. The first is through economies of distribution and production, realized by the ability of advertising to increase the size of the market for the firm, and possibly the industry as a whole. Second, advertising may save the firm, industry, or both, substantial dollars in the marketing communications budget. Finally, the manufacturer's advertising may lower the consumer's cost of search for brand and product information, as well as the selling costs of the retailer distributing the manufacturer's brand. In all cases these effects are difficult to quantify with any precision; however, this problem does not mean these effects of advertising—effects that help lower market prices—are insignificant.

Economies of Scale in Production and Distribution

The business community has long argued that advertising has made possible the national markets that allow large-scale production and lower manufacturing costs. Furthermore, as noted in the quotation by Ornstein (p. 19), the ability of advertising to allow the manufacturer to exploit these scale economies is an important aspect of the advertising = market competition school of thought. Examples of this effect are cited by Steiner (1973) in the toy industry and by Benham (1972) in the eyeglass industry, but few empirical studies have attempted to attribute a portion of these cost savings to advertising per se. Indeed it may never be possible to untangle advertising from the other factors that lead to large-scale production and marketing. To investigate these claims, economists have often tried to remove the effect of nonadvertising factors when studying the impact of advertising on industry concentration.[7] Some of these techniques take into account economies of manufacturing, but economies of distribution, warehousing, billing, and administration are likely to be far more difficult to quantify.

To some extent large-scale manufacturing may have also been responsible for increased advertising. The shift to large-scale manufacturing is often accompanied by higher fixed and lower variable costs, leading to higher incremental revenue on incremental sales. In general, marketers have more incentive to advertise when their profit margin on incremental sales is larger. In this manner, advertising almost certainly has helped build national markets for many products. Borden (1942) found support for this contention in his extensive field studies, demonstrating that advertising, by stabilizing demand, also influenced the willingness of firms to invest in capital-intensive equipment. Advertising can reduce the risk of massive investments, especially when the investment is in limited-purpose production equipment. With more capital-intensive production, firms were found to have lower production and distribution costs.

What would happen to large, national markets if advertising were stopped? Would they revert to the regional markets of a few decades ago? Probably not, but the more important questions are whether, without advertising, new products would be able to expand as quickly to reach the sales level where various economies are substantial, and whether companies would be willing to invest in plants that require a national sales base to make them economically attractive. I suspect not. The practice of "experience curve" pricing illustrates the tendency for economies of scale to develop from cumulative volume over time. Marketers often plan for the decreased costs of production that increased volume brings and adjust their prices to reflect anticipated cost savings from larger markets and/or larger market shares. This strategy was used most successfully by Honda Motor Company to enter the U.S. motorcycle industry in the 1960s.

Because the effect of advertising on sales cannot be measured with any degree of certainty, it is very unlikely that we will be able, in the near future, to quantify the cost savings from scale economies that are attributable to advertising. Nevertheless, businesspeople seem to believe that the net effect of advertising is to lower, not raise, business costs.

Communications and Marketing Efficiency

Advertising is only one of several marketing communications tools that businesses employ; these also include sales force efforts, promotion to the trade or consumer, packaging, and public relations. Marketers have long reasoned that advertising expenditures may reduce the need for such other expenditures. Aaker and Myers write:[8]

> *Advertising is part of a total marketing program; it does not operate in isolation. Its function is usually to communicate to large audiences and it often performs this function very efficiently. Without advertising the communications function would still remain, but would probably have to be accomplished in some other way by retailers, salesmen, etc. The alternative in many situations could cost significantly more.*

Schmalensee (1972) notes that "other selling methods are usually, to some extent, substitutes for advertising," thus implying that other selling and distribution costs might be higher in the absence of advertising. Aaker and Myers (1975) and Kolliner (1963) cite data for the cookie and cereal industries and for manufacturers of industrial goods, respectively. They conclude that the higher the percentage of total marketing costs accounted for by advertising, the lower are total marketing costs as a percentage of sales. However, much of this research is plagued by methodological problems inherent in cross-sectional comparisons.[9] Without controlling for different distribution strategies, conclusions about the impact of advertising on total marketing costs are difficult to draw.

Moreover, the view that advertising serves as a substitute for other forms of selling and distribution costs is not universally accepted. Proof of the lack of substitutability is provided by the positive correlation between advertising-to-sales ratios and sales-force-to-sales ratios obtained in a study by Buzzell and Farris (1976). This study also found a positive correlation between the residuals of a regression explaining the ratios of advertising and promotion to sales and a regression explaining the ratios of sales force expenditures to sales. Again, this finding of a positive correlation does not support the substitutability of advertising and sales force expenditures.

Much of the confusion over this issue is probably attributable to the use of two separate approaches: whether the researcher (1) focuses on *incremental changes* in selling costs for a marketer within a given distribution system or (2) concentrates on the *different roles* of advertising for direct sales efforts versus the strategic alternative of selling through resellers. Any reduction of total sales force expenses due to advertising must stem from one of the following mechanisms:

1. An increase in sales volume keeping a fixed sales force;
2. An actual reduction in the number (or compensation) of salespeople because of increased advertising "pull"; or
3. A strategic change in the channels of distribution made possible by increases in advertising (thus also a reduction in the number or quality of salespeople).

With the first approach, if advertising increased the number of units sold, and sales force expenditures are relatively fixed, then sales force expenditures as a percentage of sales should decline. But all fixed costs would decline as a percentage of sales. It is not necessary that advertising be a substitute for sales force efforts for this to occur; it is only necessary that advertising increase sales.

The second approach supposes that advertising increases the efficiency of the sales force and increases sales per salesperson to the point that fewer sales personnel are required. There is some speculation in the marketing literature that advertising may accomplish this end by introducing the salesperson and making the customer more receptive to his or her presentation. It seems unlikely that an increase in advertising levels would result in significant reductions in the size of the sales force, that is, that sales employees would be fired. However, it is quite possible that firms using substantial advertising budgets to presell their products may employ less expensive "merchandisers" instead of good salespeople.

With regard to the three mechanisms, the first two relate to incremental changes in sales and marketing costs for a given marketer with a given distribution system; the third involves the ability of advertising to reduce total sales force and distribution costs. This latter possibility seems more properly treated as a major strategic issue and not a simple advertising budgeting question. Marketers serving their customers through a network of wholesalers and retailers may need to increase the amount of advertising pull, whereas those selling their products directly to end users may be able to use their normally larger sales force to communicate with customers. The classic example contrasts Revlon's strategy with that of Avon. Both cosmetic companies sell many of the same products, but Revlon sells through resellers and has substantial advertising budgets in a typical year. Avon, on the other hand, sells directly to end users in their homes and does not employ as much advertising. Studies by Buzzell and Farris (1976) indicate that marketers of consumer products who sell through wholesalers and retailers typically spend more of their sales dollar for advertising and promotion and less for sales force expenses.

It could also be argued that increased advertising allows the marketer to employ fewer consumer promotions (such as couponing, sampling, and contests). Testing this idea involves drawing very precise definitions of advertising and sales promotion, which is a formidable task.

The preceding discussion concentrated on the *intrafirm* shifts in communications expenditures that might result from advertising, that is, savings only for the firm per se. Advertising might also shift *interfirm* communications costs. Brozen argues:[10]

> *Cheaper nonadvertised products may appear on the shelf along with more expensive advertised products, but they would not be as inexpensive or might not be available if it were not for the advertising of the more expensive products. Every advertiser is aware of (and concerned about) the "free rider" effect of his advertising. That is, the advertising for Brand X creates additional sales not only for Brand X, but also for other brands of the same product. Other brands may choose not to advertise and, instead, offer lower prices, relying on the availability of the Brand X to inform consumers of the utility of the product and its availability.*

The "generic" portion of any brand advertising, therefore, may function as an unintentional subsidy for unadvertised brands. The net effect is that unadvertised brands need to spend far less for marketing communication. Since the emergence of comparative advertising, it is probably even easier for less advertised brands to take advantage of the "free-rider effect." Explicit comparisons of later market entrants to the leading brand are a relatively inexpensive way to communicate the purpose of the product, allowing the main portion of the advertisement to concentrate on differentiation features, including price. These shifts in communications costs may be substantial, but they are difficult to quantify. Their effect on the absolute market-price level of a product category certainly cannot be dismissed lightly. Low-priced private label and generic brands may not have emerged in many instances without this advertising cross-subsidization.

In summation, it seems reasonable that advertising and other marketing costs are, as Schmalensee (1972) phrases it, "usually, to some extent" substitutes. It is by no means apparent that this substitution effect is significant for all types of firms. Any tendency that advertising may have to reduce other marketing costs is likely to be most significant for distribution strategy. Whether marketing communications costs for an individual firm would be lower or higher without advertising is a matter for conjecture.

Consumer Search Costs

A third way advertising may reduce the costs of bringing a product to consumers is through consumers themselves. If better-informed consumers are able to reduce their search costs for advertised products, then the total costs of the marketing system are reduced. And for the consumers, the *full* price of the product (time spent plus purchase price) may similarly be reduced.

Brozen (1974) gives an appropriate example about the hypothetical "cost" of a consumer search for a cough remedy. He concludes that "were it not for advertising, consumers might consult a doctor or consult a pharmacist." Without advertised remedies (known to consumers), the pharmacist could recommend a $5 remedy identical, perhaps, to a $2 remedy that would be available without advertising. "The cough remedy manufacturer may spend 20 or 30 percent of his revenues to inform him [the consumer], but that information comes to him far cheaper than from alternative sources." Also, our system of self-service retail stores would probably not exist to the extent that it does without the advertising of branded products. If retail clerks had to perform all the functions performed by advertising, costs of spreading information would undoubtedly be higher for new product introductions, product improvements, and so forth. Such examples are apt to remain hypothetical or anecdotal until appropriate measures of consumer search costs can be found. Simply because they cannot be measured, however, does not mean they are not real or significant.

Conclusions on Advertising and Costs

It is clear that, in many cases, advertising contributes to economies of scale in the production and distribution of consumer products. It is not clear, however, what the magnitude of these economies are for most products. Nor is it clear that existing products lose substantial economies of production and distribution if advertising is diminished or discontinued. It seems likely that new products might not reach the sales levels necessary for these economies as quickly, *or at all*, without advertising. But the advertising level required may not be large enough in many or most markets to be considered an important factor in reducing costs.

The proposition that advertising contributes to marketing or com-

Table 2.4   Summary of the Effects of Advertising on Costs

- Some strong arguments and empirical evidence in support of a negative relationship in certain cases, but magnitude of effects unclear.
- Level of advertising needed to reach cost savings also unclear.
- Advertising may allow firm and industry to obtain cost savings more quickly.
- Marketing efficiency from advertising mostly at industry level for brand-strategic shifts in distribution strategies of individual firms.
- Interfirm subsidization of communication costs from "generic" portion of individual firm's advertising for less advertised and private label competitors.
- Consumer search facilitated by advertising, thus reducing costs of search.
- Difficulty in measuring effects does not mean they do not exist at a significant level in many cases.

munications efficiency also has some empirical support. The strongest possibilities for achieving communications efficiency occur at the level of broad shifts in distribution strategies and situations that permit unadvertised brands to take advantage of markets that advertising has created—markets that otherwise might not exist. In addition, advertising can reduce consumer search costs and the functions required of retailers by consumers. All of these effects must be weighed against the cost of advertising itself. A summary of these effects is given in Table 2.4. We will see in Chapter 10 that one of advertising's contributions to marketing efficiency—a reduced cost to consumers of retail services, indicated by a lower retail gross margin—can be measured. This contribution of advertising to marketing efficiency is an important consideration for any conclusion on the effect of manufacturers' advertising on absolute market prices.

Manufacturers' Advertising and Absolute Market Prices

It is always the case that advertised brands sell for more than their unadvertised counterparts, even allowing for any superiority in advertised brand quality. But this is simply an observation of the relative prices of different kinds of brands, which is quite consistent with the possibility that in the absence of advertising the absolute prices of all brands in the category might be higher. And of course, many of the imitative private labels might not exist at all.[11]

As noted above and already made clear, the issue is whether or not advertising raises the average price level for the product category as a whole—that is, the weighted average of brand prices, with the unit market shares as weights. The important question is what the price level would be without advertising. Would the average price of a jar of mayonnaise, for example, be more or less if Hellman's and others did not advertise? The problem is obvious: Any direct measure needs a standard for comparison. How do we find a price standard with no advertising? And even if perfectly competitive prices can be found, how do we remove all other influences and isolate the effect of manufacturers' advertising on the absolute market-price level?

The available evidence is based, necessarily, on indirect tests. The applicability of this evidence relies on a priori, debatable notions of how the economic world works. Steiner, as we shall see in the next chapter, delineates the effect of advertising on market prices according to the percentage of industry sales acquired by private labels and the spread between the relative prices of nationally advertised and private label brands. Others have drawn implications from the effect of advertising on retail gross margins.

Arguments for Higher Prices

The commonly heard consumer argument for why manufacturers' advertising must raise the product price level is that "somebody must pay." The underlying assumption comes from the old economic adage, "There's no such thing as a free lunch." If a company spends money to advertise its brand, it must be recompensed with a higher price to the consumer than firms that do not advertise. If a product category has a high level of manufacturers' advertising, therefore, it will have a high market price. Furthermore, advertising persuades consumers to demand certain brands, raising the price manufacturers can charge for the brand. Again, the greater the amount of advertising in a product class, the greater the average price level. *These are arguments of opinion.* No consideration is given to other determinants of the advertising level; advertising is seen in isolation from the communications mix available to firms and the information mix available to consumers.

More well-founded arguments evolve from game theory and industrial organization theory. One applicable concept from game theory is the prisoner's dilemma, a type of non-zero sum game where, simple stated, the members of the game can all be better off if they can agree on, and enforce, a common strategy. Above some optimal level of advertising expenditures (a level that depends on certain product market characteristics),[12] all the firms in a product market are more efficient, as is the market itself, if they can all agree to reduce their advertising outlays. However, if all of them cannot be counted on to cut their budgets, those who do not cut them may gain at the expense of others. This results in the firms' advertising more than they would like, with competitively wasteful efforts. Because communication and competition costs are higher than they need to be, profits may be reduced, consumer prices raised, or both.

For example, the prisoner's dilemma situation may have occurred in the cigarette industry before the ban on television advertising. The ban may have helped the manufacturers increase their profits through reducing costs, and may have even helped to keep the market-price level down. Teel and associates (1979) report that the cost efficiency of advertising increased dramatically in the cigarette industry after the broadcast ban. At least for the immediate subsequent years, the ban may indeed have reduced excessive, cost- and price-increasing competition.

Similar in its implications, the argument from industrial organization theory (The Market Power School—Table 2.2) builds on the notion of increasing barriers to entry through product differentiation. It is held that if a firm has less competition from firms outside its particular market—firms whose entry into the market would increase competition and lower prices—it can charge higher prices. The aggregate effect is a higher price for the entire product market as well.

Arguments for Lower Prices

The commonly heard business argument for why manufacturers' advertising lowers the average market-price level is its ability to increase market efficiency. Historically the rise of mass transportation allowed for expansion in the size of a firm's market. Mass production and mass distribution then became feasible, with their concomitant scale economies. But for them to be successful, mass communication was the necessary antecedent—the most efficient way to reach a broad geographical range of prospective buyers.

Of the available communications methods, advertising is regarded by the business community as the cheapest way of letting consumers know about a product, the most efficient tool of competition in mass markets that have many brands in each product category, and the most effective method for manufacturers to obtain distribution for their products (as retail turnover is increased). Moreover, advertising can reduce the risk of capital-intensive investments, especially when the investment is in limited-purpose production. These investments can result in decreased production or distribution costs. Since the price of a product must reflect its manufacturing and marketing costs, advertising, as the most efficient marketing method for many products, allows the average price of a product category to be lower than it could be if less efficient marketing tools were employed.

Other arguments from industrial organization theory (the Market Competition School—Table 2.2) address the benefits provided by advertising as a form of information and competition in a market.

This view maintains that advertising eases entry into a product market for new firms, resulting in more firms, more competition, and a lower market price. Furthermore, it is argued, advertising stimulates the firms' desire to introduce new brands because the firms can quickly announce the new characteristics to a large market. Not only do more brands per firm create more competition, but also innovations, especially process innovations, can reduce the cost, and therefore the price, of that brand. The result may be a lowering of the absolute market-price level.

Empirical Studies

With few standards of comparison, empirical studies on the effect of advertising on absolute market-price levels are difficult to undertake. Maurizi (1972), Benham (1972), and Cady (1976) found retail advertising associated with lower market prices in the gasoline, eyeglass, and prescription drug industries, respectively. In each case the researcher investigated a situation in which one market area had advertising and another market area had no advertising. The markets with advertising had lower retail prices.

The English Monopolies Commission compared the level of prices of chocolate and cocoa mixes in the United Kingdom (intensive advertising) and Europe (little advertising), concluding that manufacturers' advertising led to lower market prices. The Commission also studied the United Kingdom soap industry (detergents), announcing that the packaging, branding, and advertising of soaps caused a substantial decrease in both retailer mark-ups and prices.

Excepting implications drawn from Reekie's work (described in this chapter in the empirical section on "Comparing Relative Prices"), only Steiner has done further work of any note on this relationship. In his historical study of the United States bicycle industry (1978a), he documented how advertising, along with other factors, led to dramatic reductions in the retail market price in the early decades of this century. His detailed examinations of the toy industry (1979) in the United States, Canada, Australia, and France have shown continually how advertising can lower the market price in an industry. For example, in U.S. cities with no television advertising of toys, the toys studied sold for $5.00, whereas in U.S. cities where spot television advertisements were used, the toy that occasionally went on sale for $4.49 now sold regularly for $3.49, with a $2.00 sale price. In France toy advertising was not allowed at all until a limited lifting of the ban late in 1975; the prices of the toys subsequently advertised—many of which had been sold for years—dropped quickly. The explanation offered by Steiner for these occurrences is that the increased turnover for the retailers, and the greater sales of the manufacturers' brands, subsidized a *reduction in the retailers' gross margins*. Steiner does note, however, that this relationship between manufacturers' advertising and the absolute market-price levels is not generalizable to every product market (such as the aspirin market). His model and the past research on the advertising–gross margin relationship are presented in the next chapter.

Summary

Two schools of economic thought have debated whether advertising rises or lowers product prices. The traditional model asserts that the firm uses advertising to persuade consumers, change their tastes, and increase market power, leading to higher profits and prices for the firm and the industry as a whole. The other school of thought views advertising as a source of product information to consumers, thereby fostering increased market competition, lower profits, and competitive prices for the firm and industry. We have seen that neither model is consistent with all of the empirical evidence.

Figure 2.1 summarizes the overall pattern of the evidence on advertising and prices. The empirical evidence indicates that, in general, advertising *decreases* factory price sensitivity, allowing higher relative prices for the manufacturer, but *increases* retail price sensitivity, reducing the price premium of the advertised brands sold

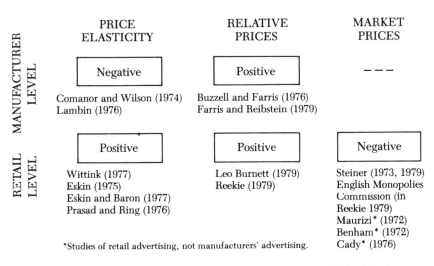

	PRICE ELASTICITY	RELATIVE PRICES	MARKET PRICES
MANUFACTURER LEVEL	Negative Comanor and Wilson (1974) Lambin (1976)	Positive Buzzell and Farris (1976) Farris and Reibstein (1979)	– – –
RETAIL LEVEL	Positive Wittink (1977) Eskin (1975) Eskin and Baron (1977) Prasad and Ring (1976)	Positive Leo Burnett (1979) Reekie (1979)	Negative Steiner (1973, 1979) English Monopolies Commission (in Reekie 1979) Maurizi* (1972) Benham* (1972) Cady* (1976)

*Studies of retail advertising, not manufacturers' advertising.

Figure 2.1 Relationship of Advertising to Price Elasticity and Price Levels.

to consumers by the retailer. However, because the comparability of different brands is uncertain, due to differences in product quality and other intangible factors, translating studies on price sensitivity to conclusions about relative price levels must be based on some assumptions. We are therefore often testing the validity of the assumptions as much as the results.

The measure generally used to gauge the impact of advertising on price is the retail price spread between advertised and unadvertised brands, but as already mentioned, it is not the correct measure. The existence of advertised brands helps keep the costs, and possibly price, of unadvertised brands down. The critical concern should be the relationship between manufacturers' advertising and the absolute market-price level for a product category, not the relative prices of advertised and unadvertised brands in the category.

To study this relationship between advertising and absolute market prices, it is important to look at the effect of advertising on business costs. We considered the possibilities that advertising may reduce the production, distribution, and/or communication costs for the firm and the entire marketing system. These effects imply that advertising may lead to lower market prices. Unfortunately we found that *quantifying these effects is difficult*. Whereas most analysts agree that in many situations advertising may indeed contribute to different types of efficiencies, possibly lowering prices, ascertaining the magnitude of these effects is nearly impossible. We are left with studies that looked directly at the relationship of advertising and market prices, shown in Figure 2.1. It should be recalled that the Leo Burnett and Reekie studies also implied that advertising lowers market prices, and that Steiner held that in some other markets (such as aspirin), advertising may raise absolute market prices.

The evidence on advertising and prices is not yet definitive. Neither model is broad enough to capture all the effects; neither differentiates between the manufacturer and retail stages of production and distribution; *neither differentiates between factory and retail prices, nor between relative and absolute price levels*. Moreover, it is not made clear whether a product's price to consumers should be adjusted to account for quality differences among products and/or should include the consumers' cost of search in choosing one of the many product alternatives available. The ability to reconcile what appears to be conflicting evidence, therefore, requires that we clarify what is meant by "price," and in so doing, develop a broader model of an economic market—a model that incorporates the distributors of the manufacturer's product. Two such "dual-stage" models are presented in the next chapter, with the retail sector developed more fully in this book. These types of models imply that the two schools of thought have been confusing different measures of price, and that the central relationship underlying the evidence on advertising and prices is that of manufacturers' advertising and the cost to consumers of distribution—the distributors' gross margin.

Endnotes

1. H. Demsetz, "Advertising in the Affluent Society," in Y. Brozen (ed.), *Advertising and Society* (New York: New York University Press, 1974), p. 67.
2. M. Hall, *Distributive Trading* (London: William Brendon & Son, 1949), pp. 125–126.
3. It should be noted that the division of economic thought on advertising into two doctrines is somewhat heuristic and oversimplified for expository purposes. These divisions represent two extreme interpretations of the role of advertising, neither of which is accepted entirely by most scholars. Still, a vast amount of research has been done to buttress one side or the other. The weight of empirical evidence, linking advertising intensity with industry profits, concentration, barriers to entry, and the like, is about equally divided between the two views. See M. S. Albion and P. W. Farris, *The Advertising Controversy* (Boston, Mass.: Auburn House, 1981), Chapter 2, for an in-depth look at the two schools, and Chapters 3, 4, and 5 for a comprehensive empirical review.
4. S. I. Ornstein, *Industrial Concentration and Advertising Intensity* (Washington, D.C.: American Enterprise Institute, 1977), pp. 2–3.
5. The price used in this framework is price per unit of quality, that is, a utility-adjusted price.
6. These studies were prepared by the Federal Trade Commission (1933), Cole (1955), Telser (1964), Marquardt and McGann (1976), Rotfeld and Rotzoll (1976), Lambin (1976), Farris and Buzzell (1976), and Farris and Reibstein (1979). See the bibliography for full citations. For a brief description of each study see P. W. Farris and M. S. Albion, "The Impact of Advertising on the Price of Consumer Products," *Journal of Marketing*, 44 (Summeer 1980), p. 23.
7. These statistical controls have not always been adequate. Comanor and Wilson (1974) are criticized by Ornstein (1977), for example, for the suspicious results yielded by their calculations of minimum efficient plant size. More specifically, economists are concerned about the *shape of the cost curve* (supply curve) for the firm: Is it linear (flat) or nonlinear (lower costs for large firms)? For a review of evidence on scale economies in advertising—flat (market competition school) or rising (market power school)—see Albion and Farris, *op. cit.*, pp. 103–114.
8. D. A. Aaker and J. G. Myers, *Advertising Management* (Englewood Cliffs, N.J.: Prentice-Hall, 1975), p. 552.
9. When comparing advertising as a percentage of marketing costs with marketing costs as a percentage of sales, either an underestimation *or* an overestimation of total marketing costs would tend to produce a negative correlation between the two measures.

10. Y. Brozen, "Entry Barriers: Advertising and Product Differentiation," in H. J. Goldschmid and associates, *Industrial Concentration: The New Learning* (Boston, Mass.: Little, Brown, and Company, 1974), p. 134.

11. R. L. Steiner in a note to Ms. Thomas of "Penny Power" from Consumers' Union.

12. For a review and new evidence on the determinants of advertising effectiveness, see P. W. Farris and M. S. Albion, "Determinants of the Advertising-to-Sales Ratio," *Journal of Advertising Research*, 21 (February 1981), pp. 19–27.

Chapter 3

ADVERTISING AND THE DISTRIBUTOR

The total effect of advertising on price is the sum of its effect on the manufacturer's factory price plus its effect on the gross margin of distribution. Neither of the two widely accepted models of the economic effects of advertising recognize this important equation. Therefore, we have criticized these models for trying to capture the many possible effects of advertising within one all-encompassing theoretical framework—*a framework that does not include the role of the distribution sector in the market*. The advertising = market power and advertising = market competition models do not delineate different roles for advertising dependent on particular market conditions or the structure of the market, in particular, the retail sector. These models are seriously incomplete.

"Truth," Oscar Wilde once observed, "is never pure and rarely simple." Unfortunately it follows that even with the greatest regard for simplicity, appropriate models may have to be more complex. Advertising may be effective only in certain product markets, not in all or in none, as the two economic models imply. As Caves notes:[1]

> *What determines in which industries high advertising outlays can serve to erect massive entry barriers? Would a great elevation of selling outlays similarly affect the market for upholstered furniture or wooden spring clothespins? Advertising outlays are profitable because they strike responsive nerves in the consumer, and we have not established rigorously what makes some nerves susceptible, others not.*

A relatively new model developed by Michael Porter addresses this question. The work of Robert Steiner, further clarified and extended by Farris and Albion, complements the Porter model. Taken together, these models have attempted to account for the

41

differences in the effectiveness of advertising by recognizing the role of distributors, especially retailers, in the sale of the manufacturer's product and dissemination of product information to consumers. By focusing on how manufacturers' advertising affects not only consumers but also the interaction between manufacturers and retailers, these models deal directly with the effect of advertising on costs, retail distribution, manufacturers' factory prices and profit margins, retail prices, and the price charged by the distributors to consumers—the gross margin of distribution. Accordingly, after presenting the two models, we review the empirical evidence on this critical relationship between manufacturers' advertising and the gross margin of distribution, which is essentially equivalent to the retail gross margin when the retailers perform the wholesale function as well (by buying their products directly from the manufacturers and either storing the products in warehouses or putting them on the retail shelves immediately). For our purposes of examining the economics of retail chains, the retailers are also the wholesalers, so the two gross margins are nearly indistinguishable.

Porter's Model

From the perspective of the Comanor and Wilson school of thought, Porter (1976) examines the structural determinants of manufacturers' profits in a particular product market. Though he agrees that advertising is a central structural determinant of profitability, Porter argues that there is no simple structural relationship between manufacturers' advertising and market power, measured by manufacturers' profits. Rather, for some types of goods, consumers are likely to seek information from the manufacturer through advertising; this demand gives the advertiser market power to increase profits.

For other types of goods, consumers seek information of a different type and from other sources, most notably the retail outlets. In this situation the manufacturer has less power vis-à-vis the retailers and consumers, and less ability to elevate profits. What has happened is that the relative bargaining power of the manufacturer as seller, vis-à-vis the retailer as buyer, has been reduced. Implications of the model are derived mostly from this bilateral market relationship between manufacturer and retailer. And although Porter focuses on the manufacturer's profits and how they are affected by the retailer's role in the market, the implication is that with a certain set amount of total profits in a product market, the retailer gets a larger slice of the pie in this type of market.

Porter defines two types of goods, convenience and nonconvenience, on the basis of intrinsic product characteristics and the character of the consumer's search for information about brands in a particular product category.[2] Furthermore, he maintains that "the characteristics of the retail channels for a product signal the relevant [essential] characteristics of consumer demand [buyer behavior] for the product." Thus he uses the *types of outlets*, convenience and nonconvenience, to characterize the distinction in types of product markets. This distinction is the crux of Porter's explanation of how and why manufacturers' advertising operates differently among various product markets.

Interbrand Choice by Consumers

Porter first considers how the buyer's demand for information and the seller's supply of information in a market may differ according to the product market. He proposes that the buyer's strategy for collecting information about different brand offerings guides the seller's choice of what mix of sales promotion devices (and media) to employ. According to Porter, the buyer's strategy depends upon:[3]

> . . . the desire of the buyer to make an informed choice; the product attributes about which information is desired; the set of product attributes about which each information source informs the buyer; the quality of each information source; the utility loss in obtaining each information source.

A buyer therefore invests in a portfolio of information, whether it is hard (consumer reports) or soft (television advertising), as determined not only by the buyer's sociodemographic group, but also by the nature of the product's attributes and the utility lost or gained by a "right" or "wrong" decision. For example, even higher-income, urban-dwelling, educated consumers may acquire information about a new soap from television advertising rather than technical print information because the utility lost by a wrong purchase is slight and a decision for such a low-priced, frequently purchased product can be corrected quickly. As attributes differ among products, so does the buyer's search for information and, therefore, the level of effectiveness of the manufacturer's advertising.

The Convenience/Nonconvenience Dichotomy

Porter divides retail outlets into two groups, convenience and nonconvenience, that reflect the nature of the buyer's choice. In the convenience goods market (products sold mostly through convenience outlets), Porter believes that the retailer has little power to differentiate the product and merely provides display space. The manufacturer, however, can differentiate the product and may do so with advertising. In this way, the Porter analysis implies, the manufacturer should be able to increase the factory price to the retailer, thereby *decreasing retail margins*. Since the size of convenience purchases is relatively small and the advertising expenditures are high, retailers accept the lower margins because of higher turnover.[4]

For the nonconvenience goods market (similar, but not identical, to shopping goods), on the other hand, the retailer is needed to provide information and differentiate the product with the store's image (in clothing, for example, Neiman-Marcus versus Macy's). In this instance the manufacturer advertises mostly to strengthen its brand name vis-à-vis the retailer to gain much-needed distribution. Porter contends:[5]

> *Whereas initial barriers to gaining access to distribution may be lower with nonconvenience outlets (as distribution is commonly selective rather than intensive as it must be, at least by area, for most convenience goods), the marginal costs of increasing distribution persist over time and probably escalate as the manufacturer's share increases.*

The manufacturer's promotional activity is directed more toward the retailers. Advertising assumes a secondary role so that factory prices are lower and *retail margins higher* than for a similarly priced convenience good.

Distinctions between convenience and nonconvenience outlets are summarized in Figure 3.1. Convenience outlets maintain little or no sales assistance (little information is provided to customers) and are densely located (distribution is intensive). Examples include supermarkets, gasoline stations, and liquor stores. The types of products sold are goods that most consumers spend little time or effort assessing before purchase. These products are generally low priced, are frequently purchased, and represent a small fraction of the consumer's budget. Little is lost by a "wrong " purchase, and the place of purchase is mainly differentiated by its accessibility. The consumer finds little gain in making price and quality comparisons as compared with saving time. Since there are many buyers continually in the market, the use of mass media is efficient as well as effective. The main source of consumer information, therefore, is advertising.

On the other hand, nonconvenience outlets offer moderate to high sales assistance to the customer and are selectively located. Examples include furniture stores, appliance stores, and automobile dealerships. For the kind of products these outlets carry, consumers are willing to invest time in gathering information, much of which is obtained from the retailer. Comparison shopping is more important

OUTLET
CHARACTERISTICS   CLASS OF RETAIL OUTLET

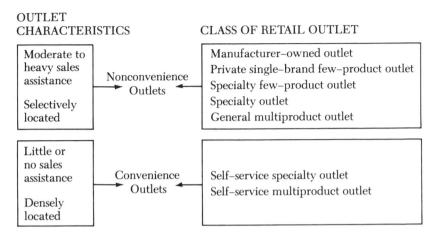

Figure 3.1 **Taxonomy of Retail Outlet Classes.** According to Porter, moving from top to bottom of the figure, the retailer's contribution to product differentiation decreases; the retailer's product line becomes less specialized; the retailer's market power decreases relative to the manufacturer's. *(Source: Porter, 1976, p. 24. Reprinted by permission of Harvard University Press.)*

and more feasible because the purchase (infrequently purchased, high-priced items) can be delayed. Price and quality comparisons may offer a substantial gain, and a poor choice can cause a substantial loss. The retailer is sought out by the consumer for the on-the-floor assistance that can be provided. Consumer loyalty may develop for a retail outlet just as it can for a particular manufacturer's brand. Furthermore, the consumer's search costs may be reduced by the outlet itself. Loyalty allows the consumer to search within the store rather than from store to store, and rely on what the consumer considers to be the good taste of the outlet. Consequently the retail outlet can bargain for and capture a larger percentage of the total market profits from the manufacturer, essentially through a higher margin.

Generally, therefore, the level of ultimate product differentiation affects the potential, lump-sum profit margin for the particular product market. This is illustrated in Figure 3.2. The figure shows proportional contribution to product differentiation, with the shaded area representing the retailer's contribution. The overall height of the block represents the ultimate product differentiation, or product differentiation as perceived by the consumer. With the assumption of a certain cost structure, it can be extrapolated that *the level of total profits in a product market is a proxy not only for profit margins but for retail prices as well.* Manufacturers of convenience goods tend to follow a "pull" strategy, with the reward of a higher per-

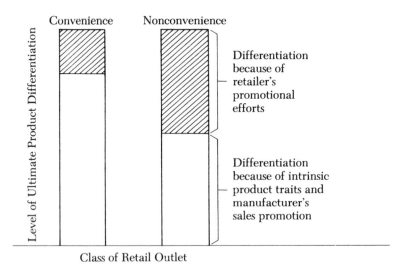

Figure 3.2   Manufacturer and Retailer Contributions to Differentiation in Convenience and Nonconvenience Goods. *(Source: Porter, 1976. Reprinted by permission of Harvard University Press.)*

centage of the total profits in the product market (higher factory prices), whereas manufacturers of nonconvenience goods tend to follow a "push" strategy, which allows retailers a higher percentage of the total market profits (higher margins).

These strategies are not the only strategies that firms can follow. Rather, each is dictated by the nature of consumer demand for both the particular product category and information about the brands in question. Though Porter's model is constructed primarily to explain the difference between the two types of product markets, Porter does recognize that variations in firms' marketing strategies within these two categories occurs. Manufacturers of convenience goods can advertise nationally, not advertise, or even produce private labels. For example, whereas Lipton advertises its tea bags nationally, Magic Mountain does not, and private label tea bags have no advertising either (although Lipton also produces many of the private label tea bags as well). In each successive case, the manufacturer receives less of the total profits in the product market; the level of ultimate product differentiation is highest for the nationally advertised brand, lowest for the unadvertised brand. Figure 3.3 depicts this situation for a representative convenience good. Total market profits and thereby, by association, retail prices are highest, Porter implies, when nationally advertised brands dominate a product market.

Essentially, the logic Porter uses to explain the variation in the manufacturer-retailer interaction *within* a type of good, such as for convenience goods (Figure 3.3), is the same as that used to explain the difference *between* Porter's two classifications of goods, convenience and nonconvenience. Porter believes, moreover, that it is in nonconvenience goods that marketing strategies abound for the manufacturer—much more than in convenience goods. These options include heavy advertising (pull), some advertising with careful selection of dealers (push), low price and low selling expense for price-sensitive goods, or use of private labels. For example, whereas Peugeot has been a large national advertiser of its bicycles, Fugi has advertised much less and is less densely distributed, Schwinn has been more a low-price brand, and private labels are sold by Sears. In succession, according to Porter, differentiation is highest with heavy advertising, decreasing slowly through selective dealers and private label brands, and is lowest for the price-sensitive goods.

Implications of the Porter Model

Porter has offered insights into the interaction between the manufacturer and retailer and the retailer and consumer that affect the

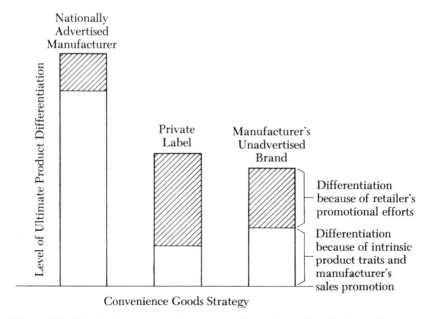

Figure 3.3 Marketing Strategy Options in Convenience Goods. Cross-hatched area represents retail promotional efforts. *(Source: Porter, 1976, p. 90. Reprinted by permission of Harvard University Press.)*

role of advertising in the marketing mix and the type of economic impacts expected. He has accounted for the variation in the effectiveness of advertising by examining the consumer's demand for information for two broad types of goods, and then operationalized this variation by using the types of retail outlets that sell the goods as a surrogate for the consumer search for product information. The basic convenience-nonconvenience dichotomy is powerful and useful. In convenience goods, the manufacturer differentiates the product, reducing the retailer's gross margin; in nonconvenience goods, the retailer contributes substantially to the value of the product and differentiates it to consumers, earning a higher gross margin.

For convenience outlets, therefore, advertised brands may have the highest relative retail prices, but also the lowest retail gross margins. Through its effects on consumers, advertising can shift the terms of trade between manufacturer and retailer toward the manufacturer. The main effect of advertising on the retailer, according to Porter, is a higher factory price for advertised brands than for unadvertised brands. As such, advertising may allow the manufacturer to increase brand sales not only without a reduction in retail prices but also *without reducing his percentage of the retail price*. These issues are addressed more explicitly by the Steiner model. Steiner extends Porter's work by examining product markets over time, with a more detailed analysis of the role of distributors in a market and the economic effects on the retailer.

Steiner's Dual-Stage Model

Robert Steiner (1973; 1978a,b,c,; 1979) is the originator of a relatively new way of viewing the effect of the manufacturer's advertising campaigns on the retail prices to consumers. As in Porter's work, Steiner's principal thesis is that the advertising = market power and advertising = market competition models have neglected the very important role of the resellers of the manufacturer's product. He believes that a careful analysis of the response of the retailers to manufacturers' advertising provides a more realistic assessment of the economic impacts of advertising. Farris and Albion (1980) have extended and refined Steiner's model to show how many of the differences between the two schools of thought can be reconciled.

The central concept of Steiner's model is that the retailer and manufacturer face different demand functions, all of which must be considered in order to understand how and why consumer prices vary among different brands and product markets. He acknowledges that retailers earn lower profit margins on items that sell quickly

than on products that move relatively slowly. Therefore, if a manufacturer generates strong consumer demand through advertising and
is able to sell more goods at higher prices to the retailer, *consumer
prices will not necessarily reflect the manufacturer's decreased price
elasticity*. Instead, because retailers still face a situation in which
consumers are price sensitive, retailers will lower their gross margins
and price to be more competitive with other retail outlets. In fact,
as Steiner maintains, "increased advertising outlays, reduced demand
elasticities, and rising or constant cost at the manufacturer's level
may be compatible with falling prices at the retail level." He uses
the toy industry (see p. 36) as an example of this proposition.

The point is that, first, the manufacturer's factory price elasticity
can be decreased by advertising, allowing higher factory prices to
the retailers. But with the strong consumer demand, retailers still
must stock the product and will compete heavily with other outlets
on the retail price so as to remain price competitive. The implication:
The manufacturer's major incentives to advertise do not include an
increase in consumer price. Rather, the manufacturer wishes to obtain the highest possible factory price and the lowest possible consumer price to achieve high sales volume. Advertising may facilitate
the attainment of *both* of these goals by its effect on gross distribution
margins. As the factory price is raised, the retail price is not raised
to the same extent because of increased retail price competition and,
consequently, a lower gross distribution margin.

Steiner illustrates these effects, as presented in Table 3.1. Note
that even though Steiner focuses on the gross distribution margin,
it is essentially equivalent for comparative purposes to the retail
gross margin. If the retailers also act as wholesalers by buying directly
from the manufacturer, then the two margins are equal; if not, as
long as the gross margin taken by wholesalers is either a constant
proportion of the gross distribution margin or independent of the
retail gross margin, no change in the analysis is necessary. Column
6 is of greatest interest; Steiner summarizes these effects as follows:[6]

> *Brand advertising reliability drives down the spread between factory
> and consumer price by increasing the elasticity of the retailers' demand
> curves and lowering their unit operation costs. Hence, although brand
> advertising is associated with higher rates of return and prices for
> manufacturing firms, it reduces the gross distribution margin [equiva-
> lent to retail gross margin in dual-stage model], lowers costs and
> markups for retailers, and, in this example, yields lower prices to the
> consumer.*

In general, therefore, Steiner sees three types of revenues accruing
to the manufacturer from advertising that are *unrecognized by the
single-stage model* of manufacturers and their market power. These

Table 3.1 Some Effects of Brand Advertising Intensity in a Consumer Goods Industry

	1	2	3	4	5	6	7
	Average Manufacturers' Selling Price (Each)	*Units (Thousands)*	*Total $ Volume at Manufacturers' Selling Prices (Thousands of $)*	*Average Retail Price (Each)*	*Total $ Volume at Retail (Consumer Prices, Thousands of $)*	*Gross Distribution Margin*	*Average Quality Index*
Industry with heavy brand advertising							
Leading national brands	$3.00	13,000	$39,000	$3.95	$51,316	24.0%	100
Other brands	1.70	7,000	11,900	2.93	20,517	42.0	98
Total industry*	2.54	20,000	50,900	3.59	71,833	29.1	99.3
Industry with light brand advertising							
Leading national brands	2.35	800	1,880	4.20	3,357	44.0	80
Other brands	1.96	9,200	18,032	4.00	36,800	51.0	77
Total industry	1.99	10,000	19,912	4.02	40,157	50.4	77.2

SOURCE: Steiner, 1979.

* A "total industry" price is called the "absolute price" as distinguished from a "relative price" for a brand.

revenues come from (1) increased retail penetration (the number of outlets carrying the manufacturer's brand), (2) increased dealer support, and (3) decreased gross distribution margin. These unrecognized revenues result from "increasing the size of the consumer universe by enlarging the brands' retail distribution and then, through the reduction in trade margins, of moving downward on the new market penetration demand curve to a lower retail price–higher unit volume point." These three effects vary in importance through four stages of what Steiner calls the "advertising life cycle concept." The stages are not meant to be universal; rather, they are meant to serve as a device for focusing on pivotal variables and what happens as these variables change.

Four Stages of Advertising Effects

Steiner describes several stages in the advertising life cycle concept, with different manufacturer-retailer-consumer relationships in each stage. He believes that (with numerous exceptions) the most beneficial effects of advertising for consumers appear in the early stages, with the more harmful effects in the later stages when the product category stops growing. Table 3.2 outlines the four stages. Within each of these stages he argues that five separate demand functions are relevant: two for the retailer (demand for the product category and demand for the particular brand) and three for the consumer (demand for the product category, demand for the brand, and demand for a particular retailer's services). Each demand function must be analyzed to predict the effects of brand advertising on consumer price.

Table 3.2   The Four Stages of the Steiner Model

Stage of Advertising Life Cycle	Factory Price	Retail Gross Margin	Consumer Price*	Market Penetration
Phase I—Unadvertised	Very Low	Very high	High	Low
Phase II—Initial advertising	Low	High	Medium	Medium
Phase III—Growth	Medium	Low	Low	Full
Phase IV—Maturity can yield:				
Manufacturers' brand domination	Very high	Very low	Very high	Full
Private label domination	Very low	Very high	High	Full
Mixed regimen	Low	Low	Low	Full

* These prices do not take into account scale economies. Steiner is not clear in differentiating relative from absolute price, although it is clear that Phase IV concerns absolute prices. Phases I–III deal with relative, not absolute, prices—a limitation of the analysis.

Unadvertised Consumer Goods Industry (Phase I). In this stage, manufacturers offer retailers far more competing items in a product category than it is economical to carry, and consumers exhibit no marked preference for one brand over the others. Consumers have little knowledge of any brand, and therefore, in the absence of retail distribution, a brand has scarcely any consumer demand. Thus retailers can freely substitute brands without fear of losing sales and can pressure manufacturers to cut prices in order to earn greater retailer profit margins. Manufacturers are unable to convince all retailers to distribute and support their products. As such, a major reason for lowering factory prices is to gain additional distribution.

Steiner argues that economic theory has failed to realize this crucial need of the manufacturer:[7]

> *The greatest casualty of the omission of the distribution system from the economists' model is their unstated assumption that manufacturing firms face their 100% market penetration consumer demand curves.*

At some point, of course, the manufacturer finds it better to forgo further increases in distribution and sales at the cost of reduced profit margins. A manufacturer must either stay at this equilibrium point or change strategies. As long as the manufacturer stays at this stage, the retailer can make a high profit, and the retailer's demand for the brand is more elastic than the brand demand curve at the consumer level. Shelf space is more valuable to the manufacturer than the brand is to the retailer. Consumer prices, however, are not necessarily low in this unadvertised stage, often considered ideal in economic theory. In fact, because competition between retailers is light, very high gross distribution margins are likely to be earned, and consumer prices may be high.

Initial Advertising (Phase II). Instead of remaining at an unadvertised equilibrium, some manufacturers may try to advertise their products and achieve increased market acceptance through rising consumer demand, which generates increased retail demand. If this strategy is successful, retailers discover that consumers expect them to stock the advertised brand. During this period the manufacturer finds it possible to increase the number of outlets carrying the brand without making the price concessions previously required. With a stable manufacturer's factory price, retail gross margins and consumer prices may fall, as sales and distribution grow. Economies of scale in manufacturing could, however, lead to higher profit margins for the manufacturer. The end of this stage is marked by the near fulfillment of the manufacturer's need for distribution.

Growth Stage (Phase III). In the growth stage Steiner assumes that the brand is carried by almost all retailers who typically stock such items and that consumer demand and retail turnover continue to increase. During this stage consumer prices may continue to decline, and retail gross margins may fall further. This decrease occurs because retailers begin to compete actively with each other on the prices charged on the advertised brand. The reason: Consumers use well-known advertised brands as a benchmark to compare prices among retailers. Without a known quality/price benchmark, consumers have difficulty recognizing price differences among stores. Retailers recognize this fact and discount these advertised brands to achieve reputations for low prices. And this retail price competition may expand demand still further.

At the height of the growth stage Steiner believes that some brands of convenience goods may achieve a market position such that almost 100 percent of the retailers dealing in the product category are forced to stock the brand. Intense retail price competition and large promotions may even drive the retailer's gross margin to zero. If so, the manufacturer's factory price effectively equals the consumer price, and the manufacturer faces only the consumer demand curve for the product. Retailer demand is ensured, and by the end of this stage, increased factory prices and the appearance of private label competitors are possible.

Maturity (Phase IV). At the end of the third phase, when there is little opportunity for further growth, the product may be replaced by new brands or new products with different product concepts. Any one of three outcomes is possible—what Steiner calls "manufacturers' brands domination," "private label domination," or "the mixed regimen."

Manufacturers' brand domination is seen by Steiner to parallel the outcome predicted by the advertising = market power school. A few heavily advertised products dominate the product category, and entry by rival firms is blocked. Existing manufacturers may, however, offer new brands. Consumer prices rise in response to increased advertising efforts that successfully differentiate the products further from competition. This situation results because gross margins earned by retailers are as low as possible, scale economies are exhausted, and increased product usage per capita is unlikely. An oft-cited example is the aspirin market, in which manufacturers' brands command very high price premiums and private label products hold less than five percent of the market.

The second outcome is private label domination, in which almost all of the market is held by private labels. Steiner argues that in this instance, the very high gross margins accruing to retailers result in consumer prices slightly below the prices in the manufacturers' brand domination scenario, but above prices in a mixed regimen.

The mixed regimen market has been referred to as the "battle of the brands" in the marketing literature. In this situation, chain stores effectively challenge manufacturers' brands with their own private label products. Retailers negotiate very low factory prices from manufacturers for private label brands and provide their own brands with favorable shelf space and local advertising support. Steiner proposes that the resulting competition between national and private label brands tends to keep factory prices and consumer prices of the national brands at what are considered reasonable levels. The retail prices of the advertised brands are lower than prices would be without advertising because of the continued low gross margins earned by the retailers. An example used is the replacement tire business, in which 50 percent of the market is held by private labels.

Steiner further maintains that for consumer prices to be at a minimum, two types of comparison must be made easy for the consumer. The first is comparison of prices of competing brands in a store, that is, *intrastore* comparisons. This comparison is facilitated by nationally known advertised brands that can serve as a comparative standard. For instance, Heinz catsup serves as the price competition for the A&P or Safeway private label catsup. The second set of comparisons that consumers need are prices of comparable products, from one store to another, that is, *interstore* comparisons. Since consumers may not be able to adequately compare A&P with Safeway private labels—there may or may not be quality differences between the two—the existence of advertised, widely distributed brands is again required. To use the previous example, Heinz catsup sold by A&P is identical to Heinz catsup sold by Safeway. The lowest prices occur when both types of price comparisons are possible.

Implications of the Steiner Model

The basic thrust of Steiner's model is, to use his own words, "the elevation of the process of consumer goods distribution to parity with with the process of consumer goods manufacturing." As a result, the price-reducing propensities of advertising, found mostly in the retail market, are not overlooked. Instead, a central element of the model is the conclusion that traditional economic theory has *underestimated* the incentives of manufacturers to advertise their products and *overestimated* the impact of advertising on prices. It is because traditional theory does not recognize that advertising increases the universe of potential purchases through expansion of distribution, increases retailer support, and diminishes the gross margin earned by the retailers—*all of which allow factory prices to increase more than consumer prices*. Therefore, with the advertising pull placing the manufacturer in a stronger position vis-à-vis the retailers, the manufacturer can realize a higher factory price, more competition on the brand's retail price, and higher unit sales volume. This set of occurrences pivots on the reduction in retail gross margin.

A major contribution of this model, overlooked by Steiner himself but developed by Farris and Albion (1980), is its ability to reconcile what heretofore has been regarded as conflicting empirical evidence on advertising, prices, and price sensitivity. The recognition that the manufacturer and retailer face different demand functions—both of which must be considered to understand how and why consumer prices vary among brands and product markets—is necessary to obtain a synthesis of the advertising = market power and advertising = market competition models. The results reviewed in the last chapter—that advertising can decrease the price elasticity for the manufacturer (selling to retailers) and simultaneously increase the price elasticity for the retailer (selling to consumers)—are entirely consistent with this model. Taken together, *the change in the two elasticities denotes a lower retail gross margin as a result of manufacturers' advertising*. A careful analysis of the impact of advertising on the retailer explains many of the inconsistencies between the advertising = market power and advertising = market competition viewpoints, and promotes a more realistic assessment of the economic impacts of advertising.

Albion and Farris (1981) have detailed some of the problems with Steiner's framework. These include: the transition from a "brand" to a "market" focus between the third and fourth stages; the determinants and viability of the fourth-stage categories for mature product categories (including some inconsistencies in the levels predicted for consumer price); and the applicability of the model to a wide range of consumer products. Still, in general, the Steiner view of manufacturer-retailer-consumer interaction provides a much richer theoretical base than previous theories for analyzing the effects of advertising on prices. As in the Porter model, the logic used to explain the difference among product categories (Porter) or in a product category over time (Steiner) can also be used to explain the variation in the manufacturer-retailer interaction between advertised and unadvertised brands in the same product category at any one time. Much work remains to implement this model, however, and some central concerns remain unsettled. More empirical tests of the model are also needed, though there is a history of studies on the relationship between manufacturers' advertising and the gross margin of distribution.

Empirical Studies

That advertising leads to lower distributors' gross margins is a matter
of common knowledge to businesspeople in consumer goods industries. Moreover, this is not a newly discovered relationship. As Emily
Fogg-Meade recognized more than eighty years ago:[8]

> *A marked characteristic of recent advertising is that it is directed to*
> *the consumer and not to the dealers and middlemen. . . . The theory*
> *is that in this way the goods sell themselves. The consumer demands*
> *them from the retail dealer, and he, from the jobber. The retail dealer*
> *thus loses his importance as a middleman and becomes a mere agent.*
> *In this way the dealer's profits can be cut down.*

Yet relatively few business researchers and economists have investigated this relationship, and when they have, the research has been
mostly anecdotal. In fact, most of the writing on this subject seems
to focus on the effect of nationally advertised products on small
retailers. Whether researchers have considered the relationship unimportant, or have overlooked it in their "single-stage" models
(models including only the manufacturers in the market), is a matter
of speculation. Whatever the case may be, difficulties in obtaining
brand gross margin data in any detail has been a significant hurdle
in this research area.

From the time of Marshall (1919), the relationship has been investigated to different extents in two distinct "waves." The first
encompassed the period from Marshall (1919) to Borden (1942); the
second began in the middle 1960s with the studies by the British
Price Commissions (in Reekie, 1979) and has continued through the
extensive work of Steiner. The British, with their pioneering work
in the distribution sector, have contributed a number of studies in
the field. The United Kingdom and United States studies have employed a variety of data bases—none necessarily "representative"
(because of data collection limitations)—that all arrive at the same
general conclusion: *Advertising reduces the distributor's gross mar-*
gin. Questions of causality have been minimized by both the lack
of theory for a gross margin–advertising relationship and the time-
series studies, which have shown that the margin reduction *follows*
increases in the advertising budget.

Three types of empirical research have appeared. Most notably,
Steiner has documented the history of a product category (1978a),
or compared a product category cross-nationally (1979) to demonstrate an inverse advertising–gross margin relationship for the product market as a whole. Many researchers in the second "wave" of
studies have made product category comparisons between markets
(interproduct) with low and high levels of advertising. And last,

brand analyses within a product category (interbrand) have been carried out. The first two types of analyses, especially interproduct, rarely surmount a common problem: inability to eliminate a variety of factors, other than advertising expenditures, that could be influencing the category gross margin. Similarly, all but one (Harris, 1979a,b) of the interbrand analyses do not account for other factors besides advertising that affect variations in brand gross margins within a product category.

Table 3.3 presents a summary of these studies categorized by type of analysis rather than author. Two points are noteworthy:

1. Often the source and characteristics of the data bases were not detailed in the research. Relevant information, however, has been acknowledged as much as possible.
2. Quite often it is not made clear whether the gross margin being discussed is the entire gross distribution margin or just the retail gross margin; often the term "dealer" or "distributor" is used. Furthermore, some authors call the margin from a vertically integrated chain (wholesaler and retailer) the "gross distribution margin"; others, the "retail gross margin"—and it is not obvious whether the "price-in," that is, the merchandise cost, being used in the data base is the price at the factory or wholesale level. However, in all but a few instances, the problem has been taken care of by some cross-checking in the literature. For the remaining cases, it should be remembered that as long as the numbers being compared were formulated consistently, the absolute magnitude of the margin is relatively unimportant for our purposes.

In addition, the following brief account of the various studies is presented as a historical cross-reference, by author, for Table 3.3. The dates enclosed by parentheses refer to the publications, not necessarily the collection of the data for the study:

1. More than 60 years ago the great British economist, Alfred Marshall, wrote briefly in *Industry and Trade* (1919) on the inverse relationship between advertising and dealers' gross margins. Noting that smaller merchants were beginning to capture sales from the larger, traditional merchants by cutting prices on branded (advertised) goods, he stated that these new turn-of-the-century dealers "were inclined to sell branded goods . . . at prices that barely covered expenses" with "the proprietors of such goods . . . selling them wholesale at relatively high prices." He further mentioned how advertising was beginning to limit the market power of the once all-powerful large distributors.

Table 3.3 Summary of Studies on Advertising and Gross Margins

PRODUCT CATEGORY STUDIES

Author	Data Base	Product Category(ies)	Description of Study
Steiner	U.S.; mostly 1880–1900—trade journals	Bicycles	Demonstrates how advertising and the change in method of distribution slashed GDM in a short period of time.
Steiner	U.S., Australia, and France; mid 1950s, early 1970s, and 1977—Toy Manufacturers of America, U.S. Census, LNA, leading chains in Australia and France	Toys	Cross-national and time-series analysis; in U.S., GDM dropped from 49% to 33% to 27–30% with A/S and advertising expenditures at 1% ($11 million), 4.8% ($80 million), and 5½–7% in 1958, 1970, and 1977; in France, no TV advertising of toys allowed and GDM stayed at 50% until a minor allowance in November/December 1975 was followed by dramatic drop in GDMs for those toys allowed to advertise; Australia has mass retailing like U.S., but without toy advertising has high GDM.
Steiner	U.S.; 1963–1973—undisclosed manufacturer information, U.S. Census, McCann-Erickson	Laundry aids	During 1963–1973, real advertising expenditures increased 90% and the GRM dropped by 29% (actual GRMs undisclosed).
EMC	U.K. and Europe; 1970	Chocolate and cocoa mixes	The U.K., with intensive advertising, had lower GRMs than Europe, which had little advertising for this category.
Reekie	U.K.; 1978—10 different four-week periods beginning in Jan., AGB's TCA, MEAL	Fast-moving, inexpensive, consumer goods	Advertising expenditures (lagged two months) preceded declines in GRMs for all but the first month.

INTERPRODUCT STUDIES

Author	Data Base	Product Category(ies)	Description of Study
Borden	U.S.; 1937–1941	Lydia Pinkham Vegetable Compound, other drug products	13.3% GDM for this highly advertised (over $1 million/year since 1920) drug product, while other drug products averaged around a 45% GDM.

NBPI	Appliances, furniture, footwear	U.K.; 1967	Appliances, with mostly brand name products, had lowest GRM; furniture, with little advertising and few brand names, had highest GRM.
NBPI	Paint, children's clothing, household textiles, proprietary medicines	U.K.; 1968	GRMs lower in advertised product categories as higher turnover and less selling effort for retailer.
EMC	Detergents, ice cream	U.K.; 1970—data submitted by Unilever	Though both products had the same manufacturer's selling costs, detergents had a 19% GRM with 2½ times the advertising as ice cream (32% GRM).
Steiner	Toys (various types)	Canada; Nov./Dec. 1972—mail catalogues	Heavily advertised toys (games and dolls) showed 12% and 41.5% GDMs for advertised and unadvertised brands as toys with little advertising (toy musical instruments) had a 48% GDM.
Steiner	Toys (various types)	U.S. and Canada; 1972—interviews with trade buyers	Found a 1:1 inverse relationship with the highest advertised toys earning a 5–10 point lower GRM than the rest.
Nelson	Basic U.S. Census major store types with further divisions for department, drug, and supermarket stores	U.S.; 1972 (but other years in data base)—U.S. Census, trade journals, and LNA	Multiple regression analysis, including various measures of advertising and other market variables; inverse relationship of advertising with GRM, but never significant.
Steiner	Toys, women's apparel	U.S.; 1974 and 1978—NRMA on large department and discount stores, LNA	Comparing toys (heavily advertised industry) and women's apparel (little advertising), toy GDM 5–11 points less than women's apparel.
Reekie	Food categories (25)	U.K.; 1978—13 weeks of ⅔ of the food sales for one food chain, MEAL	Heavily advertised (£10 million/product): 6.0%; moderately advertised (£3.5 million): 11.0%; lightly advertised (£0.5 million): 12.5%, average GRMs.

Table 3.3 *(continued)*

INTERBRAND STUDIES

Author	Data Base	Product Category(ies)	Description of Study
Grether	U.K.; 1935	454 items in 26 drug and chemical product categories	Commonly a 6–12 point differential between the category average GDM and the GDM of the well-known highly advertised brand; similar results for U.S. (San Francisco).
Borden	U.S.; 1937–1941–61 chains, including food, drug, variety, and department	12 drug and 10 grocery products	Investigated intense rivalry between PLs and LNBs; 57 of the 61 chains claimed higher GDMs on own brands than LNBs; compared PLs to the #1 and #2 LNBs in individual categories, and found much lower GDMs for the PLS in drugs (often 35 points) and usually lower GDMs (around 5 points) in food.
Preston	U.S., 1963	27 pairs of national and store brands of grocery products	Private labels have higher GRMs in 21 instances.
NBPI	U.K.; 1967	Appliances, footwear	Nationally advertised brands of footwear a 0–11% GRM, whereas unbranded had 20–35% GRMs; similar inverse relationship for appliances.
NBPI	U.K.; 1968	Proprietary medicines	Nationally advertised brands carry a before-purchase tax GRM of 18–25% as the unadvertised brands are at 25–33.3%.
Steiner	U.S.; 1971—3 different types of chain stores	Toys	Advertised brands GDMs 25 points below unadvertised brands in a department store, discount store, and small toy chain.
Elliot Research Corp.	Canada; 1972—70 stores in 6 cities for 100 toys	Toys	Using a heavy-medium-light classification of toy TV advertising, calculated GDMs of 20.2%, 31.4%, and 46.1%—a larger point differential than in a similar stratification by sales turnover.

Source	Data	Product	Findings
Steiner	U.S.; 1975—43 stores in Cincinnati, 21 brands in 7 categories	Health aids	For group of 7 health aids, GDMs of LNBs, MUBs, and PLs of 15.5%, 39.7%, and 49.2%; comparisons on individual basis of leading aspirins with their PL counterparts showed a roughly 10% GDM for the LNBs, with 10 times the advertising as the PLs (GDMs around 40%).
Steiner	U.S.; November/December 1975—same as above plus 3 LNBs and 2 MUBs, for 26 brands total	Health aids	Multiple regression explaining GDM; with a .76 R^2, the GDMs of LNBs were found to be significantly different (.001 level) than the GDMs of PLs and MUBs.
Harris	U.S.; April 1973–March 1977—one large cooperative food chain serving 450 retail stores, 275 wholesalers, and 8 selected retailers included with 6 largest manufacturers	Ready-to-eat breakfast cereals	Multiple regression analysis (82 observations) at wholesale and retail level; explaining GWM and GRM with 24 regressions: 12 for each, with 3 for each of the 4 annual periods; 4 independent variables in each regression explaining margins: advertising expenditure, proxies for handling costs and stage in the product life cycle, and a measure of unit sales (linear or logarithmic) or inventory turnover; R^2s average 0.50 with the unit sales or turnover measure contributing at least 80% of the R^2; advertising is consistently negative, but significant only 4 times, and the weakest variable (0–9% of R^2) two thirds of the time.
Reekie	U.K.; 1976 and 1977—one large manufacturer; AGB, MEAL	A fast moving, heavily advertised, frequently purchased food product	Heavily advertised: 10%; moderately advertised: 16%; lightly advertised: 19%, average GDMs.
U.K. Price Commission	U.K.; 1978	Paint (emulsion and glass)	Advertising encourages retailer to accept lower GRMs.

Abbreviations

GDM; GRM; GWM	Gross distribution margin; gross retail margin; gross wholesale margin
A/S	Advertising-to-sales ratio
LNA; MEAL	Leading National Advertisers, for U.S.; similar data for the U.K.
EMC; NBPI	English Monopolies Commission; U.K. National Board for Prices and Incomes
AGB; TCA	Audits of Great Britain Ltd.; Television Consumer Audit
NRMA	U.S. National Retail Merchants Association
LNB; PL; NUB	Leading national brand; private label; manufacturer's unadvertised brand
Points	The absolute numerical difference between two percentages

2. Ewald T. Grether (1935, 1939) worked zealously for fair trade laws (resale price maintenance) in both the United States and the United Kingdom. His many studies continually showed that, as he stated, "on the whole" . . . "very frequently" . . . "almost invariably" . . . "the better known, highly advertised brands carry smaller margins that the average of their class" . . . and "almost all the smallest margins are for highly advertised brands." He examined dealers' gross margins in both countries, before and after resale price maintenance. Though resale price maintenance considerably narrowed the margin discrepancy, the well-known advertised brands still sold at lower dealers' gross margins than the product category averages.

3. In his landmark book, *The Economic Effects of Advertising* (1942), Neil Borden compiled many case histories, most of which repeatedly illustrated that advertising reduces the distributors' gross margins. Finding a "wide differential taken upon the brands (private labels) for different classes of merchandise," he concluded that to determine any competitive pricing rules, each product category must be considered separately. His analyses of drug products (during retail price maintenance) were reproduced thirty-seven years later by Steiner, with similar findings of large margin differentials between private label brands and leading, nationally advertised brands. Borden's analyses of food products showed no differential in one product category (breakfast cereals—corn flakes only) and a slightly higher margin for the leading brands in another (canned milk), but he dismissed these as "in contrast to the margins obtained for many other products studied." Thus ended the first wave of research in this area.

4. One quarter of a century elapsed before the next surge of research appeared in the field (other than the solitary 1963 Preston study which compared supermarket margins of 27 pairs of national and store brands). As reported by Polany (1972) and Reekie (1979), the U.K. National Board of Prices and Incomes carried out some studies in the late 1960s, drawing both interproduct and interbrand comparisons. Realizing that margins must reflect various functions distributors perform, they concluded that "margins allowed in continuously advertised products . . . tend to be lower than on those products which are not new and not widely advertised, and which, therefore, have lower turnover or require more selling effort by the retailer." The Board became the British Monopolies Commission in the early 1970s and continued to examine some product categories. Finally, in 1978, the U.K. Price Commission, carrying out a

similar analysis, posited that at least within a product category (interbrand), it appeared that it is the level of sales—stimulated by brand avertising—that encourages the retailer to place a lower gross margin òn these brands than the unadvertised ones in that product category.

5. Phillip Nelson (1978), in attempting to develop empirically some of the implications of the advertising = market competition model, has produced regression results showing an interproduct inverse relationship between advertising and retail gross margin. Nelson contends that the retail gross margin is "payment for services that are substitutes for consumer search expenditures . . . the demand for this substitute increases as the demand for search increases." Therefore, the greater the level of advertising, the less search is necessary (due to greater preshopping knowledge), and the less the retail gross margin, as the retailer does less for the consumer. Nelson's data base is a collection of a variety of years (department store margins: 1964–65; drug stores: 1950–51; supermarkets: 1960; U.S. Census of Retailers, 1972), but without further explanation, he maintains "the procedure I used reduced the impact of variation in dates or sources on the calculation of gross margins." Given the circumstances and an interproduct analysis with little control for other factors, it is surprising that Nelson found any relationship, not that the relationship was statistically insignificant.

6. In this same British tradition, W. Duncan Reekie (1979) has conducted a number of different analyses: the interbrand margin variation for a food product, the interproduct margin variation for a group of food products sold at a sizeable, successful food chain, and, most interestingly, the product margin variation over time for a fast-moving consumer product. Unfortunately Reekie presents his results in two short tables and a graph, with little discussion of his research methodology. In the case of the large food chain, even though it may indeed be "representative," the "selective elimination" of 7 of the 32 product categories can be seriously questioned for sampling bias; no further reasons are given. The time-series analysis with no explanation of why that period of time. Furthermore, the graph does not clearly show the relationship asserted in the text. Still, as Reekie contends, all his analyses demonstrate an inverse relationship between advertising and gross margin.

7. Brian Harris (1979a), in his Ph.D. dissertation, designed the only comprehensive examination of advertising and gross margins. The ready-to-eat cereal market, at the wholesale and retail level, constituted the data base. The results showed an inverse,

but insignificant, relationship of advertising with gross margins at both levels of analysis, thus questioning the importance of brand advertising—independent of sales and inventory turn-over—in determining gross margins. His research design is superior to any other study. However, the analysis is of only one product category.

8. Robert Steiner (1973, 1978a,b, 1979), particularly in his un-published manuscript, "Brand Advertising and the Consumer Goods Economy," reports on a number of historical studies (especially bicycles and toys) to illustrate a fundamental principle of his dual-stage model: Advertising works to reduce the gross distribution margin. Beginning with the toy industry, in which Steiner was a principal manufacturer for many years, he has studied a variety of product categories—each with a different industrial structure—and has found continually this inverse re-lationship. His analyses cover many countries, time periods (including pre–World War II), sources of data (including Elliot Research Corp., to Cincinnati stores, to the U.S. Census, to leading chains in Australia and France), and research metho-dologies (time-series, cross-section, descriptive statistics, regression). Unfortunately he offers no comprehensive analysis of the relationship, including how it might vary in significance among categories.

In summation, it should be emphasized that many of the meth-odologies, especially the interproduct and product category analyses, are questionable, while the extrapolability of most of the results may be limited considerably. Still, all these studies have shown the ex-pected inverse relationship between advertising and gross margins, excepting a few of both Borden's and Preston's findings in food products. Critical unanswered questions remain: How strong is this inverse relationship? Which components of the relationship, such as the effect of advertising on gross margin through its concomitant effect on unit sales volume, prices, competition, and so on are most important? Is the relationship linear? Does the strength of the re-lationship vary among product categories? The remainder of this book answers these questions, with important implications for man-agers and policymakers alike.

Summary

In this chapter, two relatively new models for analyzing the economic impact of advertising on consumer price and the empirical studies on the relationship of manufacturers' advertising to the gross distribution margin have been discussed. The Porter and Steiner models recognize the role of distributors, particularly retailers, in both the sale of the manufacturer's product and the dissemination of information to consumers. These models focus on the role of manufacturers' advertising and its effects on the interactions between manufacturer and retailer and among retailers. Through the lens of these models, much of the seemingly contradictory evidence on advertising, prices, and price sensitivity can be reconciled, and the two opposing views synthesized.

Porter focuses on the ability of advertising to increase the manufacturer's bargaining power over the retailers in the market. The extent of this increased bargaining power was shown to depend on the nature of the consumer's demand for product information through advertising: The more the consumer relies on the retailer to provide product information, the less effective is advertising as an instrument of market power for the manufacturer. As such, Porter offers insights into the retailer's role in the market, maintaining that the structure of the retail sector signals the nature of consumer demand for different sources of information about a product. One of the main implications of his work is that the character of consumer demand for information may well influence the economic effects of advertising in a product market.

Whereas Porter analyzes the effects of advertising for the manufacturer at any one point in time, Steiner develops a model of the entire chain of effects of advertising in a product market over time, with added emphasis on the distribution sector and consumer prices. He points out that the motive of a manufacturer who advertises is not necessarily to increase the consumer price of the brand, but rather to increase the number (or quality) of outlets carrying the brand, the dealers' support of the brand, the brand's factory price relative to its consumer price, or some combination of all these factors. Indeed, just as advertising can increase the market power of the manufacturer and the manufacturer's bargaining power over the retailer, it can in the same circumstance, Steiner notes, increase price competition among the retailers selling the advertised brand. The result: *Advertising can decrease price elasticity for the manufacturer and at the same time increase the price elasticity facing the retailer.* Therefore, in his view, although the manufacturer's advertising may lead to a higher factory price to retailers, it does not necessarily lead to a higher retail price to consumers to the same extent. The impact of the manufacturer's advertising on the brand's gross distribution margin—a function of these two price elasticities—must be taken into account: Advertising leads to lower gross margins.

The major contribution of these models is their explicit recognition of the role of the marketing channel as more than a passive participant in a product market. As a result, with dramatic implications for measuring the effect of advertising on consumer price, the inverse relationship between manufacturers' advertising and the gross margin of distribution, a relationship with more than eighty years of scattered empirical support can be realized. However, this past evidence has been based on relatively unsophisticated methods with little understanding of the nature of the relationship:—its strength, components, shape, and variation among product categories. The next step, therefore, is to focus on the economics of the retailer and the effect of manufacturers' advertising on the retailer's decision making. Chapters 4, 5, and 6 examine the economics of the mass retailer and the reasons why brand gross margins differ among product categories. These reasons have important implications for advertising budgeters, retail managers, and public policymakers.

Endnotes

1. Preface by R. E. Caves in W. S. Comanor and T. A. Wilson, *Advertising and Market Power* (Cambridge, Mass.: Harvard University Press, 1974), p. xiii.
2. Porter assumes in his model that information gathering about brands in one product category is independent from information gathering about brands in another product category. This assumption allows the informational context of each product category to be treated separately.
3. M. E. Porter, *Interbrand Choice, Strategy, and Bilateral Market Power* (Cambridge, Mass.: Harvard University Press, 1976), pp. 96–97.
4. Porter does not explicitly consider the retailers in the market, but rather focuses on how the retail structure, as a proxy for consumers' demand for information in the market, affects manufacturers' profits. Statements concerning the retailer, therefore, have been inferred by this author from Porter's model.
5. *Ibid.*, p. 34.
6. R. L. Steiner, *Brand Advertising and the Consumer Goods Economy* (Unpublished manuscript, 1979).
7. R. L. Steiner, "A Dual Stage Approach to the Effects of Brand Advertising on Competition and Price," in J. F. Cady (ed.), "Marketing and the Public Interest," Report No. 78–105 (Cambridge, Mass.: Marketing Science Institute, July 1978), p. 145.
8. E. Fogg-Meade, "The Place of Advertising in Modern Business," *Journal of Political Economy*, 9 (March, 1901), p. 241.

Chapter 4

ECONOMICS OF THE MASS RETAILER

The profitability of retailers in an industry is an important aspect of the ultimate impact of manufacturers' advertising on retail pricing behavior. Yet little research has been done to further our understanding of the economics of the retailer, particularly in the United States.[1] Rather, marketing researchers have looked at the marketing channel in terms of the manufacturer's strategy or else focused on specific situations in distribution management. Economists have implicitly assumed that all distributors are passive participants in the market—operating as a derived demand of consumer wants satisfied by manufacturers' products. As noted by Caves and associates, these models have become increasingly incomplete with the rise of mass retailers:[2]

> *This picture of retailing is increasingly inadequate. The chain retail store has risen as the retailing sector's answer to the large manufacturing firm . . . The chain's bargaining power can shape the way that manufacturers distribute and market their products and can provide a check against manufacturers even without the exercise of conventional monopoly power. Thus the retail stage is of central interest . . . as it has the power to influence significantly conduct and performance in the manufacturing sector.*

Furthermore, the power of mass retailers is important to recognize in ascertaining not only the most profitable competitive strategy for the manufacturing firm, but also the ultimate effect of a manufacturer's policy (such as advertising) on the market outcome (the retail price). And as we demonstrated earlier, the price of the retailer's services to consumers—the retail gross margin—is a critical variable in the effect of advertising on price in a product market.

In these next three chapters we look at the mass retailer (the chain store) and focus on why and how the price of retail services varies among product categories and for brands within a category. For example, to understand why Bumble Bee tuna has a lower retail gross margin than a Hershey's candy bar, two phenomena must be explained: why canned tuna has a lower average retail gross margin than candy bars and why Bumble Bee has a lower gross margin than other canned tunas. In so doing we will isolate the impact of advertising on the retail gross margin among brands within a product category—called the *interbrand* relationship of advertising and gross margin. "Gross margin" will always refer to the "average retail gross margin" and "advertising" to "manufacturers' advertising" unless otherwise stated.

To understand the nature of this relationship, we first describe the retailer's economic environment, essentially the revenues, costs, and competition. After this discussion, the model formulation for the analysis of product category and brand gross margins is presented to introduce the descriptive model of the next two chapters and the empirical work to follow. Whereas the model has been constructed to apply most generally to mass retailers of consumer, convenience goods, *the retail supermarket is used as the prototype*. The supermarket is the quintessential mass retailer, commonly part of a large regional or national chain. Furthermore, food is a class of products that is important to all consumers, accounting for over one fifth of all retail sales and over one seventh of all retail outlets in the United States. And over 60 percent of all food sales are made by retail chains—stores usually vertically integrated backward into wholesaling, that is, stores that buy directly from the manufacturers and then warehouse the goods or sell them immediately to consumers—so it can be assumed that the retail gross margin is essentially equivalent to the gross margin of distribution. Accordingly, the empirical tests of our model use supermarket products as the data base and the retail gross margin as the measure of the cost of distributors' services to consumers.

The Mass Retailer

The supermarket retailer must make a variety of decisions, not uncommonly on as many as 12,000 items stocked at the store. Each individual decision depends on other store decisions and on actions taken by the retailer's competition. Moreover, all decisions are influenced by the retailer's goals. Within this framework marked by interdependencies in decision making, it is important to understand the operations of the mass retailer.

To simplify our model of the mass retailer, some assumptions are necessary. In no instance does removing an assumption or group of assumptions seriously affect the conclusions or implications drawn from the model. Rather, the assumptions are drawn to maintain the realism of the model while eliminating what are felt to be unnecessary complications that would sidetrack the discussion into areas that are, for our purposes, of secondary importance. In this vein, assumptions are made about the structure of the distribution channel, firm ownership, the retailer's goals, the primary retail decisions, and the nature of competition.

First, it is assumed that the manufacturer sells a brand directly to the retailer, who sells directly to the consumer. This assumption makes the retail gross margin essentially equivalent to the gross margin of distribution, so we need not be concerned with the economic behavior of wholesalers in the product markets. As previously mentioned, in mass retailing, chains are often vertically integrated into wholesaling, so the assumption of no wholesaler in this model should not be a serious omission. The chain commonly has its own warehouse (true for our data base) and either stores its products or immediately puts them on the retail shelves. Accordingly, only two prices are involved in the distribution channel—the factory price and retail price—as the chain buys directly from the manufacturer. The factory price, therefore, is approximately equal to the retailer's merchandise cost,[3] and these two prices, which represent the retailer's buying and selling price, can be used to compute the *gross margin:* the difference between the retail price (such as 50¢) and the factory price (such as 40¢) as a percentage of the retail price [that is, $(50¢ - 40¢)/50¢ = 10¢/50¢ = 20$ percent gross margin]. Wholesalers can be included in the distribution channel as long as the wholesale margin is independent of the retail gross margin on a product. For the most part, wholesale margins are independent of the sale of a particular product to a retailer, as these margins commonly depend on the size of a retailer's total order for many products from a wholesaler, not the size of an individual product order.

Second, it is assumed that the retail firm owns self-service outlets already constructed in a particular geographic market. The decision of outlet size, therefore, is eliminated. Moreover, it is assumed that each store in the chain makes individual, independent decisions, as would any independent firm. In other words, potential coordination of store policies within a retail chain is not an issue. This assumption prevents the possibility that one of the outlets would carry out a policy that might maximize the firm's profits, but not that particular store's profits. For example, the chain may be able to buy a particular product in quantity at a very low price. This product is then ware-housed and sold at all the chain's outlets—even though certain outlets would not individually choose to carry this product. In short, this assumption allows us to examine the retailer's policies, such as prod-uct selection and pricing, without having to worry about any differ-ences in decision making between the retail chain as a whole and any one outlet; each outlet (and retailer) is assumed to be repre-sentative of the entire retail chain.

Finally, it is assumed that the retailer maximizes *profits*, a term defined shortly. To maximize store profits, the mass retailer must make a variety of interdependent decisions about product mix, pric-ing, space allocation, and customer services. These decisions appear in Table 4.1. It is assumed in the analysis that some decisions are more prominent than others. The product-mix decision, that is, the selection of which product categories (such as pickles) and which brands (Vlasic pickles) to carry at the store, is important for both category and brand selection. Pricing is more important for each brand than for each product category, because once the retailer has priced each brand (Vlasic, Heinz, Cain's, private label, and so on), the price of the product category is simply the weighted average (with the unit volumes as weights) of the prices of the various brands carried in that category. Conversely, once shelf space has been al-located for each product category, the allocation of shelf space among the brands is a secondary consideration—particularly as compared with the pricing of each brand.[4] Table 4.1 offers a logical order of the decisions, considering the inherent simultaneity of decision mak-ing. Customer services are of relatively minor importance for our

Table 4.1 The Mass Retailer's Decisions

Product Mix
  • What and how many product categories to carry
  • What and how many brands to carry in each product category
  • What and how many items to carry of each brand

*Space Allocation**
  • How much space to allocate to each product category
  • How much space to allocate to each brand in each product category
  • How much space to allocate to each item of each brand

Customer Services
  • What kinds of services to provide
  • How much of each service selected to provide

Pricing
  • How much to charge for each item

---

* Subcategories are where and how to display items, brands, and product categories.

purposes; even if they are not, they can be assumed to be deter-mined independently. Accordingly, we are interested in the profit-maximizing decisions of the mass retailer primarily in terms of the selection of product categories and their brands, the shelf space allocated to each product category, and the pricing of the brands carried.

Retail Profit Maximization

The goal of the retailer should be to maximize the *total contribution* to fixed costs and profits of the store's entire product mix, that is, of all the products in the store. *Contribution* is defined as the retail price less the variable costs of the product in question and may be used to apply to an item, brand, product category, or even, as in this instance, all the products carried by the retailer. (The term *direct product profit* is often used by retailers instead of contribu-tion.) A product's *net margin* is used in a similar sense, except that net margin is measured as a percentage of sales, whereas contribution and direct product profit are not. For example, if a product sells for $2.00 with variable costs of $1.90, the contribution (or direct product profit) is 10¢ per unit; the net margin is 5 percent [($2.00–$1.90)/$2.00 = $0.10/$2.00 = 0.05 or 5 percent]. "Total" signifies the number of units sold, rather than a per unit measurement, in a given time period. So, if 100 units are sold, the total contribution of the product is $10.00 (100 × $0.10 = $10.00). For the store, after deducting the total variable costs from total revenue, the total con-tribution is left over to "cover" the store's fixed costs, with the amount remaining termed total net profit (before taxes). Therefore, when it is acknowledged that the retailer is maximizing *profits*, it is said with the concept of *contribution* in mind.

While difficulties do not usually arise for the retailer in computing the contribution of the entire store, assigning variable costs to individual products is not so easy. Because many of these costs apply to more than one product, assigning costs other than the merchandise costs to any particular product can be difficult. Employees shelve many products, for instance, making it difficult to accurately assign labor costs to individual products. Furthermore, in the long run certain components of overhead need to be allocated to individual products. Most allocation methods, based on product contribution, therefore, depend on the contribution not only of that product but of the other products as well. For example, utilities are used by all the products in the store. Consider the implications in assigning these costs to two dry packaged goods: If the contribution of one declines, not only is the overhead burden reduced for that product, but the burden must be increased for the other dry packaged good. When a store carries more than 12,000 individual items, the feasibility and complexity of this method becomes overwhelming, particularly since the long-run contribution of any one product cannot even be computed until overhead is assigned to *all* the products at the store.

Including only merchandise costs in the profit calculations results in the retailer's maximizing gross, not net, margin. The difference between gross and net margin—critical in calculating a product's contribution—is found in costs other than the actual cost of the merchandise. As such, some imputation of the variable costs associated with individual products is essential for determining the relative profitability of different products. A number of methods for arriving at this determination have been devised over the years, all far better than merely looking at a product's gross margin, even if the method is as simple as assigning costs to products on the basis of unit or dollar sales, gross margin, shelf space, and the like. A brief review of the literature on these methods is worthwhile, since in trying to ascertain how the mass retailer prices different products, the effect of manufacturers' advertising on retail pricing behavior depends on how the retailer tries to maximize store profits, that is, total contribution, in each individual product decision.

Review of Direct Product Profitability Literature

Beginning with the pioneering effort of the 1929 Louisville Grocery Survey (U.S. Department of Commerce, 1931), cost allocation efforts have been made by researchers. The Louisville study grouped retail operating costs into three categories, each with a different allocation method: (1) maintenance costs (rent, utilities, repairs), allocated by product's share of total inventory investment: (2) movement costs (selling, advertising, delivery, order assembly), allocated by product's share of total transactions; and (3) credit costs, allocated by dollar sales. In the 1950s and the early 1960s, Kriesberg and Lieman (1961) carried out similar analyses for the U.S. Department of Agriculture, with a division of costs into two categories, analogous to maintenance costs (indirect or overhead) and movement costs (direct or handling). Credit costs were no longer relevant, as supermarkets no longer sold on credit very often. Unfortunately, however, little effort was made by retailers to integrate this research into their decision making. As noted in the McKinsey–National Association of Food Chains Report (1962), many chains were still basing decisions on gross margin dollars.

Although the Louisville and Kriesberg studies were the first to attempt to allocate retail costs to individual products and measure product profit, it was the McKinsey–General Food Study (1963) that popularized the concept of "direct product profitability" (equivalent to "contribution"). Not only was a cost allocation scheme proposed, similar to manufacturers' standard cost accounting, but direct product profit *per measure of shelf space* (cubic feet in this instance) was considered as a return-on-investment surrogate. In addition, the study also provided a basis for relating direct product profits to the level of sales. The success of this study was shown by the number of companies that attempted to adapt this model to their own decision making.

A test of the direct product-profit criterion for supermarket merchandising decisions was reported in the Buzzell, Salmon, and Vancil study (1965). They found that retailers could "increase total profit for a product family by shifting space from historically less profitable to more profitable items, and by eliminating items with low profitability," supporting the McKinsey hypothesis that shelf space could best be allocated on the basis of direct product profit per cubic foot. They also noted that any basis for decision making should include four factors: gross margin, rate of movement, shelf space occupied, and costs attributable to the individual product. Case and Company's Cosmos system was designed to do just that, but operationally it was found that it was too difficult to keep up with all the merchandise changes, and that the operation of the system was ponderous, requiring night-long computer runs. Approximately four supermarket chains use an abbreviated version of Cosmos today.[5]

Profit Maximization for Individual Products

The literature on direct product profitability facilitates a more precise definition of profit maximization for individual products carried by the retailer. The concept of total contribution applies readily to the store's entire product mix and to individual products as well, with one important refinement: It is assumed that the pricing (more broadly, the merchandising) of each individual product does not affect the sale of any other product(s) in the store. This simplifying assumption allows us to consider profit maximization for individual products.

In reality, the mass retailer rarely can maximize the total profits of the store by optimizing with respect to each individual product or group of products. The reason is that the merchandising of certain products—that is, the pricing, retail advertising, and so on—affects the sales of other products in the store. Traffic-building products, such as Heinz catsup or many staples, are not necessarily priced to maximize profits for the individual product but rather for the store as a whole. Accordingly, because of their ability to affect store traffic and thereby the sales (and profits) of other products, they are priced below what would be predicted by any standard set by an individual profit-maximization criterion—and often priced to sell at a loss, called "loss leading." The importance of these product interdependencies is acknowledged in our analysis of retail pricing in the two chapters that follow. But first, we wish to establish a standard of what profit maximization for individual products entails; then, with this reference point, we can more clearly discuss the effect of these traffic-building abilities on the pricing of certain products. For the majority of products, however, these traffic-building abilities are slight or nonexistent, so the analysis of this section remains essentially unchanged.

As already demonstrated, contribution is a better criterion than gross margin. The retailer is concerned with how much profit is made on a product after all relevant expenses have been considered, not just the cost of purchasing the product for sale. Still, two further refinements are necessary to compare accurately the relative profitability of different products. As in the Buzzell, Salmon, and Vancil study, these refinements recognize the importance of the rate of movement, sometimes referred to as turnover, and shelf space occupied, sometimes called the value-bulk relationship, of a product. The two propositions are:[6]

1. The greater the rate of movement of a product, the greater its total contribution per unit of time, and
2. The greater the amount of shelf space occupied by a product, the less its total contribution per unit of shelf space.

These two propositions indicate that the retailer wishes to maximize the *total contribution per unit of shelf space (per unit of time)*. Some examples and the introduction of the critical concept of *opportunity costs*—essential throughout the next two chapters as well—will help illustrate these propositions.

For instance, if a supermarket retailer is deciding upon which of two brands in a product category to stock, say Dole or Libby's pineapple chunks, each of comparable size (8 ounces), contribution, and shelf space requirements, the rate of movement—that is, the unit sales per unit of time, computed in the notion of *total* contribution—becomes the determining factor. If the retailer believes, for example, that 1,000 cans of Dole can be sold in one year, but only 500 cans of Libby's, then Dole is twice as profitable to stock. Similarly, if the retailer is considering whether or not to allocate more shelf space to a roll of Scott paper towels or a bottle of Tabasco sauce, each with the same total contribution, it is more profitable to use the additional shelf space for the bottle of Tabasco sauce simply because the Tabasco sauce uses less shelf space. Whereas the decisions may be thought of in terms of the total contribution per unit of shelf space, the underlying notion in both situations is that of the *opportunity cost of shelf space* for the retailer.

Shelf space has a relatively fixed cost and is a relatively fixed resource for the retailer. The cost of shelf space, however, should be viewed not only through the accountant's concept of direct cost (the rental cost), but also through the economist's notion of opportunity costs, that is, the forgone income from a particular use of a fixed resource rather than the best alternative use. This notion tries to impute a value to the use of a fixed resource, shelf space, not simply the cost of obtaining that resource. Depending on factors such as the rental cost of shelf space and the total contribution of the store, the direct cost allocated to the space may be less than, equal to, or greater than the opportunity cost of that space. In the long run, however, a newly built store should equalize these two costs.

The notion of opportunity costs is not easy for those newly acquainted with the concept to understand, but it can best be thought of as the "pessimistic" counterpart to total contribution. Optimistically speaking, the retailer wishes to maximize the total contribution of the store by making the best merchandise selections, positioning products most advantageously on the shelves, pricing optimally, and providing the right amount of customer services. If all is done just right, the store attains the maximum total contribution possible. However, if there is just one wrong decision, the total contribution will be less than the most possible. In other words, there is some loss in contribution that was obtainable—hence, an *opportunity loss*. Conversely, the notion of opportunity costs implies that the retailer should try to minimize this opportunity loss, sometimes called the *net opportunity cost*, which is the difference between the total contribution of the best alternative use (the opportunity cost) and the total contribution realized from the current use of the fixed resource (in this instance, the retail shelf space). Minimizing costs is simply the other side of maximizing profits.

Opportunity costs can be thought of over time (the rate of movement) or at any one point in time (the shelf space required), since the cost and use of a fixed resource depends on *how long* (movement) and *how much* (shelf space) of the resource is needed. A product that "sells faster" (Dole) contributes more per unit of shelf space than a slower-moving product (Libby's), and this contribution is used to cover the costs of the shelf space. Similarly, a product that takes up less shelf space (Tabasco sauce) has lower fixed costs to cover with its contribution than one that takes up more space (Scott paper towels), since less of the fixed resource is used. Shelf space, therefore, is both a fixed cost the retailer must eventually allocate to the products carried to stay in business and a fixed resource the retailer can use for contribution to store profits from a variety of products. The greater a product's rate of movement, the less of the fixed cost of the shelf space used that must be allocated to each individual unit sold; the greater a product's shelf space requirement, the more of the fixed resource is used and the less is available for other products.

In the next chapter, when we recognize that the sales of some products, called traffic builders, can affect the sales of other products at the store, valuing shelf space in terms of the total contribution of products using that space will underestimate the value of the space used by traffic builders and, concomitantly, overestimate the value of the shelf space used by the other products. The notion of opportunity costs, however, is flexible enough to allow for this "indirect" contribution and therefore is better able to describe the underlying economics of the mass retailer.

Cost Structure

The mass retailer has two types of costs (alternatively referred to as expenses), fixed and variable, of which some may be discretionary expenditures, others not. Fixed costs do not vary in the short run with changes in output or any other variable; variable costs vary directly with output. In the short run only variable costs are attributed to individual products to determine contribution. In the long run all costs are considered variable and are attributed to the products to determine contribution. The retailer thinks in terms of *operating costs*, which includes a variable and fixed portion. In the short run, only the variable portion is considered, but in the long run, all costs need to be included so that the retail price will be high enough to cover the total costs of the store and generate a satisfactory return on equity.

With the supermarket chain store used again as our prototype of mass retailing, Table 4.2 displays the "Operating Results of Food Chains" for the years 1977–1978 and 1978–1979 (each May to April). These years were selected to correspond with the years of the data base used in the research. The calculations are based on 53 chains operating 8,021 stores in 1977–1978 and 48 chains with 4,709 stores in 1978–1979.

This table offers a detailed look at the supermarket's cost structure.

Table 4.2 **Gross Margin, Expenses, and Earnings for Food Chains (Percent of Sales)**

Item	1977–1978	1978–1979
Gross margin	21.74	21.93
Expense		
Payroll	12.34	12.23
Supplies	1.03	.99
Utilities	1.08	1.04
Communications	.08	.08
Travel	.09	.08
Services purchased	1.29	1.13
Promotional activities	.40	.31
Professional services	.06	.06
Donations	.01	.01
Insurance	.90	.88
Taxes and licenses	1.00	.90
Property rentals	1.25	1.13
Equipment rentals	.18	.14
Depreciation and amortization	.69	.81
Repairs	.61	.63
Unclassified	.97	1.19
Credits and allowances	− .59	− .61
Total expenses before interest	21.40	20.99
Total interest	.57	.61
Total expenses including interest	21.97	21.60
Net operating profit	− .22	.32
Other income and deductions		
Credit for imputed interest	.41	.42
Cash discounts	.59	.61
Other revenue	.06	.34
Total net other income	1.07	1.37
Total net before income tax	.84	1.70
Total income tax	.33	.77
Total net earnings	.51	.93

SOURCE: Cornell University, "Operating Results of Food Chains," 1978–79, p. 44.

From the 1978–1979 figures, it can be seen that over 78 percent of sales revenue is accounted for by the cost of merchandise. Of the items listed under "expense," some are variable, some fixed, and many are what is often termed semifixed, that is, containing elements of both fixed and variable costs. Keeping this in mind, we can group these costs under the headings "fixed" and "variable." The item names are abbreviated from Table 4.2:

1. *Fixed Costs*—costs that would remain even if nothing were sold:
   - Rent and utilities (2.31 percent)
   - Depreciation and insurance (1.69 percent)
   - Taxes and interest (1.51 percent)
   - Repairs (0.63 percent)
   - Miscellaneous fixed (1.35 percent)
     (communications travel, services purchased, professional services, donations)
2. *Variable Costs*—costs required to operate the supermarket on a daily basis:
   - Merchandise (78.07 percent)
   - Payroll (12.23 percent)
   - Supplies (0.99 percent)
   - Promotional activities (0.31 percent)

The fixed costs should reflect the amount of real capital utilized. It is questionable, therefore, whether the "depreciation" and "repairs" classifications are redundant. Rent is basically a fixed cost; however, warehouse space used for inventory, for instance, is easily leased so that it may be considered as nearly a variable cost. Likewise, good reasons may be advanced for including at least the discretionary portion of the "miscellaneous fixed" costs as mostly variable. Discretionary fixed costs do not necessarily vary with output, but in contrast to necessary fixed costs, they are not well defined when nothing is sold at the store and are subject to change in the short run by management policy, such as donations. With these limitations acknowledged and given the above, 7.5 percent of sales revenue went to these fixed costs in 1978–1979.

The same problems occur in trying to ascertain the percentage of costs that are variable. Some discretionary fixed costs may be part of payroll and promotional activities, especially since headquarter's activities are included in the data base. The administrative portion of the payroll, therefore, could be categorized as a fixed cost. In addition, the income tax may be considered a variable, although non-operating, cost. As a group, variable costs total 91.6 percent of sales revenue, 13.5 percent excluding merchandise costs.

This brief look at the cost structure of the supermarket retailer provides some perspective on the relative magnitudes of the different costs. Merchandise costs account for almost four fifths of the retailer's total costs and over 85 percent of variable costs. We have not attempted to determine which costs should be allocated to individual products so that the product's contribution may be calculated. Instead, we have outlined what the retailer's costs are, what decisions are required, and what is involved in maximizing profits. All of these considerations affect the retailer's pricing policy and handling of manufacturers' advertised brands. The economics of any mass retailer, however, can be'fully understood only within the context of the surrounding dynamic competitive environment.

The Competitive Environment

The reaction of competitors strongly influences the pricing policies undertaken by the retailer and the effectiveness of the policies selected. In trying to maintain current store traffic and possibly draw additional customers away from competing institutions, the retailer must measure the strategies of competitors to predict which promotions and which strategies will be most successful. Economic theory offers two extreme models of competition: perfect competition and monopoly. Placed somewhere between these polar opposites, however, is Edward Chamberlin's model of *monopolistic competition* (1933, 1962). This model is chosen as the most accurate representation of retailing in general and, in particular, supermarket retailing. But first, a brief review of some of the research in this area illustrates some of the important considerations relevant to ascertaining the type of market competition that occurs in retailing. The framework selected is crucial to one of the main tenets of the entire book: *Manufacturers' advertising increases retail price competition.*

Hood and Yamey (1951) have been the chief proponents of the view that retailing is best characterized by a perfect competition model since there is, in their opinion, free entry, difficulty in colluding due to the number of products sold at each outlet, and a large number of buyers and sellers. Their argument is based on the contention that a local retail market is extended geographically by what they call the "chain-linking" of this market with other local markets. The extent of this chain-linking depends, in their view, primarily upon two factors: (1) the mobility of consumers, which rests on the ease of transportation, and (2) the importance of locational convenience to shoppers, which is affected by the importance of the goods to be purchased and time to the shoppers. Hood and Yamey conclude that the mere counting of buyers and sellers in a local area seriously underestimates the numbers in the market.

On the other hand, as demonstrated in the studies reviewed by Havenga (1973), most researchers have agreed that retailing is best characterized by some form of imperfect competition. Lady Margaret Hall (1949), most notably, has maintained that competition in retailing is imperfect since "identical articles sell at very different prices in the same neighborhood." Her position is based on the nature of consumers' demand: Differences in tastes and the spatial character of demand limit the size of the market. Moreover, the form of imperfect competition used to describe retailing has most often been Chamberlin's model of monopolistic competition, which concentrates on the firm and its external relations rather than on any notion of a single market for some heterogeneous product. In retailing, where each store is differentiated at least by location, the number of firms in a market is not well defined. Chamberlin's model explicitly recognizes this fact.

The four conditions of perfect competition are product homogeneity, large numbers of buyers and sellers, easy entry, and perfect information. Chamberlin's model is based on the proposition that the firms in a market sell heterogeneous products—"slightly differentiated products," in his words—implying that each firm faces a downward-sloping demand curve, not the horizontal demand curve experienced by perfectly competitive firms. He states of retailing (1962) that "each 'product' is rendered unique by the individuality of the establishment in which it is sold, including its locations. . . . The factor of convenience differentiates the product spatially, . . . an impediment to others producing the same thing in the same market." Chamberlin concludes that in the long run (all costs variable), however, with relatively free entry, a monopolistically competitive market arrives at a zero profit equilibrium—that is, an equilibrium with firms making only competitive profits and having lower output and higher prices than under perfect competition. This type of equilibrium is the result of too many new firms entering the market. When too many firms are in the market, operating costs increase at each store because of decreased volume per store, as operating costs, which include fixed costs in the long run, are inversely related to volume (scale economies). Furthermore, this equilibrium result of only competitive profits (approximately equal to the firm's cost of capital) occurs because of the inability of the retailer to raise prices enough to maintain a monopolistic profit unless demand curves are completely inelastic.

Supermarket Competition

With some refinements, Chamberlin's monopolistic competition model offers a realistic framework for our analysis of the competitive tactics and pricing behavior in mass retailing. The model applies to competition among outlets on the entire line of products in the stores, on individual product categories, and on particular brands. For supermarket retailing, certain aspects of the model are more prominent than others.

Supermarket retailing is highly competitive, for stores are most commonly densely distributed and low in personal services; location, not image, is the critical store attribute to most consumers. Several factors, along with certain tactics used by supermarket retailers, however, offer the opportunity for monopoly profits in the long run as well as the short run for a typical retail supermarket:

1. The number of buyers and sellers is limited by the localized nature of the market (magnified by the importance of convenience to shoppers);
2. Entry can be deterred once a certain number of supermarkets are established in an area, as insufficient residual demand preempts another entrant of minimum efficient scale;
3. Consumers lack perfect information on the prices of all products at all stores in their area, since the average store has over 12,000 items, nearly one half of all purchases are made on impulse, prices are changed frequently, and the price of any one individual product is normally not high enough to cause consumers to go out of their way to obtain information on its price alone at each outlet in that area; and
4. Retailers have imperfect information and uncertainty on how the merchandising of one product affects sales of the other products carried.

The Chamberlin model predicts long run monopoly profits if entry is deterred. Locational entry barriers may exist in supermarket retailing, especially since realizing scale economies is critical in such a low net-margin business (Table 4.2). For example, there may be room in the market for two and one half supermarkets but not three, so that in the long run, just two survive, each securing monopoly profits. But structurally, with well-known, frequently purchased, mature, densely distributed products, supermarket retailing remains intensely competitive. To minimize this competition and increase monopoly power, the supermarket retailer uses three tactics in addition to advertising and other customer services:

1. Sells private labels, which account for 22 percent of all sales, 25–35 percent at the five largest chains (SAMI, 1975).
2. Uses "variable price merchandising"—that is, changes the prices of different products constantly, both up and down.
3. "Loss leads" products—that is, sells certain products at a loss to create a reputation for low prices and thereby increase store traffic in order to sell higher-margin products (on average, 14 items purchased per trip by shoppers—SAMI, 1975).

The first tactic, use of private labels, offers the retailer higher margins, especially necessary in product categories under heavy competition. The retailer has a differentiated offering—that is, Kroger peas may or may not be the same as Safeway peas—with competition reduced. The other two tactics are closely related and of a different nature than the use of private labels.

With competition threatening to destroy any long-run equilibrium monopoly profits, the main reaction of the supermarket retailer has been to create a situation where *a long-run equilibrium never comes*. Instead, the situation is better described as a series of short runs. Adjustment to a long-run zero profit equilibrium is avoided by the constant movement of prices on hundreds of products weekly.[7] This up and down movement of prices makes it more difficult for consumers to compare prices on the same products among stores, thus reducing the amount of information in the market. Monopolistic price distortions may exist, therefore, for different product categories at different times, in part because of this variable price merchandising.

The other tactic, "loss leading" of products, is available to the supermarket retailer only because of the opportunity for monopolistic pricing on the other products carried. Otherwise, loss leading would cause retailers to lose money. If all other products were priced at perfectly competitive levels, taking a loss on even one product would mean short-run losses and long-run insolvency. But as mentioned, consumers' information is not perfect on all prices, and retailers loss lead on different products not only because of different customers and economic structures but also because of imperfect knowledge on what the effects of this tactic are. Loss leading raises the important question to be addressed in the following chapters: How does manufacturers' advertising affect the pricing of a product?

The Model Formulation

Having presented the economic framework for our investigation of the factors affecting retail pricing behavior, we now consider the proper method for analyzing, most generally, how and why brand gross margins differ among product categories, and more specifically, how and why manufacturers' advertising affects retail gross margins among brands in a product category. In order to address these questions, the model is separated into two parts: (1) the determinants of variations in category gross margins among product categories, such as the gross margins of catsup versus pickles, and (2) the determinants of variations in brand gross margins within a product category, such as the gross margins of Heinz catsup versus Del Monte catsup. The first part of the model, product category determinants of gross margin, explains why product category pricing varies; the second part of the model, interbrand determinants of gross margin, explains why brand pricing varies and, most important, why advertising affects retail brand pricing. It is this relationship—the interbrand advertising–gross margin relationship—that is the focus of the model formulation. *The product category analysis will be used to explain why the interbrand advertising–gross margin relationship differs among product categories.*

A numerical example will help illustrate the issues at hand in the model formulation. Essentially we wish to properly specify brand gross margins and brand advertising, as well as the other independent factors correlated with brand advertising and brand gross margins. Once these variables are properly specified, the true measure of the impact of advertising on retail gross margins can be deduced and estimated statistically. This measure will be called the *margin elasticity (of advertising),* which may be broadly defined as the responsiveness of the brand gross margin to advertising. As our major concern is with gross margins, the discussion is limited to the proper specification of brand gross margins. An equal amount of space could be devoted to how to specify advertising, or any other independent brand factor correlated with advertising and gross margin, but such a discussion at this time would be largely redundant, since all of the brand variables are specified similarly. However, in Chapter 8 we will further refine the specification of brand gross margin and, accordingly, discuss the specification of advertising as well.

For instance, canned tuna may have an average product category gross margin of 10 percent, with Bumble Bee tuna sold at a 7 percent margin; likewise, candy bars may have a product category gross margin of 25 percent, with Hershey's candy bars at 20 percent. There is no problem in analyzing the variation in product category gross margins: 10 versus 25 percent. To isolate the interbrand variation, however, is not simply a matter of comparing Bumble Bee's 7 percent gross margin with the 20 percent gross margin of Hershey's. Simply stated, a brand's gross margin may be thought of as a function of its product category level, that is, 10 versus 25 percent in this instance, and its variation from that level, that is, 7 from 10 percent and 20 from 25 percent. If in our sample (here, two product categories) the product categories have the same category gross margins, then no problem exists; the sample could be considered one large product category for purposes of the interbrand analysis, as all the variations in brand gross margins are around the same product category gross margin level. However, as this is not the case, *the brand gross margins should be specified in order to be comparable among the different product categories.* Four possible statistical formulations to obtain this comparability are listed with their implicit assumptions; a more general discussion of each formulation follows. Our choice depends on what we believe is common retailing business practice:

1. Leave the brand gross margin as is (absolute formulation); this assumes that all the product categories can be considered as one homogeneous product category.
2. Subtract the corresponding product category gross margin (difference formulation); this assumes that the relationship between the gross margins of a brand and its product category is linear (additive model).[8]
3. Divide by the corresponding product category gross margin (ratio formulation); this assumes that the relationship between the gross margins of a brand and its product category is log linear (multiplicative model).[8]
4. Subtract the corresponding product category gross margin and divide by the standard deviation of the brand gross margins within the product category (normalized formulation); this assumes that the margin elasticities should be the same for all categories with symmetric distributions of brand gross margins within each product category (given equal amount of advertising among product categories).

To reiterate the central issue of the model formulation, we wish to analyze the interbrand variation in gross margins (Bumble Bee versus private label canned tuna) in a sample of many product categories (canned tuna and candy bars), each with different levels of product category gross margins (10 versus 25 percent). To isolate this variation in brand gross margins, we must separate out the part of the brand gross margin that is a function of the type of product category it is in. Formulation 1, using only the actual, absolute levels of brand gross margins, does not separate out these product category differences. Of the remaining possibilities, *the ratio formulation (3) is most indicative of retailing practices*.

Formulation 2—the difference formulation—specifies brand gross margins as *absolute* differences from their respective product category gross margins, such as −3 points (7 minus 10 percent) in the case of Bumble Bee canned tuna and −5 points (20 minus 25 percent) for Hershey's candy bars. Different levels of category gross margins are considered irrelevant for the brand measurements and consequent comparisons among product categories. However, formulation 3—the ratio formulation—measures brand gross margins *relative* to their product category levels of gross margin, that is, 70 (7/10 percent) for Bumble Bee and 80 (20/25 percent) for Hershey's. Formulation 4—normalized formulation—does not reflect either the absolute or relative magnitude of the dispersion of brand gross margins. Not only is it an unrealistic representation of the retailer's concerns, but it also does not allow us to measure the magnitude of the effect of advertising on gross margin.

The two most sensible formulations, therefore, are the difference (2) and ratio (3) specifications of brand gross margins. Each measure standardizes brand data for comparability by separating out product category influences, which are reflected in the level of the category gross margin. The major difference between these two is that the difference formulation assumes that brand and product category merchandising decisions are *independent*, whereas the ratio formulation implies that these decisions are *interdependent*. According to the literature on direct product profitability and the contribution model, the ratio measurement of brand gross margins best characterizes the mass retailer's decision criteria for brand merchandising. Furthermore, in practice as well, the ratio measure is held by retailing experts to be a more realistic representation of retailing practices.[9]

After having decided to carry a particular product category, the retailer must decide how to best manage that category. Dealing with different units of measurement, such as sales measured in dollars, volume in number of units sold, shelf space in linear, square, or cubic feet, and so forth, merchandisers manage, it is asserted, in *percentage* terms. Thus if a manufacturer's advertising of a brand, for example, has increased the store movement of that brand by a certain amount, that percentage increase should be translated into an equivalent decrease in the contribution percentage (net margin) by means of a lower retail price. And as long as unit variable costs do not vary with volume, as is commonly true, particularly in the long run, this decrease in contribution percentage is directly translated into a decrease in gross margin. The level of the brand gross margin should be, and in fact is, an important consideration of the retailer. As the category gross margin is simply a weighted average of the brand gross margins in the product category, the level of the category gross margin is, therefore, implicitly acknowledged as important, too.

In summation, having chosen this ratio formulation to measure the effect of advertising on gross margin, we now have two sets of relationships to explain the variation in brand gross margins among product categories. The first set explains the levels of product category gross margins, that is, the 10 percent canned tuna versus the 25 percent candy bar gross margin difference; the second explains the variation in the ratios of brand to category gross margins, that is, the 70 Bumble Bee tuna ratio versus the 80 Hershey's candy bar ratio. It is within this second set of relationships that we will investigate the effect of advertising on the brand gross margin—the margin elasticity of advertising. The first set of product category relationships will be shown to explain the variation in the stength and significance of the margin elasticity of advertising among product categories.

Summary

In this chapter we presented the overall framework of the economic structure and competitive environment of the mass retailer. Within this framework, we can analyze the pricing behavior of the retailer to concentrate on the effects of manufacturers' advertising on the cost to consumers of retail services—the retail gross margin. It was concluded that the proper model formulation to analyze the effect of advertising on brand gross margins, what we will call the *margin elasticity of advertising*, in a group of product categories—many with different levels of gross margins and advertising—is a measure of the *ratio* of the brand gross margin to its corresponding product category gross margin. Furthermore, the level of product category gross margins will be analyzed to explain the variation in the importance of the margin elasticity of advertising among different product categories.

In any description of the economics of the mass retailer, it is important to know what is meant by the assertion that the retailer maximizes profits. We explained the concepts of contribution and opportunity costs, which are essential for understanding profit maximization for the store and for individual products. The product's rate of movement, a factor in the *total* contribution, and its shelf space requirement, a factor in the total contribution *per unit of shelf space,* are important considerations in any attempt to maximize profts. Judgments that result in less contribution for the store than is feasible cause an *opportunity loss;* that is, a fixed resource, (shelf space), has not been used most profitably. We assumed that the most prominent of the many decisions the retailer must make to maximize profits are the selection of product categories and particular brands, the allocation of shelf space to the different categories, and the pricing of the various brands carried.

Maximizing store profits, however, is complicated by the difficulty of attributing many storewide costs to individual products. The relevant costs for calculating contribution, that is, operating costs, include only variable costs in the short run, but many fixed costs as well in the long run. Methods for assigning the various types of retail expenses to individual products were reviewed. Still, most retailers use rules-of-thumb; they have found that the complexity of the task makes the more sophisticated methods too expensive and unwieldy. Furthermore, within this already complex cost structure for individual products, the retailer must consider the reaction of competitors. We maintained that the competitive framework surrounding the economic structure of the mass retailer is best described by Chamberlin's monopolistic competition model. The model recognizes the possibility for monopolistic profits in an intensely competitive market. To reduce competition, the retailer must use a variety of tactics, including variable price merchandising and the sale of private label brands. Manufacturers' advertised brands are directly comparable among the different stores carrying the brands, thereby affecting the competition and pricing behavior of the mass retailer.

Endnotes

1. Notable exceptions in the United States include the work of Richard Holton and Robert Holdren. See the bibliography for full citations of some of their work. Bucklin and Stern have led much of the marketing research in this area. However, in general, the United Kingdom has produced the major body of research into the economics of distribution, including the excellent studies of Lady Margaret Hall (see bibliography).
2. R. E. Caves and associates, *Competition in the Open Economy* (Cambridge, Mass.: Harvard University Press, 1980), pp. 93–94.
3. Although for our purposes merchandising costs and factory price are equivalent, the retailer's accounting system may not result in equivalency between the two. Most commonly, a lack of equivalency may result due to the accounting of the manufacturer's promotions and volume discounts and the allocation of freight-in and other shipping expenses.
4. Certainly the allocation of shelf space among brands is important, although less so than the pricing of brands or space allocation among product categories. However, with the assumption that any increase in shelf space given to an advertised brand does not reduce its unit volume per shelf space footage to that of an unadvertised brand in that category, the issue of space allocation among brands does not affect the analysis qualitatively. Furthermore, it should be noted that pricing takes place on each *item* carried (such as an "8-ounce jar of Hellmann's mayonnaise"), and then is aggregated and averaged for the brand. Theoretically, however, it is not necessary for our purposes to differentiate between items and brands to explain pricing behavior.
5. The Cosmos model is described in R. C. Curhan, "A Study of the Relationship Between Shelf Space and Sales for Selected Products in Self-Service Food Supermarkets," unpublished doctoral dissertation, Harvard University, 1971. In addition, his discussion of literature was helpful in preparing parts of this review of the direct product profitability literature.
6. Throughout the book all propositions and hypotheses implicitly assume that all other factors are held constant, that is, *ceteris paribus*.

7. R. L. Steiner, "Brand Advertising and the Consumer Goods Economy" (unpublished manuscript, 1979), contains observations on this type of equilibrium.
8. Algebraically, with the specification of brand gross margin for comparisons among product categories in brackets, the difference approach assumes an additive model for the product category (GM_C) and (GM_B) gross margins: $GM_B = GM_C + [GM_B - GM_C]$. The ratio approach assumes interaction between the retailer's brand and product category pricing: $GM_B = GM_C \times [GM_B/GM_C]$.
9. Walter Salmon, an expert on retailing practices, specifically supermarket retailing, made this observation.

Chapter 5

DETERMINANTS OF RETAIL PRODUCT CATEGORY PROFITS

The total contribution of a product category is an important merchandising concern of the retailer. Product categories generate store profits in two ways: directly from the sales of items in the category itself, and indirectly by increasing store traffic and thereby the sales of other products in the store. The retailer, therefore, is interested in both the direct profitability of a product category and its potential as a traffic builder.

In this chapter we first examine the economics of two of the retailer's merchandising decisions: what product categories to carry, and how much shelf space to allocate to each category. After the framework for these decisions is described, we derive the factors that are associated with the level of profitability of the product categories—that is, more precisely, factors associated with the level of product category gross margins. These characteristics of the product categories carried by the retailer reflect the total direct and indirect contribution that a category produces for a given amount of shelf space. Underlying the use of retail shelf space to generate contribution for the store is the concept of the opportunity cost of the shelf space; this concept explicitly recognizes all the contribution of a product category to store profits.

Two classifications of category characteristics related to the level of product category gross margins are presented. The first classification, based on the assumption of perfect competition and independence in the merchandising of individual product categories, considers factors that are directly associated with the category's total contribution. The second classification recognizes monopolistic competition in retailing and the interdependence of product categories due to the ability of some categories to build store traffic more than others; factors that reflect the salience of a product category to consumers are discussed. Manufacturers' advertising, a primary determinant of variations in brand gross margins, is seen as a secondary factor in the merchandising of product categories.

The Allocation of Shelf Space

To reiterate, once the retailer has priced the brands to be carried in each product category, the allocation of shelf space among the individual categories remains as the central merchandising consideration. The prominent shelf space decision is *how much* to allocate to each category (the "where" of shelf space location is not dealt with in this discussion). Furthermore, it will be demonstrated that factors reflecting the level of product category gross margins can be viewed as deriving from the decision as to the amount of space allocated to each category.

The mass retailer selects from a wide range of product categories, some of which may be regarded as necessary offerings, others discretionary choices. The classification of a product category as necessary or discretionary depends largely on which categories shoppers expect the store to carry. For instance, a supermarket may need to carry staples such as milk, eggs, flour, sugar, and bread, whereas gourmet foods would be a much more discretionary choice. Low-calorie products, on the other hand, may be somewhere in between discretionary and necessary, depending on the clientele in the area and the type of customer the store hopes to attract. Similarly, the greater the percentage of planned purchases (such as coffee) versus impulse purchases (such as nuts) made by consumers in a product category, the more likely it is that the retailer feels the category is a necessary offering. Thus a product category considered discretionary today might not be so tomorrow or in another area, or for a different clientele. Corporate strategy as well as consumer expectations and buying habits dictate just what is necessary and what is not, and these strategies, expectations, and buying habits can change over time and vary for different stores and different regions.

Decision rules for these two types of product categories may differ. For example, a "necessary" product category must occupy a certain amount of space no matter how unprofitable it may be, whereas a "discretionary" category need not. Any comparative analysis, therefore, may be problematic and certainly somewhat more complex if done with different product category types. To simplify the analysis, two discretionary product categories are compared—that is, the retailer decides both whether to carry the category and, if so, how much shelf space to allocate to it, with a decision not to carry a category a viable alternative (0 percent, 100 percent is feasible). The analytical framework can also be used for necessary categories, however, if desired. The major difference is that a 0 percent, 100 percent space allocation decision is not feasible. To ensure against this outcome, the ordinate (vertical axis) of Figure 5.1 must be moved to the right until it is at the point of the minimum shelf space required for the necessary product category(ies). It will be demonstrated that within this analytical framework, *the shelf space allocation decision reflects factors associated with the level of product category gross margins*.

The Space Allocation Model

Figure 5.1 graphically depicts the retailer's decision in terms of total contribution and shelf space. Shelf space is measured in square feet, although *any units will do*. At this time it is easier to think of total contribution in terms of only the *direct* contribution of the product category; however, later on we will need to consider the aforementioned indirect contribution that a category may generate by means

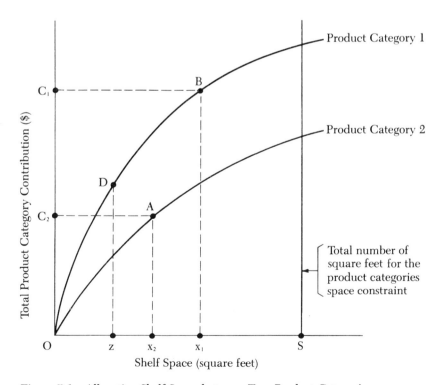

Figure 5.1   Allocating Shelf Space between Two Product Categories.

of increasing store traffic and thereby the sales of other products in the store. To capture this indirect contribution, the concept of opportunity costs of shelf space will be reintroduced. This concept is more flexible and general than that of total contribution, although the basic analysis does not change.

The retailer wants to maximize the total contribution produced by these two product categories, given a certain amount of shelf space to be allocated between them. Total contribution is the objective and shelf space the binding constraint for the retailer. The total contribution of each product category is given, determined at the brand level and then aggregated for each category, and the total amount of square feet is represented by the vertical line at point S. The two curves depict the total contribution of each product category for a given amount of shelf space allotted to that category. If the retailer requires a certain minimum total contribution per square foot in the shelf space allocation decision, this factor can be represented graphically by a diagonal line from the origin.

The representation of total contribution per square foot as a curve rather than a straight line is based on the curvilinearity of the unit sales–shelf space relationship, often referred to in the literature[1] as *space elasticity:* a diminishing marginal response of unit sales to increases in shelf space. If, instead, linear unit sales volume–shelf-space and thereby total contribution–shelf-space relationships are proposed to exist, the retailer simply carries the product category with the greater total contribution—that is, product category 1. As presented, product categories 1 and 2 may differ because of different contributions, unit sales per square foot, or both.

The retailer can maximize the total contribution of the given amount of shelf space by means of marginal analysis. Theoretically, the marginal contribution of product category 1 should be equated to the marginal contribution of product category 2 such that the sum of the amounts of shelf space used for each of the two categories equals the amount of shelf space set aside for these categories. Graphically, the slope of the product category 1 curve at point B equals that of the product category 2 curve at point A, as $x_1 + x_2 = S$, and the total contribution of the shelf space is $TC_1 + TC_2$. If the total amount of shelf space allotted to the two categories is less than z, however only product category 1 should be stocked, since up to z the highest marginal contribution of product category 2 (just beyond point 0) is always less than that of product category 1 (lowest marginal contribution up to z is at point D). If the amount of shelf space is infinite, both categories should occupy shelf space until their marginal contributions equal zero.

Operationally, the decision rule for the retailer has two steps:

1. Increase the shelf space allotted to product category 1 (the category with the greater marginal contribution just after point 0) until the marginal contribution of the last unit of shelf space is equalled by the first unit of space used by product category 2. Marginal contributions of the two product categories are equal for the first time at point D for product category 1 and just beyond point 0 for product category 2.
2. Increase the shelf space allotted to each category, keeping the marginal contribution of each additional unit of space equivalent between the two product categories, until the total amount of space has been used. This step in our example has the retailer move from point D to point B for product category 1 and from point 0 to point A for product category 2, simultaneously.

It should be clear, therefore, that in making this space allocation decision, the retailer considers the relationship between how much shelf space is occupied by a product category and what that category contributes to the store's fixed costs and profits. Herein lie the essentials of the factors associated with the level of product category gross margins: The more a factor reflects increased total contribution, less shelf space occupied, or both for a product category, *the lower the gross margin required by the retailer* to obtain the same total contribution per square foot (that is, average contribution) as from a category with characteristics reflecting decreased total contribution, more shelf space occupied, or both. This proposition, which should include the ability of a product category to increase contribution indirectly by increasing store traffic, can also be understood by recognizing the opportunity cost of shelf space.

Opportunity Costs

The concept of opportunity costs was introduced in the last chapter. We noted that opportunity costs reflect the maximum total contribution, both direct and indirect, that can be generated from a certain number of square feet of shelf space. *Shelf space is valued, therefore, by the most it can produce in total contribution from the products that could use the space.* The opportunity cost of one square foot of shelf space is called the *shadow price* of the fixed resource, that is, what another square foot of space would be worth to the retailer in terms of total contribution that the products using that square foot of space could produce. In this space allocation decision, moreover, it should be recognized that whereas the retailer is consciously maximizing total contribution subject to a given amount of shelf space, [net] opportunity costs are also being minimized, subject to the total contribution per square foot obtainable from the product categories under consideration.

For the interested reader, it should be mentioned that, in programming terminology, these two alternative formulations represent the "primal" and "dual" of the retailer's decision. All types of mathematical programming, from linear to dynamic and stochastic, are being used more and more by firms with many products that all use similar production methods. Efficiency increases have been dramatic, so it is worthwhile to present an understanding of the programming framework. In this instance the objective functions are the total contribution and the opportunity costs, subject to the binding constraints—square feet of shelf space and total contribution per square foot, respectively. The maximum of the primal, total contribution, equals the minimum of the dual, opportunity costs, in the solution of the programming problem. It is important to realize that both objective functions are fixed amounts at any one point in time, that is, the maximum total contribution obtainable and the valuation of the shelf space, the opportunity costs.

What the retailer should try to do, therefore, is minimize the difference between the amount of total contribution obtained from that space and the maximum obtainable. This difference—this loss in potential contribution—is called the opportunity loss, or net oportunity cost, of the space used. The more total contribution obtained by the retailer, the less the potential increase in contribution from an alternative use of that space; indeed, the lower is the opportunity loss. In other words, as the retailer tries to minimize this difference between what is obtained and what is obtainable, *total contribution is maximized* or, said otherwise, *the opportunity loss is minimized*. When total contribution is maximized for a given amount of shelf space, the opportunity loss is zero, as the total contribution (the valuation of the use of the shelf space) is equal to the opportunity costs (the valuation of the best alternative use of the shelf space).

Although it is admittedly easier to think of the retailer's decisions in terms of total contribution, the flexibility of the concept of opportunity costs—covering any and all contribution generated by a product—makes it a much more precise way of dealing with retail decisions, both for product categories and for brands. The concept is particularly useful for dealing with the product interdependencies critical to mass retailing. This contribution, induced by a traffic-building product category for the sale of items in other categories, is called, for lack of a better label, *indirect* contribution. When we maintain, therefore, that the retailer should try to equalize the marginal contributions of the last unit of shelf space used by each product category, they are said to include these product category interdependencies, that is, the indirect contributions of the product categories to store profits. More precisely, *net opportunity costs should be equalized*.

The powerful economic concept of opportunity costs is, in terms of economic rationale, the *raison d'être* of the total contribution–retail shelf space relationship. But for reasons of practicality and ease of understanding, the contribution formulation will be primarily used. Therefore the factors associated with the level of product category gross margins, as seen in the relationship between total contribution and shelf space, are discussed in two parts: those applying to total contribution per square foot of shelf space, and those reflecting the indirect contribution of traffic building. The first part implicitly assumes a perfect competition equilibrium, whereas the second recognizes a more realistic, monopolistic competition market outcome. Taken together, the factors explain the variation in the level of category gross margins among product categories for the mass retailer.

Perfect Competition: Independence of Product Categories

Having shown how the retailer should think about the allocation of shelf space among product categories based on total contribution, or alternatively, opportunity costs, we now assume that shelf space has been allocated. A further premise in this formulation is that retail handling expenses, though they can differ greatly among product categories, cannot be altered significantly by the retailer for any particular category. In this manner we focus on the retailer's attempt to maximize profits by examining within a competitive equilibrium framework factors that affect the retail pricing, and ultimately gross margin, of the product categories in the store.

To begin most simply, we will assume that profit maximization can be viewed separately for each individual product category—that no important interdependencies exist among product categories; that is, no category has any appreciable effect on store traffic and/or the sales of other products in the store (or alternatively, all categories have the same effect). This assumption means that the retailer needs to consider only the direct contribution of a product category in the optimization process. As explained, the retailer maximizes the total contribution for the store by means of the marginal analysis already described—by equalizing the marginal contributions of the last unit of shelf space used by each product category (Figure 5.1). In a long-run competitive market equilibrium, however, a stricter condition applies as well: *The average contributions—that is, the total contributions per square foot—should be equalized among the various product categories carried.*[2]

For example, canned tuna and canned salmon should have the same total contribution per square foot. If not—suppose canned tuna has a lower contribution (it does)—then changes in retail competition (such as higher tuna or lower salmon prices, thereby changing gross margins) should raise the total contribution per square foot for tuna and/or lower the total contribution per square foot for salmon until the average contributions are equal. In terms of Figure 5.1, tuna would be product category 2, and salmon would be represented by category 1.

That this situation does not occur, however, is because canned tuna has a greater effect on store traffic. But at this point in the discussion, with a competitive equilibrium accepted, some changes would have to take place until both marginal (on the last unit of shelf space only) and average contributions are equalized; the traffic-building effects are recognized explicitly in the next section of the model.

The competitive assumption, therefore, is one of perfect competition in retailing, an economic equilibrium that includes some profit margin above costs equal to the opportunity cost of capital. A product category with higher total contribution per square foot than others, therefore, is subject to increased retail competition, driving the total contribution per square foot down to the competitive levels of other categories in equilibrium. Based on the premise that product categories would be sold by the retailers initially at the same gross margin, the central proposition can be stated:

> *Product categories that would have higher total contributions per square foot of shelf space initially should have lower gross margins in equilibrium than categories that have lower total contributions per square foot of shelf space.*

This proposition can be stated alternatively in terms of costs, specifically, net opportunity costs:

> *Product categories with lower net opportunity costs initially should have lower gross margins in equilibrium than categories with higher net opportunity costs.*

What may seem to be a circular proposition at the outset—the lower the gross margin (a percentage of sales), the lower it seems should be contribution (a dollar amount)—needs further explanation before we examine the particular factors in question. The crux of the explanation is that in a perfectly competitive market equilibrium, all product categories must have equal total contributions per square foot of shelf space. Therefore, if a product category were to have *initially* a higher total contribution per square foot than other categories carried by the retailers, competition on that category would intensify, driving down that contribution to the competitive levels of the other product categories. Given the assumption that price competition takes place, the result is a lower gross margin for the product category once a market equilibrium is reached. Alternatively, product categories with lower total contributions per square foot would see competition abate, with higher gross margins resulting. As such, *product categories with factors* (termed *category characteristics*) *reflecting higher (or lower) total contributions per square foot should have lower (or higher) gross margins in equilibrium than other product categories.*

Product Category Characteristics

Six factors that reflect the characteristics of the various product categories carried by the retailer are listed in Table 5.1. Each factor reflects the retail shelf space required or the total contribution of a product category. Furthermore, these factors all change the product category curves in Figure 5.1 and, therefore, the space allocation decision for the retailer. Once space has been allocated, the more these factors reflect less space used and/or more total contribution for the product category occupying that space, the lower should be the gross margin required by the retailer on that category. All correlations of factors to gross margins assume all other variables are held constant, that is, *ceteris paribus*.

Retail Space Required (positively correlated with gross margins). The greater the amount of shelf space occupied by a product category, the greater the fixed cost per unit sold and, therefore, the greater is the gross margin required of that category in equilibrium for its total contribution to equal that of a product cat-

Table 5.1 Category Characteristics under Perfect Competition

Retail Space Required (+)	*Total Contribution of Retail Space (−)*
Increases with:	*Increases* with:
• Number of items (brands) carried by the store in the category	• Unit sales
• Size of items	• Retail price
Decreases with:	*Decreases* with:
• Probability of preshopping decision on purchase	• Other retail variable costs (retail expenses)

egory that uses less space. Three factors are listed in Table 5.1; two apply to the product categories carried by the retailer, one concerns consumers.

Product categories with a larger number of items carried by the retailer and/or items of a larger unit size will require more space than categories with fewer, smaller items. For instance, laundry detergents require more space than catsup both because the boxes take up more room than the bottles and because most retailers carry more separate items in laundry detergents than in catsup; moreover, the fact that more brands of detergent are carried similarly requires more retail shelf space. Also, some product categories may require more space because their items do not stack easily, especially if fragile (potato chips, for example). However, whereas size and "stack-ability" of items are beyond the retailer's control, this is not necessarily true of the number of items carried in a product category.

There are two components to the number of items carried by the retailer in a product category: the number of items per brand and the number of brands per category. The implications for the retailer differ, depending on which of these components is the more important influence on the number of items carried in the product category. The reasoning is drawn from Porter's model (Chapter 3) on the tacit negotiation of bilateral market power between manufacturers and retailers. The greater the number of items per brand carried by the retailer, the more dependent the retailer is on the brand's manufacturer, and the lower the retail gross margin should be. The retailer may have to concede more shelf space, better shelf positioning, and so forth, to the manufacturer. Alternatively, the greater the number of brands carried by the retailer in a particular product category, the less dependent the retailer is on any one manufacturer, and the higher the retail gross margin should be (limit shelf space and so forth for the manufacturer). The result: The relationship between the number of items in a product category and the gross margin is complex. Furthermore, as will be discussed shortly, the number of brands—gross margin relationship may depend on the level of manufacturers' advertising in the product category.

The third factor, the probability (percentage) of preshopping decisions by consumers on what to purchase, is also affected by advertising. If shoppers have already made up their minds before going into the store, the retailer needs to do little more than stock the product category as cheaply as possible. Less expensive space (for example, space at the end of the aisle is expensive) and less additional space are required of the retailer to display and sell the items in the product category. It should be mentioned, moreover, that this cat-

egory characteristic also reflects aspects of product salience to consumers (which will be discussed in the monopolistic competition
section later in this chapter.)

Total Contribution of Retail Space (negatively correlated with
gross margins). Product category gross margins are a function of
retail variable costs and price elasticity, both of which are reflected
in the contribution of the category. Factors leading to higher total
contributions (that is, higher retail prices, higher unit sales, or lower
retail expenses) should be offset by the retailer and competitive
forces with lower gross margins to equalize the total contributions
per square foot among product categories in equilibrium. Similarly,
factors leading to lower total contributions should be offset with
higher gross margins in equilibrium. For instance, if two product
categories differ only in retail prices or unit sales, the category with
the higher retail price (or unit sales) has a lower net opportunity
cost of the shelf space used, and therefore must have a lower gross
margin in equilibrium to equalize the total contributions of the two
categories. These product category characteristics, like preshopping
decisions, also reflect aspects of salience.

For categories that differ only in retail expenses (also referred to
as other retail variable costs, which do not include merchandise
costs),[3] a product category with higher costs requires a higher gross
margin if the categories are to have the same total contribution in
equilibrium. These higher costs may be the result of, for example,
additional handling expenses (produce), special equipment required
(deli, fresh meats), or refrigeration (frozen and chilled products). The
latter two expenses, special equipment and refrigeration, are only
directly applicable to contribution in the long run, when all operating
costs are considered variable. In each case these product categories
contribute less to the retailer's fixed cost of shelf space, resulting
in greater net opportunity costs. In equilibrium, the retailer must
compensate with a higher gross margin.

One other factor needs to be discussed: manufacturers' advertising.
*The total level of advertising in a product category should be a
secondary factor in affecting category gross margins.* Over time,
advertising may lead to lower product category gross margins, mostly
through its effects on other factors, such as unit sales and retail price,
preshopping decisions by consumers, and retail expenses. Furthermore, the effect of advertising may depend on other factors, particularly the number of brands carried by the retailer in the product
category. Advertising should be much more effective in leading to
lower product category gross margins if few brands are carried in
the category.

It is important to recognize that the effects of advertising on the retailer occur mostly at the brand level. By affecting the retail price and unit sales of a brand, advertising influences the average product category gross margin only as an aggregation of its effects at the brand level. *This aggregation, however, does not imply a simple summation.* For example, the contention that advertising increases unit sales for a product category is far different from a contention acknowledging advertising's effect on brand unit sales within a product category. The latter depends on brand substitution; the former depends on substitution among product categories, which constitutes a change in primary demand. In their survey of a number of studies on the relationship between the total amount of advertising in a product category and the total demand for that category, Albion and Farris (1981) found that the effect of advertising on primary demand, if and when it does exist, is extremely limited per se, depending on other factors beyond the marketer's control, such as favorable sociodemographic trends. The ability of advertising to affect brand sales, on the other hand, had been shown repeatedly.

Similar reasoning was advanced in Chapter 2 regarding advertising and retail price. As explained, the notion that advertising increases the relative retail price of a brand is far different than acknowledging that advertising increases the absolute market-price level of a product category. Instead, if advertising is to have an impact on product category gross margins, it may be in terms of increasing the pre-shopping knowledge of consumers about several brands in the category. Over time, advertising can increase buyer acceptance and loyalty for many brands. Because of this "goodwill" and the increased consumer familiarity with many brands in the product category, the category may then serve as a good loss leader, or traffic builder, a point to be developed next.

Monopolistic Competition: Interdependence of Product Categories

Having dealt with how certain category characteristics should affect the retail pricing, and therefore the gross margin, of product categories in a perfectly competitive market, we now focus on an essential competitive reality of mass retailing: interdependence among product categories. In this way the importance of certain products to draw store traffic and serve as *benchmarks* to consumers for a general low store-pricing policy is recognized. As Alfred Marshall noted over sixty years ago:[4]

> [retailers] . . . *were inclined to sell branded goods—as well as sugar, and some other things which many customers commonly supposed*

themselves able to judge and compare—at prices that barely covered expenses; in order that they might act as "decoys" or "leaders" for other sales.

Loss leaders, often called traffic builders if not sold at an actual loss, are an integral competitive tactic of mass retailing, and of supermarket retailing in particular. These products can be sold at a loss by the mass retailer only because that loss can be covered by the sale of other, higher-margin products at the store. In a world of imperfect information, shoppers decide rationally that it is not worth their time to compare the pricing on all low-priced, frequently purchased merchandise of interest at each store in their area every time they make a purchase. Instead, they use certain products to judge a store's overall price line. Knowing this, the mass retailer competes intensively on these products with other retailers by lowering their retail prices, usually on some subset of these products— a group that changes over time and by store. *The gross margins of these loss leaders are, therefore, lower than would be predicted in a perfectly competitive market,* with profit maximization on any one product considered separately from all others. Furthermore, the total contribution per square foot of these loss leaders should be less than the total contribution of other products in equilibrium.

National 1978 figures from *Chain Store Age Supermarkets* indicate that certain product categories are sold at a loss nationally. Product categories such as bean and whole ground coffee, granulated cane sugar, mayonnaise, and cigarettes had gross margins not exceeding 10 percent. With handling expenses (variable costs excluding merchandise costs) shown in Chapter 4 to average about 13.5 percent, these product categories appear to yield a rate of return below perfectly competitive levels. Other quarterly store figures demonstrate that in supermarket retailing the range of products used as loss leaders does indeed change over time, with different supermarkets using a different subset of these products and even changing frequently which ones are used. What determines which products best serve as loss leaders was addressed by Marshall: They are either branded, have high consumer familiarity, or both, such as brands that are in highly advertised categories and staples, respectively.

The traffic-building effect of advertising, most important at the brand level, is the central topic of the next chapter. Here it should be recognized that once we acknowledge this important effect of some product categories but not others on store sales, a perfectly competitive equilibrium with total contribution per square foot equalized among product categories is no longer a valid assumption. Another set of assumptions better describes retail competition and profit maximization: monopolistic competition with *total contribution*

plus the indirect contribution from the effect on store traffic equal-
ized per square foot among product categories in equilibrium. For
product categories with no effect on the sales of other categories,
indirect contribution is zero, and the assumption of perfect competition would still, in general, be valid.[5]

Any overall analysis of the multiproduct mass retailer, therefore,
must recognize the many possible interdependencies among product
categories and their potential effect on the equilibrium described.
Profit maximization for the store should not consider each product
category separately. As mentioned, recognition of these interdependencies implies that the equilibrium gross margins of certain individual product categories are lower than those predicted in the individual product category analysis. At the very least, the product
categories as a group should have a more skewed distribution of
gross margins than recognized previously. For instance, under the
assumption of product category independence, if all product categories had the same retail expenses and unit sales per square foot,
all should have the same gross margin. However, with the recognition of product category interdependence and the fact that the
ability to draw store traffic varies among product categories, this
equality no longer holds. Some product categories can affect the unit
sales per square foot of other categories so that these traffic builders
would have lower gross margins in equilibrium than the categories
affected. This previously unrecognized increase in total contribution
for the store is the cause of the lower equilibrium gross margin for
traffic-building product categories.[6]

The assumption of perfect competition has now been replaced by
the more realistic, monopolistically competitive description of mass
retailing. Product categories do differ in their degree of interdependency with the rest of the products in the store. The maximization
of total contribution for a product category for a given amount of
shelf space, shown in Figure 5.1, now must include the effect of the
category on other purchases at the store. Figure 5.1 can incorporate
this interdependence by shifting the total contribution curves to
include indirect contribution as well. Now total plus indirect contribution per square foot are equalized among product categories,
or alternatively, the net opportunity costs of retail shelf space are
equalized. In general, the curves should be higher or stay the same,
with the possible exception of necessary categories, such as staples
(which intersect the ordinate at negative values).

What has been recognized is what will be called a *"one-way"*
cross-elasticity among product categories: A product category may
affect the sales of another category (or group of categories), but that
other category need not do the same. For example, the merchan-

dising of fresh shrimp may affect the sale of cocktail sauce, but not the reverse. Moreover, a reduced price of shrimp is more likely to increase store traffic and thereby the sale of many products other than cocktail sauce as well. Assessing the magnitude of these effects, however, is much more difficult than determining the impact of category merchandising on the sales of that same product category. The total contribution of a product category to storewide profits and fixed costs should be harder to determine for any mass retailer because of these interdependencies among product categories. Information, therefore, is imperfect not only for consumers, who understandably do not keep abreast of all the relevant price changes on all those products at all the stores in the area, but for the retailer as well.

Given this interdependence among product categories, the proposition linking total contribution and gross margins must be refined; instead, we add a second proposition to it, one that explicitly recognizes these product category interdependencies:

> *Product categories with higher salience to retail customers should have lower gross margins than categories with lower salience to customers.*

First, it is important to define "salience"—a crucial term that is essential throughout the next chapter as well. Its importance results from the fact that *the salience of a product to consumers is the cause of the one-way cross-elasticity of that product for retailers.*

Much consumer behavior research has tried to operationalize the concept of product salience. For our purposes, *salience* refers to the consumer's recognition of and concern about the merchandising—in particular, the pricing—of a product. Product salience involves what Porter, in his discussion of the buyer information equilibrium (1976), refers to as "the desire of the buyer to make an informed choice." The greater the cost the consumer perceives in making a bad decision, according to Porter, the greater the desire to make an informed choice. Salience also concerns what Porter calls the "utility loss" in obtaining information about the product. This loss may occur from dollar outlays, search time spent, the displeasure of acquiring the information, or some combination of all of these. Similarly, salience involves the willingness of the consumer to comparison shop, based on the opportunity to make a better interbrand choice after the shopping. The more difficult it is for the consumer to make an informed interbrand choice, the less informed that consumer will be. In short, the more the consumer already knows about the product (most important, its market price) through product familiarity, advertising, or whatever, the more important the product is to the consumer; that is, the higher the proportion of the consumer's budget, and the greater the consumer's opportunity to gain from comparison shopping, the more salient is that product.

Salient product categories should have lower gross margins for two reasons. The first has already been discussed: effect on store sales. The second reason is based on retail costs (expenses) and Porter's model of bilateral market power presented in Chapter 3. Product categories that are salient to consumers because of product knowledge, however obtained, prior to shopping, require less of a selling effort by the retailer, thus reducing retail costs and the gross margin necessary to reach total contribution objectives. Furthermore, if that information has come from the manufacturers, they will receive the greater profit margin at the expense of the retailers, according to Porter's model.

Product Category Characteristics

Some of the factors discussed in the last section, such as preshopping decisions, retail price, and unit sales, also reflect product category salience. The first two factors deal with the importance of the product category to consumers, whereas the unit sales of a product category indicate its importance to the retailer—what can be called the *aggregate* salience of a product category. Furthermore, a product category's unit sales has two distinct components: the number of purchasers (household penetration) and purchase frequency. It is the number of purchasers that should affect the aggregate salience of the product category for the retailer, particularly in regard to the effectiveness of advertising. In running a price promotion, for example, the retailer is interested in how many different shoppers the promotion may affect, just as the manufacturer is concerned with how many consumers brand advertising may reach. Of course, advertising has the potential to affect salience of a product category by its impact on these other three category characteristics. Moreover, one new characteristic interacts with and affects the importance of the number of items carried by the retailer in a product category: the size comparability of items in the category, proxied by the number of different package sizes carried in a category.

Other than the number of sizes, two category characteristics[7] reflect the level of salience in a product category: the percentage of private label sales in a category and, for the supermarket retailer, the difference between selling food and nonfood products. Size comparability reflects the "utility loss" in obtaining information; items of noncomparable sizes in a product category make intrastore and interstore comparison of prices on different items in the category more difficult. The private label sales percentage in a product category indicates a response of the retailer in highly salient, intensely competitive, mature, low-margin categories. The food/nonfood division reflects "the desire of the buyer to make an informed choice"; commonly food products are more salient to supermarket shoppers, and are often the standards on which consumers compare supermarkets.

Product categories with sizes of items at noninteger multiples of each other (for example, a 6½-ounce can of tuna versus a 7-ounce can) and lack of comparability among sizes of different brands (a 6-ounce jar of French's mustard versus a 5-ounce jar of Gulden's) should make intrastore and interstore price comparisons within such categories more difficult for consumers—even with unit pricing— thus allowing retailers to obtain higher gross margins than in product categories with greater comparability.[8] Evidence of shoppers' inattention to unit pricing is plentiful, although still controversial (Carman, 1972–1973; McElroy and Aaker, 1979), including studies claiming that quite often unit prices are surprisingly higher on larger package sizes—sizes that appeal, it is commonly believed, to the more price-sensitive consumers (Widrick, 1979). Furthermore, with the advent of scanners, inaccessible and infrequent marking of unit prices, and often net rather than gross weights more relevant to consumers, price comparisons are made even more difficult for shoppers.

In these instances the "utility loss" of obtaining information within a product category is higher, due both to the increased time spent acquiring the information and to the possible displeasure of acquiring information through unit pricing. Quite often, in fact, this noncomparability among sizes of different brands is introduced into a product category by the retailer on purpose by means of private label brands. The result is that the greater the number of different package sizes carried by the retailer in a product category, the more difficult it is for consumers to compare different brands at the store (intrastore), and the more difficult it is to remember price information when comparing the price of a particular item among stores (interstore).

The effect of a large number of different package sizes in a product category on the ability of consumers to compare product prices, however, may depend on a category characteristic previously mentioned: the number of items carried by the retailer in a category. A large number of items in a product category should also make interstore price comparisons somewhat more difficult, since it becomes harder for consumers to remember exact items. Accordingly, the number of sizes–gross margin relationship may depend to some extent upon the number of items in a product category: the lower the number of items in the category, given a particular number of different sizes, the more likely is a strong relationship; that is, the greater the number of sizes/number of items ratio, the stronger the number of sizes–gross margin relationship. Conversely, a somewhat similar caveat may apply to the number of items–gross margin relationship: A stronger relationship is likely with a greater the number of sizes in the product category. If these two statements are true, it means that the more important relationship is between the number of sizes and gross margin, with the number of items–gross margin relationship a function of the number of sizes–gross margin relationship. In any case this potential interaction between the number of sizes and the number of items carried in a product category will have to be accounted for in the empirical testing.

Private label brands are offered most commonly in mature, densely distributed, and highly salient product categories on which the retailer faces intense competition, which drives gross margins down to barely cover costs. These product categories are often loss leaders, such as staples like sugar (34 percent private label share nationally) or shortening (30 percent); some are highly advertised (soft drinks). But highly advertised product categories do *not* necessarily have a high percentage of private labels: Private label brands account for under 1 percent of national chain sales in cigarettes and chewing gum—both highly advertised product categories. Steiner reviewed this advertising–private-label sales-share relationship, finding it to be "inconsistent." Better stated, what Steiner found is that private label penetration is nonlinearly related to the total amount of manufacturers' advertising in a product category—that is, high or low penetration with little advertising, moderate penetration with intensive advertising. Whereas private labels find it difficult to do well where "manufacturers' advertising is especially effective," mature product categories often have some moderate level of advertising. Any measure of a linear relationship, therefore, between the amount of advertising in a product category and the salience of a category through private labels is most probably weak.

As Borden noted (1942), retailers offer private labels "to be free from the direct price comparisons upon merchandise which consumers know to be identical." As such, retailers try to switch shoppers to higher margin private labels or, more recently, to generics. The relationship between private label penetration in a product category and gross margins, therefore, should be positive. Retailers use private labels to increase the average category gross margin in these intensely competitive product categories, which have a distinct tendency to become unprofitable. The private label brands can bestow on the retailer some market power, some product differentiation; Kroger peas and Safeway peas, for example, are not directly comparable by consumers.

However, in any statistical testing, it may be very difficult to isolate what should be a *positive* relationship between private label penetration and the average gross margin of a product category. The reason is that private label penetration is also a direct proxy for the salience of a product category, producing a *negative* relationship with gross margin in a cross-sectional analysis of a group of product categories. Our empirical results will depend on the relative strength of these two aspects of the private label–gross margin relationship, and on how well we can control for differences in salience among the product categories in our sample. For example, if all the product categories in our sample have relatively similar levels of salience, such as flour and sugar, then the expected positive relationship should appear. But whereas categories such as nuts and candy bars (low salience, high percentage of impulse purchases) are in the same sample as the aforementioned staples (high salience), our ability to control for varying levels of salience among product categories will depend on the other category characteristics used in the analysis. And since the salience of a product category is difficult to capture through these factors, a negative private label–gross margin relationship may often dominate the testing.

General merchandise products, household products, and health and beauty aids are on average not as salient to supermarket shoppers as grocery products. The 1977 POPAI/DuPont Consumer Buying Habits study (in the *1978 Sales Manual, Chain Store Age Supermarkets*) provides some evidence for this contention. This study contains category-by-category information on how supermarket shoppers actually make their buying decisions, with data showing that a higher percentage of in-store decisions ("impulse") are made for nonfood than for grocery product categories. Reasons may include differences in the nature of the product types and consumer buying habits. In general, food is considered more of a necessary, important, regular purchase. Furthermore, the amount of time it takes to consume a food purchase is typically much shorter than for nonfood products (exceptions would include for example condiments). The consumer is constantly watchful for out-of-store information on food, thereby increasing the desire to make decisions as well as the ease with which those decisions may be made prior to shopping.

In addition, it is asserted that for the most part supermarket shoppers frequent supermarkets primarily for grocery products. When comparing supermarkets, shoppers use grocery products more than nonfood products, which can be purchased at similar prices in drug and department stores. The supermarket is expected to carry grocery products, whereas stocking many nonfood products is more of a customer service, facilitating one-stop shopping. It should be much less risky, therefore, for a supermarket retailer not to carry a nonfood product category than a food category. Given this basic premise, consumers should make fewer price comparisons among supermarkets on nonfood products than on grocery products. This, in turn, should reduce retail competition among the supermarkets on these nonfood products, leading to higher average gross margins.

Exceptions to this assertion, however, are prevalent. As the assortment of products expected to be carried by supermarkets has evolved over time, many nonfood product categories (mostly fast-moving, high-volume ones) have become subject to vigorous supermarket competition; deodorants, laundry detergents, and toilet and facial tissues are a few examples. The consumer, therefore, may also expect the supermarket to carry these product categories. Different subsets of these nonfood product categories may be very salient at different points in time, with these groups changing over time as well. If so, certain groups of fast-moving, nonfood product categories will have lower gross margins than food product categories as a whole.

In summation, twelve category characteristics and their proposed relationships with the level of product category gross margins have been discussed. These characteristics, the signs of their relationships with category gross margins, and the reasons for the proposed relationship are summarized in Table 5.2. Only in the case of the private label penetration in a product category is the proposed relationship unclear.

Using the total amount of manufacturers' advertising in a product category (category advertising) as an example, we can illustrate how to read this summary table. It has been proposed that category advertising should be inversely (negatively) related to the level of category gross margins for three reasons. By affecting a number of other product category characteristics, the level of category advertising should be (1) positively related to the total contribution of retail space (which is negatively related to gross margin); (2) negatively related to the retail space required (which is positively related to gross margin); and (3) positively related to the level of category salience (which is negatively related to gross margin). The signs in parentheses in Table 5.2 denote what are considered to be secondary relationships. In the case of category advertising, therefore, its relationships with both total contribution and retail space required are of secondary importance, whereas its relationship with category salience, it is held, is of primary importance in explaining why category advertising should be inversely related to the level of category gross margins. In Chapter 7 the relative importance of all the various characteristics in explaining variations in the level of product category gross margins will be tested empirically.

Table 5.2 Summary of All Category Characteristics

Characteristic	Total Contribution of Retail Space (−)*	Retail Space Required (+)*	Salience (−)*	Proposed Relationship with Category Gross Margin
Category Advertising	(+)	(−)	+	−
Unit Sales	+		(+)	−
Household Penetration	(+)		+	−
Retail Price	+		(+)	−
Retail Expenses	−			+
Item Size		+		+
Number of Brands	(+)	+		+
Number of Items	(−)	+		+
Number of Sizes			−	+
Preshopping Decisions		(−)	+	−
Private Label Penetration	−		+	?
Food/Nonfood			+	−

Note: Signs in parentheses are considered secondary relationships.

* Relationship of column to category gross margin. For example, salience is negatively related to category gross margin; characteristics positively related to salience, such as advertising, should also be negatively related to category gross margin, whereas characteristics negatively related to salience, such as number of sizes, should be positively related to category gross margin.

Summary

The mass retailer should manage the merchandising of the various product categories carried in terms of their *total* contribution per measure of shelf space, as well as the *indirect* contribution certain categories can generate by increasing store traffic and thereby the sales (and contribution) of other products in the store. Through the lens of a model of shelf space allocation, we examined how the retailer should maximize profits. Two propositions resulted—one regarding total contribution, the other concerning this indirect contribution. Characteristics of product categories that affect this total direct and indirect contribution were then derived, to be tested empirically in Chapter 7.

The first proposition rested on the assumption that profit maximization on each individual product category promotes maximum profits for the store; that is, each category can be considered independent of all others. It was argued that this assumption implies perfect competition among retailers on each product category. Given this competitive assumption, the profit-maximizing retailer should equate total contribution per square foot of shelf space among all categories so that *product categories with characteristics that initially would lead to higher total contributions per square foot should have lower gross margins in a competitive equilibrium*. Factors discussed included retail price and expenses, unit sales (and household penetration), the number of items (or brands) carried in a product category, the size of items in the category, the preshopping knowledge of consumers, and category advertising.

The second proposition acknowledged an important reality for any mass retailer: interdependencies among product categories. The effect of certain product categories, commonly referred to as traffic builders or loss leaders, on store traffic was recognized, implying a monopolistically competitive market equilibrium. Profit maximization for the store, therefore, does not directly follow from profit maximization on each individual product category. Instead, some categories are more salient to consumers than others, resulting in a competitive price, total contribution, and gross margin lower than other, less salient product categories. As such, the retailer should equate total contribution per square foot of shelf space among all categories only after this indirect contribution from the traffic building effects of the more salient product categories has been accounted for. Factors that reflect salience include some of the previously mentioned category characteristics, as well as the number of different package sizes carried in a product category, the degree of private label penetration in a category, and the type of product category considered, which for supermarket retailers is reflected in the distinction between food versus nonfood products.

The two propositions together create a realistic framework for assessing why category gross margins differ among product categories. This framework not only explains the pricing of product categories, but also will serve to explain why the effect of advertising on brand gross margins within a product category differs in magnitude among various product categories.

Endnotes

1. Conceptual models and empirical evidence on the shelf space–unit sales relationship are provided in R. C. Curhan, "The Relationship Between Shelf Space and Unit Sales in Supermarkets," *Journal of Marketing Research*, 9 (November 1972), pp. 406–412, and R. C. Curhan, "Shelf Space Allocation and Profit Maximization in Mass Retailing," *Journal of Marketing*, 37 (July 1973), pp. 54–60. Further, it should be mentioned that there may be some nonconvexities in these curves, particularly for the first few units of shelf space allocated

to a category, that is, a "threshold" effect. But this refinement would not seriously alter our conclusions, and may not be appropriate at all for fast-moving products (our sample).

2. Recall that the analytical method behind Figure 5.1 was marginal analysis—that is, equalizing the *marginal* contributions of the last units of the two product categories. In a perfectly competitive equilibrium, however, the *average* contributions would also be equal for the two product categories, with the two category curves shifting so that points A and B both lie on the same ray from the origin. Therefore, Figure 5.1 represents a disequilibrium, since points A and B do not lie on the same ray from the origin (product category 1 has a higher average contribution than category 2).

3. Differences in factory price levels; that is, merchandise costs among product categories are assumed to be reflected in retail price levels. Propositions about factory prices, therefore, are similar to those given for retail prices, not retail expenses.

4. A. Marshall, *Industry and Trade* (London: The Macmillan Press, Ltd., 1919), p 301.

5. Strictly speaking, product categories with no effect on the sales of other categories would no longer be under the perfect competition assumption either. The reason is that just as some indirect contribution should be credited to the traffic builders, this same contribution must be subtracted from the total contribution attributed to the product categories with no effect on the sales of other categories. Accordingly, the indirect contribution for these product categories is negative, leading to higher equilibrium gross margins than predicted by the perfect competition assumption.

6. A mathematical proof of this contention is provided in Appendix 1. A partial equilibrium model is presented for a single-product and multiproduct retailer.

7. The storability of items in a product category may also reflect category salience. The contention is that product categories with items that are easily stored by the consumer at home are more readily promoted by the retailer, as consumers are more willing to make an extra trip to the store when they can "stock up" for measurable savings. This contention is not included since empirical testing was found to be ambiguous, most likely due to the subjective interpretations of the author on what product categories are more or less storable.

8. The underlying assumption for these propositions concerning the number of different package sizes is not only monopolistic competition in retailing, but also oligopoly in manufacturing.

Chapter 6

IMPACT OF ADVERTISING ON RETAIL BRAND PROFITABILITY

The relative profitability of the various brands carried by the retailer is largely dependent on pricing, unit volumes, and the relative importance of the brands to store shoppers. In particular the mass retailer must gauge the contribution to store profits generated by nationally advertised brands versus less heavily advertised regional brands and unadvertised private label brands. This choice of brands involves the effects of manufacturers' advertising on brand salience to consumers and thereby retail turnover, factory prices, and retail price competition—effects underlying the main contention of the book: *Manufacturers' advertising induces the profit-maximizing mass retailer to be willing to price an advertised brand at a lower gross margin than an identical, unadvertised brand in that product category.* In this chapter we focus on three reasons for this inverse relationship between advertising and gross margin, based on the effects of advertising on brand salience, and consider different measurements of the advertising–gross margin relationship. Essentially these measurements are of the total effect of advertising on gross margin and the effect of advertising on gross margin independent of its effect on gross margin through its effect on sales.

Although conceptually this chapter is similar to the discussion of the determinants of the level of product category gross margins, there are three important differences. First, the focus here is on retail pricing; shelf space allocation is considered secondary, so total contribution, not total contribution per square foot, is the relevant concern. Second, we are primarily interested in the advertising–gross margin relationship, so the only other factors discussed are those that have a direct impact on this relationship; those factors are brand unit sales and brand retail price. Third, we concentrate on the notion of brand salience to consumers to explain the relationships of particular factors with brand gross margins, even though all the variables can also be thought of in terms of their impact on total contribution. Two separate competitive assumptions, however, are not used, because the perfect competition assumption overlooks the very important effect of advertising on retail price competition. Rather, the factors affecting brand gross margins—most important, advertising—are all discussed in terms of monopolistic competition in retailing. The first three sections concern the effect of advertising on gross margin through its effect on unit sales, factory price, and retail price competition. Afterward, the different measurements of the advertising–gross margin relationship are examined by looking at other factors that affect brand gross margins and are related to advertising as well. All comparisons discussed are *interbrand:* among brands—advertised versus unadvertised—within the same product category. And as in the last chapter, all propositions are made with the assumption that all other factors are held constant, that is, *ceteris paribus*.

Advertising and Unit Sales

The first reason that the retailer is willing to accept a lower gross margin on an advertised brand is that advertising can increase a brand's rate of movement and inventory turnover through higher unit sales of the brand at the retail store. With higher unit sales, an advertised brand can have a lower gross margin than an unadvertised brand and still maintain the same total contribution. For the retailer, therefore, *advertising increases the retail productivity on an advertised brand*.

For this to occur, a number of economic relationships need to exist, all of which are fairly common in most product markets. First, advertising must increase the brand's unit sales at the store; second, the rate of movement at the store should be higher on an advertised brand than on an unadvertised brand; and third, the inventory turnover at the store should be higher on an advertised brand than on an unadvertised brand. Increased rate of movement and higher turnover are the two components of increased retail productivity. Here we are referring to *reducing the retail costs (expenses)* associated with a brand through the effect of advertising on brand unit sales at the store. In particular, the retail costs are primarily the fixed costs per unit sold of the brand, which includes the opportunity cost of retail space. Let us first consider the implications of increased unit sales, without which increased rate of movement and inventory turnover are not possible.

Increased Unit Sales

That advertising may increase the unit sales of a brand is well rooted in microeconomic theory. However, since the actions of manufacturers marketing competing brands can affect the impact of a brand's advertising on its unit sales, we assume that competitors' actions remain unchanged. For example, if Heinz decides to increase its advertising of Heinz catsup, any effect on unit sales may be seriously mitigated by an increase in the advertising budgets of Hunt's or Del Monte for their brands of catsup. Accordingly, given this assumption, advertising should have some effect on the total market demand for a brand, with an increase in the quantity demanded at any given price.

The situation is more complicated, however, for ascertaining the effects of advertising on the unit sales of an advertised brand at any one particular store carrying the brand. If there are other retail stores that carry the brand or that potentially may carry the brand, an increase in unit sales does *not* necessarily translate into an increase in the brand's unit sales at the representative outlet, which is defined as the average outlet carrying the brand—what we have referred to as "the retailer." Certain assumptions are required about the retail distribution of the brand, that is, about the effect of advertising on retail penetration. Penetration is defined as the average commodity volume of a brand; that volume is the weighted average of the number of outlets carrying the brand times the number of units each outlet carries (or sells, assuming no inventory build-up). In short, advertising increases the unit sales of the brand at the representative outlet as long as the increase in sales is not fully translated into sales for other stores that did not carry the brand prior to the advertising.

An increase in retail penetration can result from an increase in the number of outlets carrying the brand, the number of units of the brand carried by a representative outlet, or both. If there is no increase in the number of stores carrying the brand (and inventory per unit sold), then the increased retail penetration from the increase in consumer demand for the advertised brand is fully translated into an increase in the brand's unit sales at the store. It is very possible, however, that advertising will increase the number of outlets carrying the brand at some point. Therefore, for retail penetration to be increased, essentially *the percentage increase in stores carrying the brand needs to be less than the percentage increase in the unit sales of the advertised brand.* In addition, the representative outlet must not lose sufficient relative market share of the brand after the increase in advertising to offset entirely its percentage increase in the market unit sales of the brand.

These conditions for advertising to increase unit sales of a brand at each representative outlet are not very strict. Excepting the atypical store, there would not be, on average, a large loss in the relative market share of the brand at the store after advertising. Similarly, a large percentage increase in stores carrying the brand would also not occur. For instance, if advertising were to double the yearly demand for a brand, say from 100,000 to 200,000 units, and there were 100 stores with equal brand market shares selling the brand before the advertising (1,000 units each, for example), then less than 200 stores must be carrying the brand after the advertising for there to be an average increase in store sales. And if there is no change in the number of stores carrying the brand, but there is a shift in average market shares, the change would have to be from 1% (1,000/100,000) to less than 0.5 percent (1,000/200,000), a highly unlikely occurrence for any representative, average outlet. Rather, an increase in unit sales for the retailer should result from an increase in the total market demand for a brand, caused by the manufacturer's advertising.

Increased Rate of Movement

An advertised brand will have a higher rate of movement as long as the increase is in *unit sales per unit of time*—no matter what period of time is used. On the other hand, if advertising merely affects the timing of demand, then an increase in unit sales for a particular time period, a common result of retail cents-off promotions, need not translate into an increased rate of movement. Since we have assumed that shelf space is equally apportioned among brands, the amount of space used is not a consideration. But even if it were not, all that is necessary is that *the advertised brand not use proportionately (to unit sales) more shelf space than the unadvertised brand*, all things being equal.

Research on the relationship between shelf space and unit sales, most notably by Curhan (1972, 1973), has investigated how the amount of shelf space given to a product affects its unit sales, but not how unit sales affect shelf space allocation. This research indicates that the amount of shelf space given to a brand does not increase proportionately with the brand's unit sales at the store. Furthermore, in supermarket retailing, brands are shelved by the case; the breaking up of a case is disastrous for profits due to space and labor costs. There is rarely any backroom stock except for promotional items. This "case plus" method of stocking—shelf refills done a case at a time so that after a refill, at least one case is on the shelf—means that the faster-moving, advertised brand may possibly occupy even less shelf space on average than an unadvertised brand since at any point in time, less of the case of the advertised brand is on the shelf. Proprietary studies of the margarine market in Germany demonstrate this relationship: Advertised brands use less shelf space at any one point in time than unadvertised brands. More commonly, however, as shown by the supermarket scanning data collected at the University of Chicago (proprietary at the time of this publication), advertised brands are given more shelf space, but not in proportion to their higher level of unit sales. On the basis of marketing research, therefore, the retailer should have a higher rate of movement on an advertised brand than on an unadvertised brand, which permits the advertised brand to have a lower gross margin and still be as profitable.

Higher Inventory Turnover

This contention is similar to that of increased rate of movement, the difference being that the higher rate of movement is viewed in terms of inventory costs rather than use of shelf space. The effect here is that an advertised brand has a lower number of units of inventory for a given number of units sold at the store than an unadvertised brand. This higher inventory turnover translates into lower inventory costs for the retailer as long as *inventory does not rise proportionately with unit sales.*

Optimally, inventory should not rise proportionately with unit sales but, rather, according to the economic order quantity (EOQ) inventory formula with the square root of dollar sales. With a minor revision, this frequently used formula serves as strong evidence that, at the very least, inventory should not rise proportionately with unit sales.[1] Therefore, on this basis as well, an advertised brand should be more profitable than an unadvertised brand because less of the retailer's money is expended on the carrying costs of inventory—a critical concern in inflationary times of higher interest rates. Again, as with increased turnover, the implication is that the retailer can price an advertised brand to remit a lower gross margin than an unadvertised brand and realize comparable profits on either brand.

Advertising and the Manufacturer's Factory Price

Whereas the effect of advertising on the unit sales of a brand at the store reflects an increase in total contribution for the retailer generated by the manufacturer's advertising, the effect of advertising on factory and retail prices results in lower total contribution—that is, increased factory prices and increased retail price competition, leading to lower retail gross margins. The retailer is willing to accept the higher factory prices and compete more intensely on the retail prices of advertised brands because of the effect of advertised brands on store traffic. Because of the higher salience of advertised brands to consumers, the retailer is willing, albeit is forced, to carry these brands, even though the factory price charged is higher than on unadvertised brands. As Marshall noted:[2]

> *They [the retailers] had little defense against the selling cheaply of those few branded goods, which had already so strong a hold on the public, that a refusal to handle them would simply drive away customers.*

This result is the second reason for an inverse advertising–gross margin relationship: *Advertising forces the retailer to be willing to pay a higher price to the manufacturer for an advertised brand than for an identical, unadvertised brand.* In effect, advertising allows the manufacturer to charge the retailer a higher price—an increase in retail variable costs that the retailer is willing to accept because of the importance of advertised brands to store sales. Through this effect, advertising decreases the retailer's profitability on a brand.

Underlying this contention is the understanding that *advertising decreases the price elasticity of the retailer's demand for the manufacturer's brand*, thus representing a decrease in the factory price elasticity. It can then be reasonably assumed that the manufacturer raises the brand's price within a certain period of time in response to this decreased elasticity of demand from the retailer. This effect of advertising on factory price sensitivity was reviewed in Chapters 2 and 3 and requires further discussion.

Porter's model of bilateral market power in convenience goods documented the potential of advertising to shift the terms of trade between manufacturer and retailer. Advertising, it is maintained, can confer increased monopoly power on the manufacturer through its effects on consumers. The marketing channel responds to the consumer so that the manufacturer may enjoy increased bargaining power over the retailers. As the manufacturer tries to attract more customers (advertising pull) and increase brand loyalty among its customers through advertising, the retailer is forced to stock the manufacturer's brand to satisfy store shoppers.

On the other hand, unadvertised brands, with less brand loyalty and fewer customers, are easily substituted for one another by the retailer. For example, the supermarket retailer may be able to replace Hunt's with Del Monte catsup, but most likely can ill afford

not to stock Heinz. In general, catsup purchasers who buy Heinz
are less willing to switch to another catsup (they are more brand
loyal, as documented in the Simmons *Target Group Index* data) if
the supermarket does not carry Heinz than are purchasers of Hunt's.
A store that does not stock Heinz, therefore, is more likely to lose
customers (and more consumers purchase Heinz) than a supermarket
that does not stock Hunt's. And in a multiproduct enterprise, where
the average customer purchases 14 items, a loss of customers translates into the loss of sales for the supermarket of more than just
some catsup. In short, other brands cannot be as easily substituted
by the retailer for an advertised brand as for an unadvertised brand
(or a less heavily advertised brand). Not only is the advertised brand
differentiated to the customer, but it is therefore differentiated to
the retailer as well.

Manufacturer-Retailer Intrabrand Competition

This advertising pull—the increased consumer demand from the
manufacturer's efforts—indirectly affects the retailer, as depicted in
Figure 6.1. The manufacturer's advertising affects the competition
and bargaining between the manufacturer and retailer over the price
the manufacturer can charge the retailer for the brand. The first of
two types of brand competition to be described, this competition
is called *manufacturer-retailer intrabrand competition*. The other
type of brand competition, which will be discussed second, is among
retailers selling the same brand, called simply *retail intrabrand
competition*.

To illustrate this point, reconsider Heinz, which is in a very different position when bargaining over the factory price with a retail
supermarket than is another catsup manufacturer. Since the retailer
cannot so easily substitute another brand for Heinz as for Hunt's,
the elasticity of the retailer's demand for the more heavily advertised
brand (Heinz) has been decreased relative to that for the less heavily

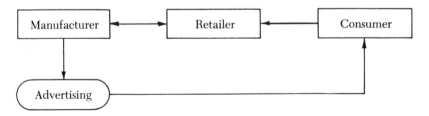

Figure 6.1   Indirect Effect of Advertising on the Retailer. The two-way arrow
between manufacturer and retailer represents manufacturer–retailer intrabrand
competition.

advertised brand. Heinz should be able to bargain for and receive a higher price, to a large extent because of the consumer goodwill developed from advertising. Evidence on this relationship of advertising with both factory price elasticity (negative relationship) and relative factory prices (positive relationship) was cited in Chapter 2.

In summation, it has been argued that advertising allows the manufacturer not only to increase brand sales, given a retail price, but also to increase the brand's factory price without necessarily affecting a change in the retail price. Unless the retailer raises the price of the advertised brand proportionately by the same amount as the manufacturer has raised the factory price, the advertised brand must have a lower gross margin than an unadvertised brand. In effect, the manufacturer captures an increased percentage of the retail price of the advertised brand—*a hidden effect of advertising* often overlooked by manufacturers. As a result, an increase in the factory price of an advertised brand causes a smaller change in consumer demand than if the increase had occurred for an unadvertised brand, which carries a higher retail gross margin.

From the retailer's perspective, total contribution dollars from the sale of manufacturers' advertised brands need to be protected. The increase in factory price is treated as an increase in inventory carrying cost. But although the advertised brands are more expensive for the retailer, they are also more productive. The higher factory price for advertised brands may be offset by the higher rate of movement and inventory turnover. If we assume that the retailer equates the total contribution of brands, then the decreased gross margin should be entirely offset by the increased unit sales. For the profit-maximizing mass retailer, however, *this offset need not occur*. Instead, the increased salience of advertised brands to consumers requires that the retailer carry these brands *even if they generate less total contribution than unadvertised brands* because of the effect of advertised brands on store traffic. Moreover, the retailer prices advertised brands differently than unadvertised brands because of this increased brand salience. The strength of these different effects will depend on how important the brand is to the manufacturer (is it one of a multiproduct line?) and to the retailer (are there other equally important advertised brands?).

Advertising and Retail Prices

There are two effects of increased consumer brand salience on the mass retailer. As mentioned, the first is that the retailer is forced to carry these brands. Second, since consumers typically use these more salient, often highly advertised brands as benchmarks for the store's pricing policy on all products, the retailer tends to compete heavily on the prices of these brands. Therefore, whether the retailer is or is not as profitable on advertised as on unadvertised brands, as determined by the two previous effects on advertising on unit sales and factory price, the question remains: How does advertising affect retail pricing policies? It will be argued that, in fact, *advertising causes retailers to be more price competitive on an advertised brand than on an identical, unadvertised brand*.

As early as Alfred Marshall (1919), researchers recognized "advertising's propensity to invigorate competition among retailers." Neil Borden investigated the struggle for brand control between manufacturers and distributors in the 1880s, commenting that:[3]

> *Experience has shown them [wholesalers and retailers] that the handling of well-known manufacturers' brands has often led to keen price competition among these brands within the trade, with resultant reductions in trade margins. . . . [They] require dense distribution and hence stocking by directly competing distributors, [so that] the fierce price competition which is likely to occur in both the wholesale and retail channels brings a shading of list prices and a consequent narrowing of trade margins.*

In setting advertising budgets, however, most manufacturers have neglected this important *hidden effect* (to them) of advertising on everyday retail price competition. The retailer sets a price based on costs and price elasticities, which are a function of competition. The effects of advertising on retail costs and factory price elasticity have already been discussed. Its effect on retail price elasticities—which are determined in part by the cross-elasticities of the brand with the other brands carried by the retailer—can be viewed through its effect on retail intrabrand competition, that is, the competition among retailers on the sale of the same manufacturer's brand. This competition focuses on the retail price charged to consumers.

By examining the effects on the mass retailer of lowering the price of a brand, and how the effects differ for an advertised versus an unadvertised (or similarly, a less advertised), brand, we will demonstrate that *advertising increases retail intrabrand competition*, thus reducing the retailer's monopoly power in the sale of the brand, and gross margin, and, most probably, the net margin. Advertising, it is argued, increases the retail price sensitivity of the brand, as reported in Chapter 2. Even so, with this downward pressure on the gross margin and total contribution of an advertised brand, it is maintained that the retailer should carry the brand because of its importance in maintaining and, quite possibly, increasing store sales.

Retail Pricing

Retail pricing, in particular supermarket pricing, involves two distinct components of the retail price: a regular, everyday price and a promotional price. Profit-maximizing retail pricing requires setting an optimal distribution of temporary prices over time—what has been called "variable price merchandising." This pricing method helps free the retailer somewhat from interstore price comparisons by consumers because it increases the difficulty for consumers to compare among stores the frequently changing prices on the same items. Accordingly, the discussion involves the benefits of both a low promotional price and a low everyday retail price. For our purposes, effects can be thought of as a result of either, with little modification in the analysis over any given time period. Therefore, the retail decision behind this third effect of advertising on the retailer is: How much should the retailer charge for Brand A? The corollary is: How often and how much should Brand A be promoted at a reduced retail price? Given the factory price, this decision determines the gross margin. The decision should be made considering the costs, competition (and their prices), unit sales, and gross margin of not only Brand A, but of *all* the products in the store.

The interdependence of the merchandising of Brand A with that of the rest of the products sold in the store is an essential reality of multiproduct, mass retailing: The retailer needs to maximize profits on the sales of the entire product mix in the store. The sensitivity of the sales of other products in the store to the price of Brand A depends upon how consumers perceive Brand A. Do they notice the price of Brand A relative to the competition, and do they care? The notion of product salience, developed in the last chapter, should be kept in mind throughout the discussion. The main contention is that advertising increases a brand's salience to consumers, called its "product recognition" by Reekie (1979), "which also depresses margins. Thus advertised brands . . . come under increased competitive pressure through improved product identification." The retailer, moreover, should be willing to accept these depressed margins because these advertised brands can serve as traffic builders and improve storewide sales and profits by attracting more shoppers to the store—shoppers who will then buy, the retailer hopes, higher margin brands as well.

Once the retailer has taken into account the competitive price of Brand A and the store's cost structure, the central pricing question then deals with *whether or not to lower the price of Brand A*. That is:

1. How beneficial is it for the retailer to price Brand A below the competitive market price level?
2. How will a price reduction and a policy of a low retail price of Brand A affect storewide profits?
3. How will competitors react to a lower price on Brand A?
4. Will the effects be different for an advertised Brand A than for an unadvertised Brand A?

The first three questions are similar in kind; they focus on the effects on retail profits of lowering the price of Brand A, which must acknowledge some type of competitive response. The last question is our main concern. The answer is "yes"; the question remains "why." First, it is useful to present the effects of a price decrease of Brand A on the retailer, with competition held constant; then, the difference between an advertised and unadvertised Brand A is discussed. The section concludes with a more explicit consideration of the nature of competition among retailers on advertised brands and competitive responses.

Table 6.1 shows the more important possible effects of a decrease in the price of Brand A for the supermarket retailer—our prototype of the mass retailer. Butter is used as an example. The advertised brand is represented by Land O Lakes butter, and the unadvertised brand by Hood's butter. The effects on the store's current and potential customers are included in Table 6.1. A number of assumptions made to simplify the analysis should be made explicit:

1. The retailer is deciding only how to price Brand A; all other store decisions have been taken care of, including the pricing of all other store products.
2. As an analysis of one brand in a supermarket, competition is also assumed fixed.
3. The manufacturer of Brand A makes only Brand A for supermarkets.
4. The purchasing of nonsupermarket products and aggregate savings remains unaffected.

The first two assumptions isolate the analysis to one brand's price at one store. The last two assumptions reduce the number of effects and avoid some unnecessary complications. The third avoids the problem of a change in retail price affecting the sales of that manufacturer's other supermarket products—a necessary consideration with firms like Kraft, Heinz, and Campbell's. The last assumption avoids the complication of shifts in consumer expenditures among different types of retail outlets and away from consumer savings. None of these assumptions should affect significantly the conclusions

Table 6.1   Impacts of a Decrease in the Price of Brand A (Butter) for the Supermarket Retailer

CURRENT CUSTOMERS

Brand Competition in the Product Category
1. Effects on purchase of butter
   a. Buy more of Brand A and less of other brands
   b. Buy more of Brand A today and less tomorrow
   c. Buy more butter

Customers' Purchases of Supermarket Products
2. Effects on purchase of other supermarket products
   a. Buy less of substitute products (margarine)
   b. Buy more of complementary products (bread)
   c. Buy more products today and less tomorrow
   d. Buy more of other products in the store

POTENTIAL CUSTOMERS

Store Competition on Supermarket Products
3. Effects on store traffic
   a. Attract customers from other supermarkets to buy Brand A
   b. Attract customers from other supermarkets to buy other products at the store

derived. Any effect from relaxing these assumptions, moreover, would be to strengthen the conclusions in most cases.

Table 6.1 separates the effects of a price decrease into three categories containing nine different effects. The first two categories of effects concern the current, established clientele at the representative supermarket. The first category deals only with the sale of butter: manufacturers' brand competition and the percentage of the supermarket customer's dollar spent on butter. As shown, one group of effects from a price reduction is to increase the amount spent by current customers on Brand A (or butter) at the expense of other brands, other time periods, and/or other supermarket product categories. The increase in units purchased may be the result of Brand A (or butter) being purchased more frequently, as frequently but in larger sizes, or some combination of both. Effect 1b is very common with temporary price reductions, which change the pattern of purchase. On an annual or semiannual basis, however, a temporary price reduction generates a lower average retail price, with 1a and 1c as important possible results. In this regard, it should be recognized that an increase in dollar sales from the price reduction assumes that the downward retail price elasticity is greater than one.

The second category of effects concerns other store products: those related (2a and 2b) and those unrelated (2c and 2d) to butter through consumption. The effect is to increase the buying power of the Brand A customer at the store because of the price decrease in Brand A. The same basket of supermarket products can now be purchased for less. Substitute products become relatively more expensive, whereas complementary products can now be purchased and consumed at a lower *joint* cost; that is, Brand A–buttered bread is now cheaper, so the savings can be spent on other store products.

The third category of effects involves potential customers who are currently shopping at other supermarkets. The possibility that the Brand A price reduction may draw customers to the store from other supermarkets is at the heart of competition among mass retailers: *the opportunity to transfer customers (and thereby sales and profits) from one store to another by a price reduction on one product or a subset of products, but not all products*. The potential problem for the store is the "cherry-picking" phenomenon—new customers purchase only the promoted product(s) at the store (3a). It is assumed in this analysis that once at the store, new customers buy more than just Brand A—a reasonable, realistic assumption in the mass retailing of low-priced, freequently purchased, convenience products—so that effect 3a leads to effect 3b. Otherwise, the efficacy of loss leading in mass retailing would be sharply curtailed.

As the store's sales objectives are to increase its share of the market among current customers (that is, their dollars spent on supermarket products) and increase its total share of customers, three effects are of central concern. They are normally the strongest and capture most of the effect of a price decrease of Brand A for the outlet. Furthermore, these effects are reliable indicators of the strength of other effects. Reflecting the competition among manufacturers' brands (1a) and the competition among supermarkets (3a and 3b), they can be rephrased as:

1a—Given the brand market shares of butter at the store, the reduction in the price of Brand A will increase its market share at the expense of the other brands of butter at the store.

3a and 3b—Given the store's market share of customers in the relevant supermarket retail market, the reduction in the price of Brand A will increase that store's share of supermarket customers.

The question remains of how these effects will differ between an advertised and an unadvertised brand. The more effective the price reduction in increasing store sales (and profits), the more incentive the profit-maximizing retailer has to lower the price and undercut the competition. Effect 1a signals that the price reduction has been noticed and acted upon by shoppers in the store, as does 3a among potential customers; effect 3b translates into more store traffic, sales, and profits. Eliminating our assumptions and considering all the effects only strengthens the arguments to follow in most cases: For instance, 2d (an effect among present customers which is analogous to 3b among potential customers) is critical to the store's objective to increase its share of market among present customers. It should not be one of the stronger effects, however, and its inclusion would only increase the additional contribution to the store from a price decrease for Brand A.

Retail Intrabrand Competition

The consumer behavior underlying the concept of product salience is that consumers notice more easily and appreciate more readily a low retail price (or purchase reduction) on an advertised brand than on an unadvertised brand. Accordingly, consumers generally recognize and appreciate a low market retail price on Land O Lakes butter more than on Hood's butter. The increased salience of advertised brands to consumers causes *more retailers to carry them*— whatever their individual profitability—whereas the increased potential effectiveness of a price decrease increases the retail intrabrand competition on advertised brands.

Similar to Figure 6.1, Figure 6.2 diagrams the effect of manufacturers' advertising on the price competition among retailers on an advertised brand (dark two-way arrow) and on the price competition

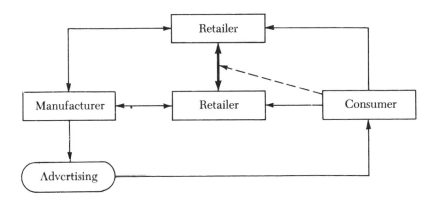

Figure 6.2 Indirect Effect of Advertising on Retail Intrabrand Competition. The dark two-way arrow between retailers represents retail intrabrand competition. The two two-way arrows between manufacturer and retailers represent manufacturer-retailer intrabrand competition (Figure 6.1).

between manufacturer and retailer over the transfer price (factory price) of the brand (both two-way arrows). It is maintained, therefore, that advertising affects not only each outlet's purchase situation, that is, its bargaining power vis-à-vis the brand's manufacturer, but also the market in which each store sells its products. The retailer competes intensively on the price of these salient brands because of their ability to affect store traffic—a one-way cross elasticity—and thus hopes to make up for the thin margins on these brands with larger margins on other, less salient brands sold at the store.

To substantiate this claim, it is necessary to answer two questions concerning how the three effects (1a and 3a and 3b in Table 6.1) of a price reduction differ for the retailer between an advertised and an unadvertised brand. The questions concern aspects of the salience of a brand to the consumer: Will the consumer notice? Will the consumer care?

Will the Consumer Notice?   For a price reduction to be noticed by shoppers in the store, a point-of-purchase display is sufficient; to draw store traffic, the supermarket can advertise the price reduction. A price reduction, therefore, is easily communicated to consumers by the retailer whether the brand in question is advertised by the manufacturer or not. However, for consumers to recognize that a brand carries a low retail price relative to the competition at the outlet, they need to know the average market retail price of the brand, which is similar to a list price, for the particular geographical market. This type of knowledge requires a different source of information, as the price comparison is no longer within one store at one point in time. It is maintained that *this interstore information can be acquired more readily for advertised brands*, thus facilitating interstore price comparisons for consumers.

Consumers may learn of the average market price of a brand through retail advertising or their own search and word-of-mouth. Manufacturers' advertising, however, rarely carries retail price information on supermarket products. Instead, it normally tries to raise the consumer's brand awareness and recognition of certain product characteristics deemed beneficial by the manufacturer to brand sales. Price information is carried in retail advertising, but only for the "specials." Therefore the main source of price information for the consumer must be search.

Consumer search costs among the various stores in an area are reduced by advertising, for advertising increases the number of outlets carrying a brand and the numbers of buyers of the brand. As advertising increases the brand's unit sales in the market, higher retail penetration follows, reflected in increased unit sales at each store and, quite probably, more outlets carrying the advertised brand than an unadvertised brand. This increase in the number of outlets carrying the advertised brand is a result of not only more buyers—which would occur unless the increase in brand unit sales were totally from old customers purchasing more (a highly unlikely situation)—but also the outlet's inability to substitute other brands for the advertised brand as easily, due to higher brand loyalty and salience. Marginal search costs are reduced for the Land O Lakes shopper, as it is easier to obtain information by word-of-mouth from other Land O Lakes purchasers (more of them) and more convenient to comparison shop among supermarkets since more stores carry Land O Lakes than Hood's butter.

Will the Consumer Care?   Certainly the two questions of "notice" and "care" are not entirely separable. The more a consumer cares about the price of a brand, the more its price and product attributes are noticed. The question of noticing a low market retail price at the store was discussed in terms of the relative ease for the shopper of gaining access to the necessary information. Being aware of and sensitive to a low market retail price (or price reduction) makes the retailer's competitive efforts more effective. In our definition of product salience, we can recall that the relevant aspect of this "relative ease" is what Porter calls the "utility loss" from obtaining brand information. The question of caring about a low market retail price at the store can be seen as the consumer's being sensitive to a low market price—what Porter calls "the desire to make an informed choice." In this regard, two contentions are made here, the first relating to effect 1a and the other to effects 3a and 3b.

1. A low market retail price at the store is more effective on Land O Lakes than on Hood's butter, in terms of both stimulating purchase by Land O Lakes purchasers and precipitating brand switching, as Hood's purchasers are more price conscious.
2. A low market retail price of Land O Lakes at the store is more effective in increasing store traffic, as consumers appreciate that low price more than any price reduction on Hood's.

Neither contention is necessarily intuitive, so further explanation is warranted.

The first contention concerns the current customers at the store, both Land O Lakes and Hood's purchasers, and the total *market* demand for the two brands. To understand it, we must first make a distinction between two types of price elasticity: *upside* elasticity and *downside* elasticity. Similar to contentions made by Moran (1978), this assertion maintains that *advertising can decrease the elasticity of Land O Lakes (the advertised brand) above the market retail price while at the same time increasing the elasticity below that level.* As Steiner (1979) notes:

> *The very fact that consumers know the approximate price of a well-known brand that is important to them causes its demand curve below that level to become extremely elastic in response to a temporary price reduction . . . . At the same time, the leading national brand's demand curve, that obtained when it is selling at its everyday price, tends to be relatively inelastic upward from its prevailing everyday price.*

In Steiner's terms, these "leading national brands" are normally the highly advertised brands.

Given these two very different effects of advertising on retail price elasticity, the result is a kinked *market* demand curve for the advertised brand. Land O Lakes purchasers should be comparatively insensitive to an increase in the relative retail price of Land O Lakes butter caused by an increase in the price of Land O Lakes or a decrease in the price of Hood's butter at the store, but more sensitive to a decrease in the relative retail price of Land O Lakes, caused by a decrease in the price of Land O Lakes or an increase in the price of Hood's. Similarly, purchasers of Hood's, with greater upside elasticity and lower downside elasticity than Land O Lakes purchasers, should respond in surprisingly the same manner: They are more sensitive to an increase in the relative retail price of Hood's, that is, price of Hood's up or price of Land O Lakes down, and less sensitive to a decrease in the relative price of Hood's, that is, price of Hood's down or price of Land O Lakes up, at the store. Accordingly, the advertising of Land O Lakes has also put a "kink" in the market demand curve for Hood's. Both Land O Lakes and Hood's purchasers, therefore, should be more sensitive to a price cut by the supermarket retailer on Land O Lakes than on Hood's butter, as shown in Table 6.2.

The decreased upside price elasticity of demand of the Land O Lakes purchasers reflects their brand loyalty, often referred to as a decreased cross-elasticity of the brand with other brands and commonly associated with manufacturers' advertising. These consumers are mostly concerned with Land O Lakes butter, not Hood's, but also do appreciate a good price on Land O Lakes. This increased downside elasticity of the Land O Lakes purchasers—the increased upside elasticity of the more price-conscious Hood's purchasers, who care more about the retail prices of butter at the store—reflects how manufacturers' advertising may increase retail intrabrand price competition by increasing the salience of the brand to consumers. Moreover, price discounts on the advertised brand are also commonly

Table 6.2   The Effects of Advertising on Retail Price Elasticity of Market Demand

	Sensitivity of Land O Lakes Purchasers	*Sensitivity of Hood's Purchasers*
Land O Lakes		
Price increase	Less (upside)	Less (downside)
Price decrease	More (downside)	More (upside)
Hood's		
Price increase	More (downside)	More (upside)
Price decrease	Less (upside)	Less (downside)

NOTES: All increases and decreases are relative to approximately the market retail price level. The terms "less" and "more" are comparable within each cell only.

announced by retail advertising, which increases downward retail price elasticity as well.

The second contention (Land O Lakes butter is a better traffic builder) concerns *store*, not total market, demand and is more simply explained. When the retailer attempts to draw more customers to the supermarket, a low retail price is not valuable to the potential store customer for the savings on that brand alone (effect 3a in Table 6.1), but rather as *an indication, a price-point, of an overall store policy of low retail prices* on average for the entire consumer shopping basket of supermarket products. With too many products and price changes for the consumer to inspect all prices, and the potential monetary savings low relative to the time spent acquiring the interstore information, a low retail price on the "right" products can give the supermarket a reputation for generally low retail prices.

These "right" products are generally those more salient, well known to the consumer, and often the advertised brands (exceptions are staples, which are not heavily advertised). Carried by most supermarkets, these brands often become the instrument of comparison shopping by consumers, whether the consumer is a purchaser of Land O Lakes or Hood's butter. Price promotions are more expected by the consumer for the low-price brands: private labels, generics, lesser-known manufacturer's brands. Price promotions on the well-known name brands, however, are more appreciated as an unexpected savings, and are thought of as a benchmark of dollar savings for the shopper at that store. It is these brands on which supermarkets compete the most intensively in their hope to offset any loss in margin on these promoted advertised brands by sales of other higher-margin products a shopper is likely to buy while in the store.

Conversely, a high retail price on these brands at the store can give the supermarket a reputation for generally high retail prices. The result should be an increase in the traffic-building potential of the brands at other stores, since these brands now have a relatively low retail price at the other stores. For store demand, therefore, these advertised brands should have a more elastic demand curve at *all* levels of retail price than unadvertised brands, with no kink.[4] The evidence of Eskin (1975), Eskin and Baron (1977), and Wittink (1977), discussed in Chapter 2, further substantiates this relationship between advertising and the retail price elasticity of the store demand curve.

Retail Competition and Competitive Responses

The question of how the retailer should price a brand has been examined so far primarily in the context of the retailer free from any competitive responses. It has been argued that advertising increases the salience of the brand to consumers and that the retailer competes intensively on the advertised brand by lowering its retail price (and gross margin) in order to increase store traffic. That advertising increases retail intraband competition was discussed mostly in terms of the retailer and the store's customers, not the competitive conditions. Steiner (1979) argues that advertising increases retail intrabrand competition, as demonstrated by its effects on the four conditions of perfect competition:

1. *Large numbers of buyers and sellers:* Advertising increases the number of outlets carrying the brand and the number of buyers.
2. *Easy entry by firms:* New outlets commonly carry branded merchandise for the most part, as they have yet to establish their own goodwill.
3. *Perfect information:* Product information can be disseminated through advertising, but as explained, information is mostly collected through consumer search, the costs of which are reduced for consumers because of condition 1 (above).
4. *Product homogeneity:* The more differentiated the product, the less differentiation is available to the retailer; that is, Land O Lakes butter is Land O Lakes butter no matter where it is purchased, but is Kroger butter the same as Safeway butter?

Given these assertions and the monopolistically competitive environment of the mass retailer, the question of the competitive response to a retailer's price decrease of Brand A in this environment remains to be answered. The loss leading of Brand A at the outlet may indeed draw store traffic from competitors, but will not the other supermarkets retaliate by lowering their retail prices of Brand A as well, leading to an inelastic market demand curve at all prices? And if they do, will not the effects of this price decrease be mitigated for the average store—in fact, will not *all* supermarkets lose on this brand, resulting in a "prisoner's dilemma"?[5]

This question was asked and briefly answered in the last chapter with regard to product categories that are loss leaders, such as flour. The answer is that the other stores will not necessarily all lower their retail price of Brand A, as there are many Brand A's. Those brands that are good loss leaders, proposed to be mostly the well-known, highly advertised brands, change over time, with individual stores alternating those promoted through constant daily and weekly specials. It is fair to assume that whereas some brands may be better traffic builders than others, each store has its own opinion of which brands are the best to promote at a particular time in a particular market, depending on the current shoppers, the shoppers it hopes to attract, and the promotions of competitors.

Accordingly, with the large number of these brands, the analysis of the individual store selling a particular Brand A may closely approximate the reality of the situation: In a retail market so heavily dominated by price competition as a means of differentiation among the stores, evidenced in supermarket retailing, it is the price competition on advertised brands, which reduces their gross margins and total contributions, that is central to the profit-maximizing mass retailer's strategy. The increased salience of these brands, moreover, leads to lower gross margins than for brands with lower salience to consumers. This concept of salience is also the theoretical link between other brand characteristics and the level of gross margin obtained by the retailer of the sale of a brand.

Brand Factors

Our central concern is to measure the advertising–gross margin relationship among brands in a product category. To measure this interbrand relationship in a sample of many product categories with different levels of gross margins and advertising, *we need to specify all variables as ratios of their respective product category levels,* as was discussed in Chapter 4. Accordingly, brand factors that affect this relationship, such as brand unit sales and retail price, must be specified similarly. In this manner we can isolate the various interbrand relationships from the various effects of different product category levels. Therefore, for example, we can examine the gross margins of Bumble Bee canned tuna and Hershey's candy bars and allow for the fact that canned tuna has a lower category gross margin than candy bars (and we can examine advertising and the brand factors similarly). In this discussion, however, the term "gross margin" is used for simplicity even though the more precise term is "the ratio of brand to category gross margins." The same terminology is used for the other variables as well, such as "advertising" for "the brand's share of total category advertising."

This important relationship between advertising and the retail gross margin has been called the *margin elasticity (of advertising)*: the change in the ratio of a brand's gross margin to its product category gross margin, divided by the change in the ratio of brand advertising to the total advertising in the product category.[6] Since the brand variables are already expressed as percentages of their category levels, further specifying the variables as percentage changes (empirically, a double-logarithmic specification) would be redundant. By measuring the advertising–gross margin relationship with or without factors correlated with both variables, we can estimate different relationships between advertising and gross margin. We are essentially concerned with three measures: the *total* margin elasticity (also called the total effect), the *partial* margin elasticity (also called the indirect effect, per Figures 6.1 and 6.2), and the *sales* margin elasticity (also called the direct effect). The total margin elasticity is the sum of the partial and sales margin elasticities; similarly, the total effect is the sum of the indirect and direct effects.

By including brand factors correlated with advertising as well as gross margin in the estimation equation explaining the level of gross margins, we may estimate without bias the partial margin elasticity (the slope coefficient of gross margin regressed on advertising). If no brand factors have been left out of the equation, this slope coefficient should be the same for all product categories in the sample.[7] More important for our purposes, if all those factors that directly influence a brand's total contribution are included, *the partial margin elasticity can be used to proxy the effect of advertising on retail price competition*. A "proxy," that is, an indirect measure, must be used because we have no direct method of measuring the effect of advertising on retail price competition. Since interbrand variations in shelf space have been considered negligible, as have interbrand variations in handling expenses, we will use measures of the retail dollar sales (unit sales and retail price) to isolate the partial margin elasticity. In this manner we can obtain measures of both the partial margin elasticity of advertising and the sales margin elasticity of advertising. Together, these indirect and direct effects of advertising on gross margin comprise the total margin elasticity.

In short, we will use the estimate of partial margin elasticity of advertising to infer that the retailer is pricing as if the brand has a significant one-way cross-elasticity with the other products sold at the store. The sales margin elasticity measures advertising's long-recognized ability to increase the retailer's productivity (unit sales) and contribution (dollar sales, which includes retail price). The total margin elasticity captures both effects of advertising on gross margin, measuring the total impact for the manufacturer of brand advertising on the retailer's pricing. For instance, if a 10 percent increase in a manufacturer's share of total category advertising leads to a 5 percent decrease in gross margin, possibly 60 percent of the decrease (3 percent) may be attributable to the effect of advertising on gross margin through its effect on sales (the sales margin elasticity), whereas 40 percent will then be inferred to be the result of advertising increasing retail price competition, proxied by the partial margin elasticity.

Two other brief points need to be made before we discuss the brand factors. First, factors other than unit sales and retail price can influence the partial margin elasticity estimate if these factors are correlated with advertising and gross margin. We will discuss one of these factors, brand loyalty, and show how its impact is already captured, as an intervening variable, in the sales margin elasticity estimate. Second, an effect is very different from a relationship primarily because an effect connotes *causality*. Whereas advertising may lead to lower gross margins, these lower gross margins may feed back to higher sales and still higher levels of advertising. We will measure this simultaneity, what will be called the *feedback effect*, discovering that in our sample it is quite small. Further support can be found in the only study done on the direction of this advertising–gross margin relationship, described in Chapter 3 (Reekie, 1979), which did find that reductions in gross margin *follow* increases in advertising. Claiming that advertising leads to lower gross margins, therefore, should not be misleading.

Figure 6.3 shows the system of relationships; the partial margin elasticity, the sales margin elasticity, and the total margin elasticity (the sum of the partial and sales margin elasticities) are all dia-grammed. The hypothesized signs of the various relationships are enclosed in parentheses, with all the margin elasticities of advertising expected to be negative. it should be noted that whereas advertising may affect gross margin through its effects on unit sales and retail price (the direct effect), these two brand factors also affect gross margin independently (the dotted lines). Brand loyalty, however, as an intervening variable, is shown to be reflected in the brand's retail price and unit sales, and therefore does not need to be included in the equation estimation.

In Chapter 4 we used two propositions, one dealing with a product

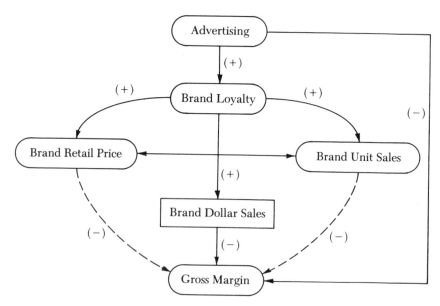

Figure 6.3   The System of Interbrand Relationships. Direction of relationships is indicated by plus and minus signs in parentheses. Partial margin elasticity (indirect effect) is represented by the solid arrow from Advertising to Gross Margin around the right side of the diagram. Sales margin elasticity (direct effect) is represented by the remaining group of solid arrows connecting Advertising with Gross Margin. The broken arrows depict relationships of brand factors, Brand Retail Price and Brand Unit Sales, with Gross Margin. Variables are circled; derived variables are boxed.

category's total contribution, the other with its "indirect" contribution, or salience, to explain the relationships of various category characteristics with the level of category gross margins. Here, only one proposition is necessary, based on brand salience, as retail price and unit sales reflect both total contribution and salience; two propositions would be redundant. Moreover, whereas previously product category space allocation and the valuation of retail space were the central issues, the primary brand merchandising issue has been maintained to be retail pricing in a monopolistically competitive environment. Finally, with retail handling expenses maintained to have minimal interbrand variation (as is the case, for example, with Vlasic versus Heinz pickles and Wise versus Cain's potato chips), but with great variation among product categories (such as pickles versus potato chips), interbrand contribution and gross margin are essentially equivalent constructs, although significantly different in many instances among product categories.

Accordingly, one proposition is offered to explain the relationship of brand factors to gross margin that affects the measurement of the margin elasticity of advertising:

> *Brands with higher salience to retail customers should have lower gross margins than brands with lower salience to customers.*

Brands factors to be discussed include brand loyalty and the brand's retail price (or average unit size) and unit sales. The importance of the brand's unit sales can also be understood by the notion of brand salience, just in terms of what may be called *aggregate* salience.

Brand Loyalty

A brand with loyal customers is an important competitive tool for retailers attempting to increase store traffic. One of the functions of brand advertising is not only to attract new customers or increase usage rates but also to reinforce the consumer's product decision. The question remains, therefore, of how much brand loyalty can be affected by brand advertising. Whereas a brand with high loyalty is very salient to consumers, it is not obvious that advertising per se increases loyalty and thereby salience to any significant degree. Albion and Farris (1981) have reviewed the research in this area, noting that most of the studies have produced insignificant results, usually because some critical variables were not included in the statistical work, such as product quality, advertising by other brands, and so forth. In general, however, the research does seem to show some positive relationship, although the strength of the relationship remains questionable. On the other hand, most research does indicate a strong positive relationship between brand loyalty and both brand retail price and unit sales. For the individual consumer, a brand's salience increases with increases in the number of units purchased of the brand. For the retailer, however, a brand's salience increases not only with the number of units purchased by each customer, but also with the total number of customers who purchase the brand— thus the term "aggregate" salience.

Brand Retail Price

The more a consumer spends on a brand, the more important the brand becomes to the consumer, thus increasing brand salience. Given a certain number of units purchased per time period, the greater the retail price (and/or average unit size) of the brand, the more the consumer spends on it. Higher-priced (larger) brands in a product category, therefore, should possess greater brand salience to consumers than lower-priced (smaller) brands.[8]

Brand Unit Sales

Assuming that the amount a consumer purchases of a brand does not depend on which brand(s) is (are) purchased in the product category—implying an equal distribution of heavy and light users interbrand—a brand's unit sales depends on its share of users in the product category. Although brand salience for each individual customer does not increase unless more units are purchased by that individual, aggregate salience as viewed by the retailer is increased by the number of shoppers who purchase that brand at the store. In addition, the concentration of users should be important to brand salience. A small core of heavy users (of margarine, for example) may lead to increased brand salience so that two brands with the same level of units sales, but a different concentration of users, may still have different levels of brand salience.

Summary

In this chapter we discussed why the mass retailer is willing to price an advertised brand so as to obtain a lower gross margin than on an identical, unadvertised brand in the same product category. Three reasons derived from the retailer's cost structure and pricing policy were given to support this contention of an inverse relationship between advertising and gross margin among brands:

1. By increasing brand unit sales for the retailer, manufacturers' advertising increases the retail productivity on an advertised brand.
2. Advertising forces the retailer to accept a higher price from the manufacturer for an advertised brand.
3. Advertising causes retailers to be more price competitive on an advertised brand.

In the first instance, advertising affects the brand's retail costs; in the latter two, advertising increases the brand's salience to consumers, since they tend to use advertised more than unadvertised brands as benchmarks of the store's pricing policy. Figure 6.4 illustrates these two types of effects of advertising: on costs (unit sales) and on salience (factory and retail price). It was pointed out, moreover, that in ascertaining the effect of advertising on the retail price elasticity of market demand (reason 3 above), we must be careful to differentiate "upside" and "downside" elasticity. It was held that advertising can decrease the retail price sensitivity of consumers for the brand above the average market retail price through increased

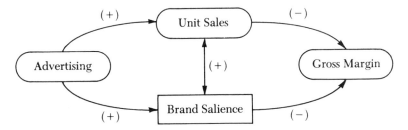

Figure 6.4   Effect of Advertising on Brand Gross Margin. Concepts are boxed; variables circled. Brand factors would appear as affecting brand salience and as affected by advertising. The two–way arrow represents the possibility of including the unit sales variable in the notion of aggregate brand salience.

brand loyalty. On the other hand, we argued that advertising can also increase retail price elasticity below the average market retail price of the brand, as retailers respond to the situation by competing intensively on the brand to draw store traffic. The price elasticity of the market demand curve for the advertised brand, therefore, is affected by both the consumer's response to advertising and the retailer's response to the brand's salience to consumers. For each individual retailer, however, the advertised brand has a more elastic demand curve at all prices, as a price rise signals a low relative price at other stores, resulting in a potential loss of store traffic. Whereas the retailer will advertise the low relative prices at the store, other retailers will do the same for their low-priced brands as well.

As in the last chapter, the brand's salience to consumers is an important underlying concept. If advertising does indeed increase the salience of a brand to store customers, retailers are forced to stock the brand and to keep prices on it low to maintain and attract store traffic. It was held that advertising increases the one-way cross-elasticity of a brand with the other products in the store since consumers are more apt to use an advertised than an unadvertised brand to compare store pricing policies. We argued that this occurs because it is easier for consumers to know the average market price of an advertised brand and because, in general, they appreciate a lower price more on an advertised brand. Accordingly, the pricing of an advertised brand has a greater effect on the sales of other products at the store: The more customers are attracted to the store, the more probable it is that the sales of other products will increase as well.

The effect of advertising on gross margin is referred to as the *margin elasticity of advertising*. By including brand factors that affect the level of brand gross margins and are correlated with advertising, we were able to separate out three types of margin elasticities, each representing a different type of effect of advertising on gross margin. The brand factors necessary for the estimation of these different elasticities are brand unit sales and retail price. In this manner we will be able to estimate: (1) the sales margin elasticity—the direct effect of advertising on gross margin through its effect on retail sales (our proxy for the brand's total contribution since handling expenses are assumed to vary little interbrand); (2) the partial margin elasticity—the indirect effect of advertising on gross margin through its effect on retail price competition (proxied by this residual of what is *not* advertising's effect on the brand's total contribution); and (3) the total margin elasticity, the total effect of advertising on gross margin (the sum of the sales and partial margin elasticities). The partial margin elasticity of advertising is our proxy for the one-way cross-elasticity of a brand with the entire retail product mix.

In the next three chapters we will test empirically this model of retail profitability. Specifically, we will concentrate on measuring the margin elasticity of advertising and determining why it may vary among product categories. To do so, we examine the determinants of variations in category gross margins and brand gross margins for supermarket retail data, which include mostly food products. The empirical work demonstrates the importance of this inverse relationship between advertising and gross margin among brands, and how the strength of this relationship varies systematically with product category characteristics related to the level of category gross margins. These results can then be used to develop important managerial and public policy guidelines.

Endnotes

1. The EOQ formula is EOQ $= (2D{\cdot}s/c{\cdot}i)^{\frac{1}{2}}$, where D is yearly demand (dollar sales), s is the setup cost per order, c is the unit variable cost of the item, and i is the cost of carrying inventory as a fraction of inventory. D and s vary directly and c and i inversely with the amount of inventory kept on hand. D can easily be separated into $p{\cdot}q$ to obtain a formula with unit sales (q) recognized explicitly.
2. A. Marshall, *Industry and Trade* (London: The Macmillan Press, Ltd., 1919), pp. 301–302.
3. N. H. Borden, *The Economic Effects of Advertising* (Chicago, Ill.: Richard D. Irwin, 1942), pp. 35, 39.
4. I am indebted to my discussions with Tom Nagle for clarification on this point—that advertising increases the retail price elasticity of the brand at all levels for store demand, while causing a kinked market demand curve for the brand, with increased retail price elasticity downward but decreased price elasticity upward.
5. The recent situation in the airline industry regarding transcontinental routes is a good example of the prisoner's dilemma. If the airlines could collude and price normally, all would be better off; however, if one company undercuts the

others, that company gains while the others all lose substantially. The result is that all price very low and all lose, but not as much as with incomplete collusion. Tacit collusion is even more complex on the short-haul routes since the competitors are very different types of companies with different goals and strategies—for example, New York Air versus Eastern.

6. Mathematically, the expression for the partial elasticity is: $-(\delta GM_B/GM_C \div \delta A_B/A_C)$. The negative sign gives the elasticity a positive value so that the concept can be discussed in absolute terms. The total margin elasticity is expressed similarly, as a total derivative. Using GM for the ratio of the brand to category gross margin, A similarly for the brand's share of total category advertising, and X for brand factors (retail price and unit sales as percentages of category levels), it is (without the negative sign): $dGM/dA = \delta GM/\delta A + (\delta GM/\delta X) \cdot (\delta A/\delta X)$.

7. Since category characteristics affecting gross margins, advertising, and the other brand variables are controlled for by the use of ratios, any remaining heterogeneity in the sample must be the result of differences among product categories in the interaction of advertising and gross margin. These differences are addressed in the discussion of category gross margins: the margin elasticity of advertising is greater in product categories with characteristics reflecting lower category gross margins. A detailed discussion is presented in Chapter 7.

8. This contention assumes either that consumers of items in the product category have the same level of income or that their marginal utility of income is equal in this situation.

Chapter 7

EMPIRICAL ANALYSIS OF RETAIL PRODUCT CATEGORY MARGINS

To determine the relative importance of various product category characteristics associated with the different levels of category gross margins requires statistical testing. In this chapter we test the relative strength of the characteristics described in Chapter 5 to uncover those factors most significantly related to the level of category gross margins. Both cross-tabulation and regression analysis are applied to a 1978 sample of 51 supermarket product categories. The results indicate not only the most important category predictors of gross margins, but also those category characteristics that best explain *why the effect of advertising on retail brand gross margins differs among product categories.*

Before we discuss the empirical results, we will present an overview of some of the more important aspects of the structure of the empirical testing in this and the following two chapters. This introduction describes why the product category characteristics associated with gross margins explain the magnitude of the impact of advertising on brand gross margins, the specification of advertising and the other independent variables, and the different data bases used. In addition, we review our a priori hypotheses of how the independent variables (product category characteristics) should be related to category gross margins, holding all other factors constant.

Throughout the empirical analysis of Chapters 7, 8, and 9, sections are included that begin with "in summation" to summarize the findings and, where appropriate, to mention briefly their practical importance. A more detailed discussion of the importance of the findings is reserved for the last chapter. (Readers who do not wish to spend too much time on all the empirical results can therefore read just these sections with no loss of text continuity.) However, readers with minimal statistical background may still wish to look at the cross-tabulations or graphs for a general overview of the relationships between gross margin and one or two other variables at a time. Readers with further background can refine their understanding of the relationships involved by examining the multiple regression analysis. The regression analysis allows us to determine which variables are most important in explaining the level of gross margins, and the possibility of nonlinear specification(s)—introduced in Chapter 5—is tested using an analysis of the residuals in the regression. Finally, the stability of the product category results is examined using 1977 data, 1978 subsamples, and a national sample.

Structure of the Empirical Tests

Before presenting the statistical results in this and the following two chapters, we need to explain how the two parts of the theoretical model, the product category and brand analyses, are related. In other words, how can this analysis of category gross margins help us to determine why the interbrand advertising–gross margin relationship—the margin elasticity of advertising—differs among product categories. A short discussion then follows of all the independent variables to be considered, the specification of advertising, and the sample(s) used.

Two propositions were presented in Chapter 5 to explain why retail gross margins may vary among product categories. The first proposition stated that product categories with lower retail total contributions per unit of shelf space than other categories should have higher retail gross margins in a competitive equilibrium. The second proposition focused on the potential of the merchandising of one product category to affect the sales of other products in the store. Product categories with higher salience to consumers, it was argued, should have lower gross margins than categories with lower salience, as retailers compete more intensively on the sale of items in these product categories in order to maintain or increase store traffic. The concept of product salience was defined to include the consumer's desire (involvement) and ability to make an informed interproduct choice.

The analysis of retail brand gross margins in Chapter 6 focused on the notion of product salience. The central proposition held that advertising can increase the salience of a brand to consumers and, through three effects (on unit sales, factory price, and retail price competition), cause the retailer to price an advertised brand so as to accept a lower gross margin on it than on other, less advertised or unadvertised brands in the same product category. Accordingly, two brand factors were proposed to help explain this effect of advertising on brand gross margins: unit sales and retail price. At the heart of the brand analysis, it was maintained, lies the bilateral market relationship between manufacturer and retailer. By examining certain aspects of how manufacturer and retailer each respond to the competitive environment and the nature of consumer demand, we can connect the two parts of the theoretical analysis, relating the category characteristics associated with product category gross margins to the strength and significance of the margin elasticity of advertising.

The proposition, therefore, is that the more the retailer "adds value" to the final product sold to consumers (proxied, for example, by the level of retail expenses associated with the sale of the product) and the less consumers care about (or are able to find out about) any price differentials on a brand among stores, the weaker the effect of advertising on retail brand gross margins. In other words, *product category characteristics that reflect higher category gross margins should also reflect lower margin elasticities*. The retailer need not respond to the manufacturer's advertising as much when:

1. The retailer incurs additional costs by carrying the product category (such as freezer space for ice cream).
2. The retailer has increased bilateral market power in dealing with manufacturers because of some action(s) or situation dictated by consumers (such as carrying an increased number of brands in a product category).
3. Consumers are not as sensitive to the terms of sale of the product category (such as being less price sensitive to impulse goods than to loss leaders).

The theoretical model accounts for conditions 1 and 3 above. Porter (1976) derived the second condition in terms of the manufacturer's profit margin for a broader range of products—convenience versus nonconvenience goods—as discussed in Chapter 3. As will be demonstrated in the empirical analysis to follow, the second condition is also applicable to a more narrow range of convenience products (supermarket products), but only in certain situations. First, however, we need to identify which factors are most strongly and significantly related to the level of product category gross margins. Then in the following chapters we will test the relationship between these category characteristics and the margin elasticity of advertising, that is, the effect of advertising on brand gross margins.

Independent Product Category Variables

The theoretical analysis of product category gross margins, presented in Chapter 5, suggested twelve independent category characteristics that should be related to the level of category gross margins. In addition, it was proposed that two relationships between category characteristics and gross margins may depend on the level of two other product category characteristics, that is, the number of brands in a category on the total level of advertising in the product category, and the number of items in a category on the number of sizes in the category. All but one of these product category variables (the number of purchasers in a category, called "household penetration," which is subject to confidentiality requirements here) were tested empirically for a relationship with the category gross margin. Each of the remaining thirteen product category variables is listed below along with a brief review of how it is measured, its predicted relationship with the category gross margin (in parentheses), and the reason(s) for the proposed relationship, *holding all other factors constant*.

1. *Category Advertising* (negative relationship). The term "category advertising" refers to the total amount of brand advertising in a product category, measured as a four-year total amount (discussed in more detail after the descriptions of the other variables).
   Hypothesis: Over time, advertising may lead to lower category gross margins, mostly through its effects on other variables (such as preshopping decisions and retail expenses).
2. *Unit Sales* (negative relationship). Measured as the number of cases sold of an item times the number of items per case, then aggregated for each brand, and then for the product category.
   Hypotheses: The more units sold in a product category, the less is the opportunity cost of the space used by the category and, therefore, the lower the gross margin required by the retailer to obtain a total contribution equal to that of other categories with lower unit sales; also, the more consumers spend in a product category—especially the greater the number of purchasers (household penetration)—the greater the aggregate salience of the category to the retailer and, therefore, the lower the gross margin charged by the retailer.
3. *Retail Price* (negative relationship). Measured as the dollar sales of an item divided by the unit sales of the item, then aggregated and averaged for each brand, and then for the product category.

Hypotheses: Similar to those for unit sales (the greater the retail price, the lower the opportunity cost of the space and the greater the salience).

4. *Retail Expenses* (positive relationship). Measured as a dummy variable (value of 1 for product categories considered to have high retail expenses; value of 0 for all others); specifically referred to in Chapter 5 as "other retail variable costs." Seven product categories are deemed to have high retail expenses in the sample of supermarket products: cheese, cottage cheese, frozen dinners/entrees, frozen orange juice, frozen seafood, frozen vegetables, ready-to-serve (chilled) juices.[1]

   Hypothesis: The greater the retail expenses associated with the sale of a product category, the greater must be the category gross margin for the retailer to obtain a total contribution equal to that of other categories with lower retail expenses.

5. *Item Size* (positive relationship). Measured both as a dummy variable and as a continuous variable (in ounces, although difficult to compare product categories with items easily measured in ounces—canned peas, for example—with those that are not, which include items in most household product categories—facial and toilet tissues, for example). For the dummy, eight product categories in the sample are considered to have large items (value of 1; value of 0 for all others): dry cat food, dry dog food, flour, sugar, detergents, disposable diapers, paper towels, toilet tissues. For the continuous measure, we used the size of an item times the number of units sold of the item, then aggregated for each brand and for the product category, and then divided by the number of units sold in the category.

   Hypothesis: The greater the average size of items in a product category, the more space is used by the category and the greater must be the category gross margin for the retailer to obtain a total contribution for the space used by the category equal to that of other categories with smaller items that use less space.

6. *Number of Brands* (positive relationship). Measured by counting the number of brands sold by the retailer in a product category.

   Hypotheses: The greater the number of brands carried in a product category, the more space is used, and the higher the gross margin required (similar to item size); also, the greater the number of brands carried in a product category, the less the retailer depends on any one manufacturer, thereby increasing the retailer's bilateral market power and ability to capture a larger gross margin at the expense of the manufacturer's margin.

7. *Number of Items* (positive relationship). Measured by counting the number of items sold by the retailer in a product category.
   Hypotheses: The greater the number of items carried in a product category, the more space is used, and the higher the gross margin required (similar to item size); however, the greater the number of items carried per brand, the more the retailer depends on that one manufacturer, thereby decreasing the retailer's bilateral market power and ability to capture a larger gross margin (assumed to be of secondary importance).

8. *Number of Sizes* (positive relationship). Measured by counting the number of different package sizes sold by the retailer in a product category.
   Hypothesis: The greater the number of different sizes carried in a product category, the more difficult it is for consumers to make price comparisons, both intrastore among brands and interstore on any particular brand(s), since additional time is required to compare intrastore and more information is needed to compare interstore. The result is less retail price competition within the product category, higher retail prices, and higher retail gross margins than in categories with fewer different sizes of items.

9. *Preshopping Decisions* (negative relationship). (Measurement described in more detail in Appendix 2.) Formally called "preshopping specifically planned purchase," this variable measures the percentage of supermarket shopping, brand-specific decisions made by consumers before shopping (approximately the opposite of the percentage of impulse purchases).
   Hypotheses: The greater the percentage of preshopping decisions in a product category, the more salient is the category to consumers, and the lower the gross margin; also, the greater the percentage of preshopping decisions in a product category, the less additional (or "more expensive," such as end of the aisle) space is required by the category. Therefore, a lower gross margin can be accepted by the retailer to still obtain the same total contribution as in other categories with lower percentages of preshopping decisions.

10. *Private Label Penetration* (ambiguous relationship). Measured by the percentage of the dollar sales of a product category accounted for by private label brands.[2]
    Hypotheses: The greater the percentage of private label sales in a product category, the more mature, densely distributed, and salient is the category to consumers (lower category gross

margin); on the other hand, the greater the percentage of private label sales in a product category, the more the retailer is able to increase the overall average gross margin for the product category (higher category gross margin) through the sale of the higher margin, private label brands.

11. *Food/Nonfood* (positive relationship). Measured as a dummy variable. Ten product categories are considered to be nonfood (technically called "household products," with a value of 1; food products, 0).

   Hypothesis: Food products are more salient to supermarket shoppers than nonfood products, so that given a greater ability to build store traffic, food product categories should on average have lower gross margins than nonfood categories.

12. *Item × Sizes* (negative relationship if 7 or 8 in the analysis). Measured by multiplying the number of items sold in a product category times the number of different package sizes in that category.

   Hypothesis: The fewer the number of items carried in a product category, the stronger is the relationship between the number of sizes and the category gross margin. Because price comparisons among a large number of items in a product category are already difficult for shoppers, the number of different sizes makes less of a difference than when there are fewer items carried in the category.

13. *Category Advertising × Brands* (negative relationship). Measured by multiplying the four-year total amount of brand advertising in a product category by the number of brands sold in that category.

   Hypothesis: The greater the level of advertising in a product category, the less the retailer is able to increase bilateral market power (and category gross margin) by carrying more brands in the category.

Specification of Advertising

To conclude this discussion of the independent category variables, it is important to consider in more detail the specification of advertising—a subject that has continually plagued researchers. Because it controls for dollar sales, the advertising-to-sales ratio is the most commonly used index, but the measure is by no means universal or perfect. Most important, the advertising-to-sales ratio has the problem that both the numerator and denominator should be negatively correlated with gross margin (measured as a percentage of sales also), thus confounding the two different relationships. Sales can be controlled for in our analysis by the use of other variables in the cross-tabulations and regressions. It should be mentioned that the advertising-to-sales ratio was tried and was persistently positively related to gross margin, primarily due to the sales denominator.

Our model suggests that it is the *total amount of advertising dollars over time* that affects the retailer's pricing behavior. In the product category analysis, therefore, the measure is an absolute amount. The question then becomes how to specify this total, often called a "goodwill" measure of advertising, which is referred to as "category advertising" throughout for simplicity.

Three measures were tried in the analysis before we decided to use the simple total four-year dollar amount (1975–1978 for the 1978 data). We found, as did Cable (1972), that the R^2, F, and t statistics were relatively unchanged, with a slight change in the magnitude of the coefficients, by the three alternative specifications. These three specifications are:

1. A one-year measure;
2. A four-year measure, taking into account some decay rate of advertising; and
3. A four-year total measure.

The one-year measure of category advertising has a .97 correlation with the four-year total measure and a .95 or higher correlation with the four-year measure including various decay rates. The various four-year measures, with and without a decay rate, are also highly correlated to approximately the same degree. The advertising-to-sales measure, however, has only about a .4 to .45 correlation with these dollar-amount measures. The question of which measure to use depends on what is assumed to be the appropriate decay rate of advertising for these supermarket products. If it is felt that the decay rate is relatively short, then a one-year measure is sufficient; if it is believed that the decay rate is long, the four-year total measure is more appropriate.

The problem of the decay rate of advertising has been a highly controversial subject among researchers. The two sides of this debate argue essentially about whether repeat purchase behavior should or should not be attributed to advertising. The former, the long decay rate, is the view held by Clarke (1976); while the latter, the short decay rate, is maintained by Palda (1964).

Clarke's survey of 70 studies (1976) showed that calculations of a 90 percent duration interval of advertising (the time after which only 10 percent of the effects of advertising remain) ranged from 0.8 to 1,368 months. Various studies of the cigarette market alone yielded estimates ranging from 17 to 677 months, whereas studies of low-priced grocery products resulted in estimates from 0.8 to 416 months! On the basis of these findings, it is difficult to decide what is the "correct" decay rate. As already stated, a few different decay rates were chosen arbitrarily, with little change in the analysis. Given the arbitrariness of any decay rate selected, and the particular importance of goodwill (that is, the loyalty or patronage) built up over many years for highly advertised, fast-moving supermarket product categories (our sample), the four-year total measure was used. When we speak of "category advertising," therefore, it is with this measure of advertising in mind.

The Data Base

The primary data base used is for one medium-sized supermarket chain for 1978. Operating data were available for each SKU (stock-keeping-unit—that is, item—such as a 14-ounce bottle of Heinz catsup), including retail and factory prices, unit sales, promotions, and gross margins. Data from 1977 were also used, for comparative purposes, but these data are not as complete as those for 1978. In addition, product category data were available on a national basis and were used for comparative purposes; these, too, are not complete, and little data have been collected on a brand-by-brand basis. Fortunately, *the chain selected is very representative of all other supermarket chains*. The representativeness of the data base and further descriptions of the product categories, brands covered, and data sources, are given in Appendix 2 and Appendix 3.

Using a minimum store sales-share criterion of 0.5 percent, 52 product categories (505 brands) were selected. Accordingly, the data base consists of mostly *fast-moving, highly salient product categories*. Butter was then excluded from the sample because its 1978 chain data were representative of neither national averages nor chain averages in other years for this product category. The omission of butter had little significant effect on the category findings,[3] leaving 51 product categories (488 brands) that cover over two thirds of the chain's sale of products that are stored in their warehouses. Moreover, results were computed in all instances using only 50 product categories, with cigarettes omitted. Cigarettes is the only product category affected by state and excise taxes. With extremely high advertising expenditures (per advertising data from *Leading National Advertisers*), a very large number of items, and a lack of price variation among brands, it is an outlier on many regression planes. The results reported are for the 51 product categories, but any significant changes because of cigarettes—especially in our analysis of the ten nonfood categories—are noted.

Statistical Overview

The purpose of a cross-tabulation analysis is simply to provide an overview of the data and to indicate what general results to expect from the multiple regression analysis. The cross-tabulation method selected calculates the means of one variable, in this instance the category gross margin, for different subsamples of categories dependent on the level(s) of one or two other variables, called *criterion variables* in this and the following two chapters. For example, using category advertising as the criterion variable to divide the sample of 51 product categories in half (26 product categories in one subsample, 25 in the other), the cross-tabulation results would show the two mean gross margins—one for each subsample. One mean gross margin would be the average of the 26 category gross margins in the subsample of product categories with the 26 lower levels of category advertising; the other mean gross margin would be the average of the 25 category gross margins in the subsample of product categories with the 25 higher levels of category advertising. The two subsamples would be referred to as "low category advertising" and "high category advertising," with "low" and "high" denoting "below the mean" and "above the mean," respectively. This cross-tabulation method of analysis amounts to a one-way analysis of variance.

Any cross-tabulation results must be interpreted with caution, just as those of any simple regression: *Other factors that are not included in the analysis may affect the results*. For instance, a weak relationship may appear between category gross margin and the number of brands in a product category, but when other factors that may confound the relationship are included in the analysis, such as category advertising, a stronger relationship appears. By just looking at the number of brands–gross margin relationship, therefore, we may overlook the fact that the relationship of advertising to the number of brands and gross margin has complicated attempts to measure a relationship between the number of brands in a product category and category gross margin.

A few preliminary points need to be made before looking at the results shown in Table 7.1. First, Table 7.1 shows the mean gross margins for various subsamples of the 1978 chain data. These subsamples were selected by using as criterion variables those independent variables, that is, category characteristics, just reviewed (except the multiplicative variables, category advertising times brands and items times sizes). The (D) denotes a dummy variable; otherwise, these criterion variables are used to divide the sample of 51 product categories into halves and thirds.[4]

Second, the mean gross margins shown are *unweighted* averages. For example, using category advertising as the criterion variable, approximately $125 million of advertising (over four years) divides our sample of 51 product categories into 26 low advertising categories and 25 high advertising categories. By adding up the gross margins of the 26 low advertising categories and dividing by 26, we calculate a mean gross margin for this subsample of 15.18 percent. Similarly, we derive a mean gross margin of 14.29 percent for the "high" advertising subsample. The results show, therefore, that product categories with high levels of advertising do have lower gross margins than categories with relatively low levels of advertising, but not by very much, as expected. However, if the mean gross margins were *weighted* (using the unit sales of product categories as weights), the numbers in Table 7.1 would change. Fortunately, assuming that unit sales is negatively correlated with the category gross margin, and knowing that, excepting a few categories, the unit sales of product categories varies little in our sample, the changes are slight and commonly strengthen the results.

Third, all cross-tabulation tables in the book are meant to be read down, not across. Looking at the first two entries—category advertising and unit sales as category criterion variables—we see that for category advertising, the relationship between it and the category gross margin is negative if the sample is split in half (15.18 percent down to 14.29 percent from low to high levels of category advertising), but inconsistent when the 51 product categories are divided into three groups based on the levels of category advertising (14.12 percent up to 15.44 percent, and then down to 14.68 percent). No such change occurred for unit sales as a criterion variable, which has a consistent, though relatively weak, negative relationship with gross margin. In this regard, comparisons can be made up and down for any one category criterion variable, such as category advertising, but not across two or more criterion variables. For instance, the 14.12 percent mean gross margin for the 17 product categories with low category advertising is *not* comparable to the 15.84 percent for the 17 categories with low unit sales. The reason: They are two different groups of 17 product categories. What may be roughly compared among category criterion variables, however, is the relative change in mean gross margin from low to high for each of the criterion variables.

The Cross-Tabulation Results

Having dealt with the preliminaries, we can now look at the information offered by Table 7.1. *All but three of the variables have the predicted relationship with the category gross margin.* The number of sizes has a very strong positive relationship with category gross margins; that is, product categories with a large number of different package sizes have higher gross margins on average than categories with a small number of package sizes. The results are similar for the level of retail expenses. Likewise, the percentage of preshopping decisions made in a product category by consumers shows a strong negative relationship with gross margin. The three unexpected results occur for the food/nonfood dummy, private label penetration, and item size criterion variables. Based on these results and a look at our sample, more discussion of these three findings is appropriate.

In our sample of 51 product categories, 10 are household product categories; these nonfood categories have a lower mean gross margin than the food categories. This finding contradicts our theoretical proposition that nonfood products on average should have higher gross margins than food products because of their lower salience to supermarket customers. Moreover, as shown in Appendix 2, samples based on national data and all the nonfood product categories carried by the chain do show our proposition to be correct. Our finding, therefore, is caused by *sample selection.* We did note previously that in the evolution of the supermarket's product line, some nonfood product categories can and do become just as salient as nearly any food category. What happened is that *our criterion for selecting product categories for the sample (a minimum store-sales share) captured many of the most salient, highly advertised nonfood product categories.* The food sample, on the other hand, is more representative of food products in general. This potential bias in the selection method should not be of concern. It should, however, be kept in mind throughout the empirical analyses because any conclusion about nonfood product categories may only apply to a special, low gross margin, highly salient subset of nonfood categories.

The results of the private label penetration criterion variable should be no cause for alarm at this point either. What is continually shown in the cross-tabulation results is that even though the retailer can and does raise the category gross margin through increased sales of the higher margin, private label brands, the gross margins of these product categories still remains below that of other categories with a lower percentage of private label sales. The reason for this finding is that the categories with a relatively high percentage of private

Table 7.1   Mean Gross Margins Dependent on the Level of Product Category Criterion Variables

Level*	Category Advertising	Unit Sales	Dollar Sales	Retail Price	Item Size†	Item Size (D)†	Retail Expenses (D)
Low	15.18 (26)	15.08 (25)	16.33 (26)	15.30 (25)	16.14 (25)	15.63 (43)	13.97 (44)
High	14.29 (25)	14.43 (26)	13.10 (25)	14.21 (26)	13.40 (26)	9.97 (8)	19.63 (7)
Low	14.12 (17)	15.84 (17)	14.91 (17)	15.58 (17)	15.48 (16)		
Mid	15.44 (17)	15.26 (17)	16.54 (17)	14.00 (17)	16.32 (17)		
High	14.68 (17)	13.13 (17)	12.79 (17)	14.66 (17)	12.61 (18)		

	Number of Brands†	Number of Items†	Number of Sizes†	Private Label Penetration	Preshopping Decisions‡	Food/Nonfood (D)
Low	13.81 (28)	12.48 (26)	12.22 (26)	14.90 (25)	17.26 (20)	15.31 (41)
High	15.88 (23)	17.11 (25)	17.37 (25)	14.60 (26)	13.26 (21)	12.42 (10)
Low	12.29 (13)	11.67 (16)	11.25 (15)	16.93 (16)	18.49 (13)	
Mid	15.41 (22)	15.08 (17)	14.45 (19)	13.99 (18)	14.08 (13)	
High	15.82 (16)	17.17 (18)	18.16 (17)	13.49 (17)	13.35 (15)	

NOTES: The numbers in parentheses are the number of observations (product categories) used to compute the mean gross margin in the cell. All gross margin numbers are percentages. All numbers are unweighted averages.

The mean gross margin for the 51 product categories is 14.8 percent; the median is 15.2 percent.

* "Low," "Mid," and "High" correspond to the value of the criterion variable. These values are selected to equalize as much as possible the number of observations in each cell. The values vary among criterion variables.

† These criterion variables are in terms of "small," "medium," and "large."

‡ For 41, not 51, product categories.

label sales are the highly salient, highly price competitive, mature product categories with particularly low gross margins on the nationally advertised brands. The retailer's attempt to increase the category gross margin by selling private label brands closes the gap between the high and low private label penetration product categories, but does not overcome it. *The private label sales percentage measure, therefore, serves as a proxy for the salience of a product category.* If differences in salience among the categories were controlled for by some other variables, or a group of product categories with equivalent levels of salience to consumers were examined (such as our household product category sample), then we would expect a positive relationship between private label penetration and category gross margins. We will make this test later in the chapter and find these assertions to be correct.

The most disturbing finding is the general inverse relationship between item size and the category gross margin, especially for the item size dummy. This counterintuitive *intercategory* result (the average size of a package of flour versus the average size of a bottle of steak sauce, for example) appears repeatedly throughout the analysis. Since the variable is a proxy not only for space used (hypothesized positive relationship with gross margin) but also for retail price (hypothesized negative relationship with gross margin), we controlled for the value of items in more complex cross-tabulations, but the direction of the results remained the same. The one logical explanation for this finding is similar to that for the food/nonfood dummy, that is, the sample selected. For the dummy variable, six of the eight large size item product categories are highly advertised; all are fast-moving, highly salient commodities (sugar and flour are the only two not highly advertised). For the continuous item size variable, in addition, the large decline in gross margin occurs between medium and large sizes. It may be that we have not been able to control for certain aspects of the salience of product categories with large items, and would not find this result if the sample included some slow-moving (low store-sales share) categories as well.

It should also be recognized that in the statistical analysis there is no explicit measure of the amount of shelf space used by the different product categories. This absence affects, for example, the strength of the unit sales criterion variable: There is a weak inverse relationship with gross margin except when the number of items (or package sizes) is included in the analysis—controlling, in effect, for the amount of space used by a product category. Furthermore, as these relationships and all the analyses of category gross margins show only correlation, not causation, particular relationships may be confounded. In the case of the average retail price of a product category, we proposed that it has a negative relationship with the category gross margin (higher retail price, lower gross margin for same contribution); however, by reversing the causality, we would posit a positive relationship (higher gross margin leads to higher retail price). Fortunately, this problem is minimal in most instances.

In summation the results as a group are as predicted. Variables hypothesized to be an important source of variation in gross margins among product categories are strongly and consistently related to category gross margins. By examining different subsamples of the 51 product categories based on the level of the category characteristic tested, we found a strong positive relationship between the category gross margin and the number of items, the number of sizes, and the retail expenses in a product category; a strong negative relationship appeared, as expected, between gross margin and the percentage of preshopping purchase decisions made by consumers in a product category. We argued that the sample selection process, however, resulted in a group of highly salient household product categories with lower gross margins than food categories, and similarly, a sample of very salient product categories with large items. And as expected, category advertising showed a generally weak inverse relationship with the category gross margin. For any further analysis and for confirmation of these findings, we need to test the relationships of these independent variables with gross margin by means of multiple regressions. This method will allow us to examine which are the most important explanatory factors of the variation in the level of category gross margins under a variety of conditions.

Multiple Regression Analysis

The purpose of the multiple regression analysis is to isolate the relationships of particular independent variables with the category gross margin and to determine which variables best predict the variation in the level of gross margins among the product categories in the sample. Also, by analyzing the residuals of the regressions, we can see the shapes of certain relationships—in particular, whether they are linear or nonlinear. Overall, *the results of this analysis reinforce the cross-tabulations*. The most important explanatory variables are again shown to be the number of different package sizes in a product category and the level of retail expenses for a category. In addition, two multiplicative variables are found to be important: the number of items times the number of package sizes in a product category and category advertising times the number of brands in a category. The latter is shown to be essential to specify properly the relationship between the number of brands in a product category and the category gross margin. These findings have important managerial and policy implications, which are covered briefly here and in more detail in Chapter 10.

Table 7.2 displays the simple correlation coefficients of the variables with both category gross margin and category advertising. It should be noted how in a fairly small sample of 51 product categories, one category (in this instance, cigarettes) can affect the entire analysis. Accordingly, care has been taken throughout the analysis to analyze residuals, plots of correlations and regression planes, and the like. No analysis would change perceptibly with a slight change in the sample unless noted—for example, by removing cigarettes from the sample. All relationships have been checked and crosschecked. The discussion here, however, is limited to the more important points, with a minimum of technical discussion.

Table 7.2 indicates that there are strong correlations of five product category variables with category gross margin—number of sizes, retail expenses, item size, preshopping decisions, and private label penetration. Each variable has a significant relationship with gross margin, as tested by the F statistic in each simple regression. The number of sizes alone explains over 21 percent of the variation in gross margins among product categories! The number of brands shows a weak relationship with category gross margin, but its strong correlation with category advertising portends the importance of the multiplicative term, category advertising times brands.

Table 7.2   Correlation Coefficients of Product Category Variables with Category Gross Margin and Category Advertising

Variables	Category Gross Margin	Category Advertising
Category Advertising	−.12	—
Unit Sales	−.06	.11
Retail Price	−.15	.63*
Dollar Sales	−.17	.75*
Item Size	−.28	−.05
Item Size (D)	−.37	.05
Retail Expenses (D)	.35	−.16
Number of Brands	.13	.72*
Number of Items	.08	.70*
Number of Sizes	.46	.02*
Private Label Penetration	−.25	−.26
Preshopping Decisions	−.33	.24
Items × Sizes	.20	.20*
Category Advertising × Brands	−.09	.93
Food/Nonfood (D)	−.21	.39

* These correlation coefficients are all heavily determined by cigarettes. Within cigarettes, reading from top to bottom, they are .19, .18, .83, .38, .32, and .46, respectively.

Table 7.3 Correlation Matrix of Product Category Variables

	Unit Sales	Retail Prices	Item Size (D)	Retail Expenses (D)	Number of Brands	Number of Items	Number of Sizes	Private Label Penetration	Preshopping Decisions	Items × Sizes	Category Advertising × Brands
Unit Sales	1.00										
Retail Price	-.34 (-.45)	1.00									
Item Size (D)	-.12	.16 (.27)	1.00								
Retail Expenses (D)	-.00	-.04	-.17	1.00							
Number of Brands	.24	.25 (.02)	-.07	-.14	1.00						
Number of Items	.34 (.44)	.31 (-.21)	-.12	.02	.46 (.33)	1.00					
Number of Sizes	.17	-.22	-.13	.11	.23 (.32)	.33 (.61)	1.00				
Private Label Penetration	-.04	-.12	-.00	.10	-.26	-.26	-.24	1.00			
Preshopping Decisions*	.13	.13	.27	-.22	-.00	.11	-.31	-.02	1.00		
Items × Sizes	.34	-.14	-.02	.09	.33	.65 (.91)	.81	-.22	-.21	1.00	
Category Advertising × Brands	.17	.50	-.03	-.11	.84	.65	.06	-.18	.15	.18	1.00

NOTE: Numbers in parentheses are based on 50 observations, with cigarettes excluded.
* 41, not 51, observations (product categories).

Table 7.3 reports the correlation coefficients among eleven of the product category variables. Again, some of these correlations—such as the number of items and retail price correlation—are heavily influenced by the inclusion of cigarettes in the sample, so that these correlations are presented for a sample of 50 categories, excluding cigarettes, where appropriate. Strong intercorrelation of variables indicates that in the multiple regression analysis, one of the heavily correlated variables will lose its significance—a significance based not on its relationship with gross margin, but on its relationship to the other variable(s) related to gross margin. Moreover, these intercorrelations suggest that the significance of some of these variables may depend upon which other product category characteristics are included in the multiple regression analysis. Most notable are the intercorrelations among number of brands, sizes, and items variables, the correlation of the number of sizes with preshopping decisions, and the correlation between unit sales and retail price. The strong correlation $(-.31)$ between the number of sizes and preshopping decisions variables, for example, results in the preshopping decisions variable losing significance in any multiple regression that includes the number of package sizes as an explanatory variable. Accordingly, we must be careful that any results we use as evidence for managerial and/or policy implications are not caused by other independent product category variables not included in the analysis.

The Regressions

The multiple regression results using only linear specification of variables are presented in Table 7.4.[5] The results are very similar for regressions on a sample without cigarettes, with the item size dummy less significant. As mentioned, the preshopping decisions variable is never significant when the number of sizes variable or the retail expenses dummy is included in the regression. *Only the number of sizes, retail expenses and item size dummies, and the private label penetration variables are always significant.*

A variety of relationships that require brief discussion were found in the analysis. Whereas the number of sizes and retail expenses dummies dominate the results, the number of brands, number of items, and category advertising variables are significant only under certain circumstances. These circumstances involve the relationships between the number of individual items and number of different package sizes in a product category and between the total amount of category advertising and the number of brands in a category. Shortly we will introduce two nonlinear terms that isolate these

Table 7.4   Multiple Regression Equations Explaining Product
Category Gross Margins (n = 51)

Intercept	Category Advertising	Unit Sales	Retail Price	Dollar Sales	Item Size (D)
13.53[a]	−.117E-7[c]	−.971E-6[c]	0.072		−3.966[b]
(2.29)	(.889E-8)	(.669E-6)	(1.194)		(1.803)
13.68[a]	−.904E-8[b]	−.883E-6[c]			−4.114[a]
(1.61)	(.485E-8)	(.540E-6)			(1.725)
13.51[a]	−.344E-8			−.102E-5	−3.970[b]
(1.67)	(.775E-8)			(.843E-6)	(1.804)
12.60[a]					−4.255[a]
(1.42)					(1.754)
13.55[a]		−.733E-6[c]			−4.526[a]
(1.55)		(.538E-6)			(1.744)
13.93[a]				−.851E-6[b]	−4.287[a]
(1.60)				(.502E-6)	(1.719)

The significance of the regression coefficients is tested using a one-tail t test.
The significance of the coefficients of multiple determination is tested using
the F test. Standard errors and corrected R^2s are in parentheses.

[a] Coefficient is significant at the 99 percent level.
[b] Coefficient is significant at the 95 percent level.
[c] Coefficient is significant at the 90 percent level.

Retail Expenses (D)	Number of Brands	Number of Items	Number of Sizes	Private Label Penetration	R^2*
4.432[a]	.1775[c]	.0083	.2246[b]	−.0677[b]	.487[a]
(1.900)	(.1070)	(.0193)	(.1100)	(.0390)	(.390)
4.545[a]	.1588[b]		.2460[a]	−.0688[b]	.485[a]
(1.831)	(.0935)		(.0938)	(.0381)	(.415)
5.102[a]	.1238	.0017	.2163[b]	−.0655[b]	.472[a]
(1.928)	(.0987)	(.0184)	(.1110)	(.0394)	(.386)
4.576[a]			.2724[a]	−.0624[b]	.414[a]
(1.863)			(.0919)	(.0381)	(.377)
4.473[a]			.2929[a]	−.0621[b]	.440[a]
(1.844)			(.0919)	(.0376)	(.391)
4.748[a]			.2589[a]	−.0700[b]	.449[a]
(1.829)			(.0904)	(.0376)	(.401)

* Throughout this and the following chapter, R^2s are given. For those desiring the corrected R^2s, they can easily be computed as equal to $1 - (1 - R^2)(n - 1)/(n - k)$, where n is the number of observations and k the total number of variables. For large samples, the difference between the two measures is negligible. Here, with a small sample and many variables, the corrected R^2s are listed in parentheses under R^2s.

relationships. At this point, however, the analysis indicates that the relationships of these product category variables with gross margin may depend on certain characteristics of the categories examined. In addition it should be noted that, whereas the item size dummy variable is significant in the regressions, the continuous measure of item size is not. It seems that this variable (along with private label penetration) is a direct proxy of the salience of a product category, which dominates our attempt to measure the space used by the category.

In summation, the most important implication of these findings concerns the number of different package sizes carried by the retailer in a product category. There seems to be little question that for this fast-moving, high unit-volume sample of supermarket product categories, in all situations and controlling for all other factors, this variable is strongly and significantly related (directly) with the level of gross margin in a category. As predicted, it appears that the greater the number of different sizes in a product category, the more difficult it is for consumers to compare brand prices. For policy-makers, this evidence strongly suggests standardization of package sizes within product categories. As for retailers, they are urged to carry as many different sizes as possible in a product category and, as already done in many cases, package private labels (and generics) in different sizes than manufacturers' advertised brands. However, it must be remembered throughout the empirical analysis that the results are produced from *cross-sectional analysis*. Any implications drawn, therefore, must remain tentative unless we are certain that all independent effects on gross margin are included in the analysis. The underlying relationships may be more complicated than they appear.

Two other variables are of interest, but do not necessarily have a linear relationship with gross margin: the number of brands and percentage of private label sales in a category. Both are methods by which retailers can increase their bilateral market power vis-à-vis manufacturers and obtain higher gross margins. However, as we investigate the linearity of these relationships, we see that the ability to increase gross margins in either of these ways may be limited.

Nonlinear Specifications

In the theoretical model, we proposed that two multiplicative terms should be important to specify properly the relationship of the number of items and package sizes in a product category with gross margin, and the relationship of the total amount of category advertising and the number of brands in a category with gross margin, respectively. To test for these nonlinearities and others, we analyzed the residuals of the multiple regressions.

The residuals were plotted against the regression fit and the individual variables to test for these possible nonlinearities. The residuals do show a distinct pattern when plotted against the number of items, the number of sizes, and the number of brands, but no other explanatory variables. Without a clear theoretical mandate for nonlinear or polynomial terms for any of the other variables, none of these results are shown. Some nonlinear specifications helped; others did not. For example, nonlinear (including logarithmic) specifications were tried for the percentage of private label sales in a product category with only a marginal increase in significance and a small decrease in the relationship of the residuals with the variable. However, two multiplicative terms, *number of items times number of sizes and category advertising times number of brands*, helped reduce substantially the relationships between the residuals and the number of items and number of package sizes and between the residuals and the number of brands, respectively.

To recap briefly, the theory concerning the number of items and sizes carried by the retailer in a product category holds that given a certain number of items in a category, the greater the number of different package sizes in that category, the more difficult it is for shoppers to compare prices at the store and remember the price per package size for price comparisons among stores. The effect of the number of sizes carried in a product category, therefore, should be weaker in categories with a large number of items than in those with a small number of items, since comparison shopping is more difficult in a category with a large number of items regardless of the number of sizes. This should be of particular importance for low-involvement products, such as those sold in supermarkets.

Empirically, not only the analysis of residuals but also the division of the sample into groups supports this contention. Dividing the sample of 51 product categories in half, based on the number of items in a category, shows the number of sizes regression coefficient (relating the number of sizes to the level of category gross margins) to be over four times as strong (.63 versus .14) in the subsample of categories with a small number of items for the 51 categories as in the subsample with a large number of items. Moreover, the number of sizes variable is significant at the 99 percent level, explaining by itself 30 percent of the variation in gross margin in the subsample of product categories with a small number of items; in the other subsample, the number of sizes variable is insignificant, explaining less than 5 percent of the variation in gross margin. This difference in the number of sizes regression coefficients between the two subsamples is significant, as indicated by the Chow test for equality of coefficients in regressions.

Discovered in the multiple regression analysis, the significance of the number of brands variable depends primarily on whether or not the level of category advertising is also included as an explanatory variable. Given this evidence and the pattern of the residuals with the number of brands variable, a multiplicative term—category advertising times the number of brands in a product category—was tried. The inclusion of this term in the regression analysis had little effect on the residuals with respect to category advertising, but substantially reduced the distinct pattern of the residuals with the number of brands variable. Furthermore, if the sample of 51 product categories is divided in half on the basis of the level of category advertising, the number of brands variable is significant at the 99 percent level in the subsample of categories with low category advertising, but insignificant in the other subsample; this difference in regression coefficients is significant (Chow test).

The theory behind these results, and the category advertising–number of brands–category gross margin relationship, is diagrammed in Figure 7.1. The relationship between the number of brands in a product market and the total amount of advertising in a product category has been discussed and tested empirically in the literature (Farris and Albion, 1981): The greater the number of brands in a market (holding the number of firms and sales constant), the more messages the firm needs to influence consumer demand, given the increase in choice. The other two relationships have already been explained. Most important (other than the obvious aforementioned impact on shelf space required), the greater the number of brands the retailer carries in a product category, the greater the bilateral market power (and gross margin obtained), as the retailer depends less on any one manufacturer. Therefore, the number of brands has a positive relationship with category gross margin *independent* of its effect on category advertising, but a negative relationship with category gross margin *through* category advertising.

Leaving either one of the variables out of the analysis biases the

Figure 7.1   Category Advertising—Number of Brands—Category Gross Margin Relationship.

coefficient of the other down (for number of brands if category advertising is left out of the regression) or up (for category advertising if number of brands is not included). However, as indicated by Figure 7.1, our main concern is with the number of brands–category gross margin relationship, since the number of brands precedes category advertising in the chain of effects on gross margin. The use of the multiplicative term allows us to isolate these relationships and establish an important managerial implication for retailers—an implication concerning *the differential impact of the number of brands carried in highly advertised versus less advertised product categories*. This implication will be discussed shortly.

Table 7.5 presents the multiple regressions explaining category gross margins with the two multiplicative terms, number of items times number of sizes and category advertising times number of brands. The first three regressions use both nonlinear terms, the fourth and fifth just number of items times number of sizes, and the seventh and eighth just category advertising times number of brands. The sixth and ninth regressions include no nonlinear terms and can be compared with the others, such as the third with the sixth regressions, to demonstrate the importance of the nonlinear terms. The magnitude of the coefficients of the variables in regressions with a nonlinear term, however, is not necessarily directly comparable to the magnitude of the coefficients in regressions without a nonlinear term. This warning is particularly important for the number of items, number of sizes, number of brands, and category advertising coefficients, as well as variables strongly correlated with these four variables.[6]

From all the regressions that were run, we found that the significance of many of the variables—item size dummy, category advertising, unit and dollar sales, number of items—depends upon which other variables are included in the multiple regression. In particular, category advertising is rarely significant if the category advertising times number of brands interaction is included in the regression, and is insignificant in many of the regressions run but not shown in the table. However, when the other independent product category variables are controlled for, *category advertising does appear to be a source—albeit a secondary source—of variation in category gross margins*. The number of items variable, on the other hand, is significant only when the number of items times number of sizes multiplicative term is included in the regression analysis. This finding suggests that it is the number of different package sizes in a product category that is the more important explanatory variable of the level of category gross margins. As a group, *the results continually stress the importance of the multiplicative*

Table 7.5   Multiple Regression Equations Explaining Product Category Gross Margins, with Nonlinear Terms (n = 51)

Intercept	Category Advertising	Unit Sales	Retail Price	Item Size (D)	Retail Cost (D)	Number of Brands	Number of Items	Number of Sizes	Private Label Penetration	Items × Sizes	Category Advertising × Brands	R^2
6.031[a]	-.733E-8	-.102E-5[b]	-.4932	-1.288	4.959[a]	.5244	.0894[a]	.6621[a]	-.0263	-.0059[a]	-.694E-9[a]	.670[a]
(2.45)	(.107E-7)	(.550E-6)	(.9899)	(1.684)	(1.576)	(.1248)	(.0247)	(.1469)	(.0340)	(.0015)	(.266E-9)	(.588)
3.491[a]		-.784E-6[c]			5.325[a]	.5796[a]	.0884[a]	.7120[a]		-.0061[a]	-.930E-9[a]	.645[a]
(1.66)		(.478E-6)			(1.494)	(.1159)	(.0191)	(.1337)		(.0012)	(.183E-9)	(.597)
4.738[a]	-.123E-7[c]	-.901E-6[b]			4.983[a]	.5500[a]	.0977[a]	.7034[a]	-.0252	-.0064[a]	-.665E-9[a]	.662[a]
(2.01)	(.909E-8)	(.491E-6)			(1.532)	(.1203)	(.0218)	(.1363)	(.0335)	(.0013)	(.261E-9)	(.598)
8.703[a]	-.255E-7[a]	-.971E-6[c]	-0.292	-0.943	4.445[a]	.3126[b]	.0797[a]	.6689[a]	-.0532[c]	-.0056[a]		.612[a]
(2.43)	(.872E-8)	(.589E-6)	(1.056)	(1.797)	(1.673)	(.1014)	(.0262)	(.1571)	(.0346)	(.0015)		(.527)
7.750[a]	-.284E-7[a]	-.897E-6[b]			4.490[a]	.3366[a]	.0862[a]	.6989[a]	-.0516[a]	-.0059[a]		.608[a]
(1.73)	(.697E-8)	(.523E-6)			(1.616)	(.0919)	(.0226)	(.1450)	(.0338)	(.0013)		(.544)
12.51[a]	-.151E-7[b]	-.994E-6[c]			5.002[a]	.2179[b]	.0168	.2115[b]	-.0663[b]			.426[a]
(1.62)	(.752E-8)	(.624E-6)			(1.928)	(.1051)	(.0195)	(.1124)	(.0403)			(.348)
11.54[a]	.446E-8	-.102E-5[c]	-0.078	-4.429[a]	4.867[a]	.3492[b]	.0125	.1937[b]	-.0458		-.588E-9[b]	.529[a]
(2.46)	(.122E-7)	(.649E-6)	(1.161)	(1.767)	(1.859)	(.1382)	(.0189)	(.1080)	(.0397)		(.312E-9)	(.426)
12.38[a]		-.864E-6[c]		-4.403[a]	4.821[a]	.2862[a]		.2279[a]	-.0570[c]		-.372E-9[a]	.518[a]
(1.59)		(.522E-6)		(1.658)	(1.772)	(.1164)		(.0912)	(.0365)		(.144E-9)	(.452)
13.32[a]		-.829E-6		-4.481[a]	4.614[a]	.0328		.2855[a]	-.0583[c]			.443[a]
(1.64)		(.554E-6)		(1.761)	(1.881)	(.0665)		(.0939)	(.0388)			(.381)

The significance of the regression coefficient is tested using a one-tail *t* test. The significance of the coefficients of multiple determination is tested using the *F* test. Standard errors and corrected R^2s are in parentheses.

[a] Coefficient is significant at the 99 percent level.
[b] Coefficient is significant at the 95 percent level.
[c] Coefficient is significant at the 90 percent level.

terms, the number of different package sizes, and the level of retail expenses. If any of these variables are dropped from the regression, the change in R^2 is significant (Chow test).

Other functional forms were tested, including semi-log and double-log specifications to minimize the effect of outliers, with improved significance only for the private label penetration variable. The R^2s are higher, but in any case, the R^2s of linear and logarithmic specifications are not comparable. Moreover, with the dependent variable, category gross margin, already expressed in percentages, logarithms may be redundant. And with no clear theoretical mandate to the contrary, a linear form for the regression equation should suffice.

In summation, the number of different package sizes in a product category again dominates all other explanatory variables of the category gross margin. If this variable is removed from a regression, the drop in R^2 averages .250! The number of items times number of sizes multiplicative term is also very important (contrast regressions five and six), and improves the explanatory power of many of the other variables in the regression. The policy and managerial implications of this finding have already been mentioned. The critical new finding conerns the interaction of the number of brands carried in a category with the level of category advertising. The inclusion of this interaction term (category advertising times the number of brands) in a regression increases the magnitude and significance of the number of brands coefficient.

As already mentioned, retailers may try to raise their bilateral market power (and gross margin) by increasing the number of brands carried in a category. However, given the aforementioned caveat applicable to cross-sectional analysis, this evidence suggests that their ability to do so may depend on the level of category advertising (multiplicative term). If the level of category advertising is high, it appears that all a retailer may do is increase the shelf space used and decrease the total contribution per square foot. This problem is increased if one firm (Procter and Gamble, Kellogg's, and so on) manufactures many brands in the product category—a situation more prevalent in categories with a large amount of advertising (cereals, candy bars, detergents) than in categories with a lesser amount of advertising.

On the other hand, in categories with a lower level of advertising, the number of brands carried by the supermarket retailer may indeed be a very important source of increased market power. This finding implies that we modify our understanding of the relationship of the number of brands in a category with the gross margin: In product categories with a relatively low amount of category advertising, retailers can more easily become less dependent on any one manufacturer, thereby increasing their own bilateral market power, by increasing the number of brands (including private labels) carried in the category. As always, however, this potential to increase bilateral market power (and gross margin) must be carefully weighed against a possible decrease in unit sales per square foot, particularly if the rates of movement on these brands are low. And if there is a relatively large amount of advertising in the category, manufacturers dominate the market (consumers demand particular brands), and the retailers have less chance of even increasing their bilateral market power in this fashion.[7]

The Stability of the Results

The stability of the empirical results based on the 1978 chain data was tested on the 1977 chain data, the food and nonfood 1978 chain subsamples, and 1978 and 1977 national data. Most important, we found that the percentage of private label sales has a positive relationship with the category gross margin in the nonfood subsample, and that the retail price and preshopping decisions variables are important explanatory variables in the national sample. These findings are expected, however, given that the nonfood product categories have similar levels of salience and the national sample is missing key explanatory variables, such as number of sizes and private label penetration, so that the included variables may serve as proxies for the missing variables. Otherwise, *the previous findings are reaffirmed*.

The results based on the 1977 chain data are very similar to those shown in Tables 7.4 and 7.5. Category advertising is a somewhat weaker explanatory variable of gross margin, and the private label penetration variable, still inversely related to gross margin (as a proxy for variations in salience among product categories), is always significant at the 99 percent level. The R^2s are higher as all other variables are slightly more significant: .534 without nonlinear terms, .786 with.

Food and Nonfood Subsamples

Table 7.6 provides the correlation coefficients of the various category characteristics with the category gross margin for the food and nonfood subsamples. No retail expenses dummy is shown because all the so-called high expense categories are in the food subsample. Similarly, no preshopping decisions variable is used as it was available

Table 7.6 Correlation Coefficients of Product Category Variables with Category Gross Margin for Food and Nonfood Subsamples

	Category Gross Margin		
	Food (n = 41)	*Nonfood* (n = 10)	*Nonfood** (n = 9)
Category Advertising	.07	−.26	−.12
Unit Sales	−.02	−.73	−.72
Retail Price	−.11	−.17	.12
Dollar Sales	−.07	−.39	−.66
Item Size (D)	−.25	−.66	−.78
Number of Brands	.22	−.23	−.06
Number of Items	.26	−.21	−.02
Number of Sizes	.49	.31	.25
Private Label Penetration	−.37	.58	.55
Items × Sizes	.28	−.02	−.05
Category Advertising × Brands	.03	−.25	−.11

* Nonfood subsample, excluding cigarettes.

for only two of the ten nonfood categories. We must be cautioned, however, not to overgeneralize from the nonfood subsample results as the number of categories included is so small. Moreover, because of this difference in number of product categories between the two subsamples, 41 versus 10 (9 excluding cigarettes), *the magnitudes of the correlations are not directly comparable*. As a guideline, a variable with about a .20 correlation in the food subsample or a .45 correlation in the nonfood subsamples is significant in a simple regression of gross margin. The two most striking results from Table 7.6 are the difference between the food and nonfood subsamples for the private label penetration variable and the many differences between the nonfood subsamples with and without cigarettes, necessitating that any conclusions about these household product categories, be checked using both subsamples.

Multiple regression analysis was performed on each of the subsamples, although our analysis was necessarily restricted for the nonfood subsamples because of limited degrees of freedom (partial least squares used). As would be expected, the food subsample contains relationships relatively similar to the entire sample. The one important difference is for category advertising, which has an even weaker relationship with gross margin unless the number of brands (.9 correlation with advertising) is included in the regression analysis. Here the importance of category advertising in explaining variations in category gross margins appears to be less than found previously, particularly in the less salient, slower-moving product categories.

Considering that the sample selected includes the fastest-moving supermarket product categories, the effect of category advertising on category gross margins seems limited—at least limited to its more long-term effects on other category characteristics that influence the level of category gross margins. In the nonfood subsample, which includes all very fast-moving, highly salient categories, the effect of category advertising on gross margin is more pronounced.

Before we discuss the two most important findings from this analysis, it is important to reiterate the difference between these food and nonfood subsamples. Certainly the selection method used (store sales-share minimum) relegates the analysis to fast-moving, highly salient categories; the relationships found may be quite different for slower-moving categories, and a sample of both high- and low-volume categories may produce a different group of results. But as mentioned, the nonfood categories selected are on average even more salient and faster-moving than the food product categories. The non-food product categories average $262 million ($155 million excluding cigarettes) of category advertising (four-year total), whereas food categories average only $74 million. Accordingly, to a large extent the nonfood-food comparison is between highly advertised, highly salient product categories and less heavily advertised, less salient product categories.

Having acknowledged this difference, we can easily understand the results for the subsample of the category advertising–number of brands interaction term and private label penetration in the regressions on category gross margin. In the food subsample, the interaction term performs as in the entire sample. But in the nonfood subsample, the inclusion of this term has little effect on the category advertising or number of brands regression coefficient. This result reaffirms our previous analysis: Retailers may be capable of increasing their bilateral market power by carrying a greater number of brands in less heavily advertised categories, but not to the same degree in heavily advertised categories. Almost all nonfood categories are heavily advertised. We would therefore expect this relationship to be even stronger for a sample of slower-moving product categories.

Throughout all the regressions for the subsamples, the private label penetration variable has a significant *negative* relationship with gross margin for the food subsample—that is, the percentage of private label sales in a product category proxies the level of salience of the category—and a significant *positive* relationship with gross margin for the nonfood subsamples—that is, private label sales increase the average product category gross margin. Considering that the nonfood product categories all have similar levels of salience and the food categories do not, these two findings should be expected.

Private labels do raise the average category gross margin for the retailer; the problem is as has been stated, that it also proxies the level of category salience (private labels are more easily introduced into mature, salient product categories). This problem should be even greater for a sample that includes both high- and low-volume product categories.

In summation, the results of the food and nonfood subsamples reaffirm our interpretations of previous findings. In particular, category advertising remains a secondary determinant of product category gross margins, mostly affecting gross margins through other variables related to category gross margins. Moreover, retailers may be able to increase their market power by carrying more brands, but not necessarily in the heavily advertised categories. And researchers must be careful to control for product salience when measuring any relationship between the percentage private label sales in a product category and category gross margin.

National Sample

The results using the national data suggest that another variable may be important in explaining product category gross margins: the average retail price of a category. This variable was never significant in any analyses performed on the chain data. Moreover, the pre-shopping decisions variable is significant as well.

National category gross margins for 50 of the 51 product categories averaged 19.0 percent in 1978, compared with 14.8 percent for the chain from which our observations came. Data were not available for the number of brands, number of items, and number of sizes in a product category, but an assortment variable (items/brands/sizes) was. Furthermore, it was felt that the chain's retail prices could be used in the national data analysis because, although the chain's prices may be below the national average, there is no reason to expect that the *relative* prices among product categories differ substantially between the two data bases. This assumption was not made, however, for the private label penetration measure, which was also not available for the entire national data base.

The national results are very similar between the two years, so only the 1978 results are reported here. Cross-tabulation analysis of the national data also produced results similar to those shown for the chain data in Table 7.1. The most important findings from the national data analysis, as shown in Table 7.7, are the surprising significance of retail price, the significance of the preshopping decisions variable, and the weakness of the relationship between category advertising and category gross margin, independent of dollar

Table 7.7   Multiple Regression Equations Explaining National Product Category Gross Margins, 1978 (n = 50, 40*)

Intercept	Category Advertising	Retail Price	Dollar Sales	Item Size (D)	Retail Expenses (D)	Assortment	Preshopping Decisions	R^2
19.34[a]	.616E-8	−1.408[c]	−.0023[c]	−2.478[c]	9.137[a]	.0265[b]		.502[a]
(1.39)	(.550E-8)	(1.093)	(.0015)	(1.654)	(2.128)	(.0146)		(.445)
20.06[a]		−2.250[a]		−2.220[c]	7.444[a]	.0128		.473[a]
(1.25)		(0.693)		(1.654)	(1.833)	(.0110)		(.439)
18.25[a]			−.0023[a]	−2.723[b]	8.684[a]	.0322[a]		.471[a]
(1.03)			(.0007)	(1.642)	(1.858)	(.0123)		(.436)
18.09[a]	−.653E-8[b]			−2.731[c]	7.071[a]	.0196[c]		.400[a]
(1.10)	(.335E-8)			(1.752)	(1.983)	(.0120)		(.361)
24.71[a]	.926E-8[c]	−2.602[b]	−.0016	−1.042	8.662[a]	.0141	−.1330[b]	.574[a]
(3.27)	(.634E-8)	(1.317)	(.0018)	(2.266)	(2.504)	(.0171)	(.0791)	(.497)
24.45[a]		−2.438[a]		−1.084	7.062[a]	.0091	−.1260[b]	.545[a]
(2.72)		(0.724)		(2.108)	(2.031)	(.0117)	(.0730)	(.493)
20.97[a]			−.0021[a]	−2.681[a]	8.559[a]	.0282[b]	−.0854	.496[a]
(2.81)			(.0008)	(2.208)	(2.183)	(.0137)	(.0800)	(.438)
21.60[a]	−.542E-8[c]			−2.339	6.953[a]	.0165[c]	−.1140[c]	.428[a]
(2.98)	(.378E-8)			(2.346)	(2.294)	(.0134)	(.0845)	(.363)

The significance of the regression coefficients is tested using a one-tail *t* test. The significance of the coefficients of multiple determination is tested using the *F* test. Standard errors and corrected R^2's are in parentheses.

[a] Coefficient is significant at the 99 percent level.
[b] Coefficient is significant at the 95 percent level.
[c] Coefficient is significant at the 90 percent level.

* Regressions above the dashed line have 50 observations (product categories); those below have 40. Note that there is little variation in the item size dummy for the 40 observations as only four are considered to have large items.

sales. In fact, category advertising has a *positive* and often significant relationship ($P = .865$ in first regression) with category gross margin if either retail price or dollar sales is included in the regression. The evidence further shows that, whereas advertising may be an important independent determinant of brand gross margins, its impact on category gross margins is primarily through its effects on other category characteristics.

The importance of the preshopping decisions variable is not unexpected. As a proxy for the salience of a product category to consumers, as well as the consumer familiarity with the product, and for the amount of additional retail shelf space required to sell items in a category, it should have an inverse relationship with gross margin. Manufacturers have increased their bilateral market power and decreased the retailers' costs—quite possibly through advertising—so that lower retail gross margins would be expected. Most likely, this result did not appear in the chain data because the number of sizes and items in a product category proxied category salience and shelf space used better than did preshopping decisions.

The more curious finding—a strong and significant inverse relationship between the average retail price of a product category, and gross margin in the national but not the chain data—requires further comment. By itself, retail price explains about 20 percent of the variation in category gross margins; with the retail expenses dummy, 43 percent is explained; and with the preshopping decisions variable, 53 percent. The point is that in the national data the product category retail price (measured for the chain) is a robust explanatory variable even with the other very important independent variables. Its strong relationship with gross margin remains in all national samples.

By examining intercorrelations among variables (Table 7.3) and some unreported regressions, we find that in this sample of all relatively low price, low involvement, frequently purchased supermarket products, the average retail price of a product category may serve to signal the salience of the category to consumers, that is, the greater the retail price of a category, the more consumers are willing to spend time making interstore price comparisons. The difference can be thought of for this sample as that between buying a can of tuna fish and buying a candy bar. The data analysis shows that the retail price variable may reflect aspects of product category salience previously proxied by the private label penetration and number of sizes variables. These variables are available for the chain but not the national data. Accordingly, this particular finding augments a previous warning: In cross-sectional analysis, implications of findings must be drawn carefully, as the results may be drawn in a situation where critical variables have been left out of the analysis.

In summation, the tests for the stability of the results derived from the 1978 chain data validated most of the findings. The results helped us to understand better how the number of brands, items, and sizes in a product category may be thought of by the retailer, how increasing the percentage of preshopping purchase decisions made by consumers in a category should be beneficial to the manufacturers (lower retail gross margin), and why interpretations of cross-sectional statistical results must be drawn carefully.

Summary and Implications

This chapter provided an empirical analysis of the variation in the level of category gross margins among a sample of supermarket product categories. The analysis was carried out for one data base, with the results cross-checked on other data bases and subsamples. The purpose of this statistical study has been to uncover what independent product category variables are most significantly related to category gross margins, since it is believed that these category characteristics will also be instrumental in isolating why the margin elasticity of advertising varies among product categories. That analysis is carried out in the two chapters that follow.

In the empirical analysis we found that the number of different package sizes carried by the retailer in a product category and the level of retail expenses in a category are the most significant explanatory variables of gross margin. Whereas the association between the level of retail expenses in a product category and gross margin has few implications, the strong positive relationship between the number of sizes in a category and the category gross margin *at all times* is a very important finding. As mentioned, the relationship is stronger and more significant than that of any other category characteristic with gross margin, including, most notably, that of the number of brands or items in a category with gross margin. However, since the results are from cross-sectional analysis, implications must be drawn and considered with caution. Without controlling for all possible explanatory factors or establishing causality, underlying relationships could be more complex than they appear.

For policymakers, the marketing practice known as "packaging to price" arises again. The evidence here strongly advocates the standardization of package sizes within supermarket product categories. With the low-involvement nature of these products, unit pricing does not seem to have made a significant difference in terms of consumer information and choice. Indeed, this "noncomparability," limiting the ease with which the consumer can make intrastore and interstore price comparisons in a product category, may be an important source of monopolistic profits not only for manufacturers (reduced direct competition among manufacturers' brands, allowing higher factory prices), but also for the retailers. Retailers are urged by this finding to carry brands packaged at different sizes than other brands carried in the product category. In addition, retailers should make sure that their private label brands (and generics) are packaged in sizes different from the manufacturers' brands carried.

The theoretical analysis of Chapter 5 and the analysis of residuals in this chapter suggested that two nonlinear specifications could be important in explaining product category gross margins: the number of items times the number of sizes in a category, and category advertising times the number of brands in a category. Whereas these terms improved the R^2 of the regression estimation until over two thirds of the variation in gross margin was accounted for, the category advertising times number of brands term has important policy and managerial implications as well.

The category advertising times number of brands multiplicative term increased both the strength and significance of the number of brands coefficient in the regressions, but not the category advertising coefficient. In addition, the number of brands variable is strongly related to gross margin for product categories with more moderate levels of category advertising, but not for categories with high levels of category advertising. From this evidence we inferred that retailers may be effective in increasing their bilateral market power (and gross margins) by carrying more brands in product categories that are not intensively advertised; surely, high gross margins are needed for these brands if they are not fast-moving. However, this tactic may incur additional costs and lower total contribution per square foot, particularly in highly advertised categories. We can also speculate that the number of brands carried could be even more important for retailers and their profits in supermarket product categories not covered by this sample since these generally have lower sales volume and are less heavily advertised. Still, the findings do suggest that retailers carefully monitor the number of brands carried, since many may not add to the store's total contribution unless they improve the retailer's bilateral market power. *Supermarket retailers may very well be carrying too many advertised brands in a number of product categories.*

Regarding the importance of category advertising as an explanatory variable of category gross margins, these findings and others from the regression results as a group indicate that advertising per se may not have a strong effect on category gross margins—at least not in the short run. On the other hand, category advertising does appear to have a significant relationship with gross margin by impacting on a number of other category characteristics. Included are, most prominently, the number of brands carried in a category and the percentage of consumer decisions made prior to shopping in a product category. *Over time, therefore, category advertising may be strongly related to category gross margin*, but most of the effects of advertising should take place at the brand level.

These findings have important implications for manufacturers and policymakers as well. In highly advertised categories such as cereals, brand proliferation may indeed be an effective method for increasing manufacturers' profits at the retailers' expense. Regardless of the number of brands carried by the retailer in these product categories, *monopoly profits for manufacturers may affect and reduce the potential margins (and profits) for the retailers*. The retailers' response in these product categories, therefore, may be the introduction of private label brands.

Retailers always have the opportunity to increase the average category gross margins by means of more private label sales, for these brands typically are priced to give the retailer a much higher gross margin than advertised brands. Many researchers have maintained that private labels can be introduced most easily into product categories where there is a substantial amount of consumer familiarity with the product from purchase, advertising, and the like. The private labels, therefore, can be "free riders" on the advertising of the manufacturers' brands. On the other hand, in highly advertised, highly salient product categories, private labels may be limited to small shares if consumers are more "brand" oriented. It might therefore be argued that private labels are most effective in product categories somewhere between these two extremes. If we add some brand data to the category analysis of this chapter, we uncover some interesting information on this matter that has important managerial implications.

On a brand basis, our data support the contention that private labels hold a greater sales share in product categories with relatively low levels of category advertising than in categories with high levels of category advertising—13.7 versus 2.8 percent share, respectively. Given our category selection method, the "low" advertising categories actually are closer to "moderate." Similarly, the private label sales share is greater in the food subsample than in the more highly advertised, nonfood subsamples—13.6 versus 8.7 percent or 9.7 percent share excluding cigarettes, respectively. However, despite the low private label sales percentage, the retail chain is more effective in increasing its average product category gross margins through private label sales in categories with high levels of category advertising than in categories with relatively low levels of category advertising—5 versus 3 percentage-point increases in average category gross margins, respectively. Moreover, in our sample the chain is much more effective in increasing its average category gross margins through private label sales in nonfood product categories than for food product categories—13.2 versus 0.7 percentage-point increases, respectively.

The reason is that private labels are priced to obtain a much greater relative gross margin (relative to the advertised brands) in highly advertised product categories (including the nonfood categories) than in the more moderately advertised categories (including most of the food categories in our sample). It seems that in the highly advertised, highly salient product categories, it may be more difficult for retailers to sell private label brands, but the gross margins relative to the advertised brands (very high factory prices, heavy retail competition) are so much higher that on the whole, retailers can be quite effective in raising their average category gross margins. In this regard, the even larger differences in private label pricing between food and nonfood subsamples indicate that these two types of product categories differ in our data base by more than just the average level of category advertising. Instead, these results suggest that the retailer has much more latitude in the pricing of private label brands for these nonfood, household product categories than in food categories. In other words, private labels can be a very effective tool for retailers when advertised brands are priced to have very low gross margins, but in addition, they can be even more effective in nonfood product categories—at least for those in our sample (heavily advertised household categories, such as laundry detergents, soaps, and toilet tissue). We will pursue these and other contentions in more detail in the brand analysis to follow.

Endnotes

1. This dummy variable was tested for sensitivity to those product categories selected as having high retail expenses. Specifically, the chilled product categories were eliminated and other categories then included as having high retail expenses. There was no significant change in the results.

2. Technically, private labels and regional, unadvertised brands (also with high gross margins) are included in this measure. Subtracting out these regional, unadvertised brands, however, has almost no effect on the statistical results in all instances. Ninety-eight percent of the volume of these brands is accounted for by the private labels.

3. In 1978 the chain was involved in intense price competition, so category gross margins were consistently lower than the national averages and the 1977 chain averages, but usually only by a few percentage points (Appendix 2). Butter,

however, had an extremely low gross margin at the chain in 1978 of 0.3 percent, compared with 8 percent the year before and 17.1 percent nationally. Most important, this 0.3 percent category average creates a problem in the brand analysis of Chapter 8; with the denominator of the dependent variable less than one, the ratio of brand to category gross margins becomes extremely large and seriously distorts some of the regression planes.

4. 2×2 and 2×3 cross-tabulations tables using one and two category criterion variables, respectively, were computed throughout the analysis to check on particular relationships. For example, category advertising and unit sales in a 2×2 table produce four cells of groups of product categories with low category advertising and unit sales, low category advertising and high unit sales, high category advertising and low unit sales, and high category advertising and unit sales. Such tables are not reported, but no conclusions are drawn in the text that any of these computations might contradict.

5. For expository purposes, two methods were used to compute the regressions: the use of all the variables, reducing the number by dropping the insignificant variables; and the use of the most significant variables, increasing those used one at a time with a variety of combinations.

6. The units of comparison are different. For comparative purposes, either the coefficient of the variable examined in the regression with the multiplicative term or the coefficient of that variable in the regression without the multiplicative term must be transformed. For example, in Table 7.5 the coefficient of the number of sizes is .6989 in the fifth regression and .2115 in the sixth. To compare, .6989 is transformed to $.6989 + (-.0059 \times 47) = .4216$, so that *.2115* can be compared with *.4216*; or .2115 is transformed to $.2115 - (-.0059 \times 47) = .4889$, so that *.4889* can be compared with *.6989*. The improper comparison that results if this transformation is not made overstates the difference between the two coefficients. The method used, based on partial derivatives, is detailed in M. S. Albion, *The Effect of Manufacturer's Advertising on Retail Gross Margins in Supermarket Retailing* (unpublished Ph.D. dissertation, Harvard University, May 1981), p. 225.

7. An important issue here is not only the level of category advertising, but also the variation in advertising among the different firms in the product market. In other words, if the level of category advertising is high, but the variation in brand advertising among the firms is also high, the situation may be far different than if all firms advertise approximately the same amount. For an analysis of this type, see M. E. Porter, *Interbrand Choice, Strategy, and Bilateral Market Power* (Cambridge, Mass.: Harvard University Press, 1976), pp. 200–212.

Chapter 8

EMPIRICAL ANALYSIS OF ADVERTISING AND RETAIL BRAND MARGINS

To examine the impact of advertising on the gross profit margin of the various brands carried by the mass retailer requires that four questions be answered:

1. How strong is the effect of advertising on retail brand gross margins?
2. How much of the relationship between advertising and retail gross margin is the *direct* effect of advertising on brand profitability (through sales) and how much is the *indirect* effect (through increased salience leading to more intensive retail price competition)?
3. How complex is the relationship? Is it a simple linear relationship, or is there a threshold level of advertising that must be achieved before the effect is significant?
4. How does the relationship differ among various product categories and why?

In addition, it is important for us to know whether there is a strong *feedback* effect; that is, whereas increased advertising may lead to higher unit sales and lower gross margins, do the lower gross margins then lead to higher unit sales and thereby more advertising?

In this chapter we will look briefly at whether or not there is a strong feedback effect and answer the first three questions. The fourth question, which requires both the product category and brand analyses, it answered in the next chapter. The statistical analysis is based on the 1978 chain data; the 1977 results are quite similar and reinforce the 1978 results. But before this analysis, it is important

177

to discuss the specification of the two central variables of the book: brand gross margin and brand advertising. We will extend the discussion of Chapter 4 and show that with these variables specified as ratios of their respective category levels, there remain a variety of options available. The choice of which specification to use for each variable depends upon the questions to be answered.

The Central Variables[1]

Our initial question concerns how to specify the brand gross margin in a sample of product categories, many of which have different category gross margins. We established in Chapter 4 that the brand gross margin should be measured as a ratio of the product category gross margin. However, there are two ways to specify the *brand gross margin ratio* (hereafter often referred to as BGMR): the brand gross margin as a percentage either of the weighted average category gross margin—the measurement of category gross margin used in the statistical analyses of Chapter 7—or of a simple, unweighted average of the brand gross margins in the product category. We will argue that *a simple average of the brand gross margins should be used*. To calculate the brand gross margin ratio, therefore, involves dividing each of the 488 brand gross margins (expressed as percentages of sales) by the unweighted average gross margin for all brands in that product category, and multiplying by 100. By using a hypothetical example, we will demonstrate why this measure is superior and, to complement Chapter 4, why the use of merely the brand gross margin would distort the brand analysis.

The reason we should not simply use the brand gross margin instead of the BGMR is that the brand gross margin results in comparing "apples and oranges" in any pooling of the 51 product categories. A weighted average BGMR should not be used either, because of the nature of our analysis. We wish to examine the difference in gross margins between advertised and unadvertised brands. As advertised brands generally have much higher unit sales than unadvertised brands in the same product category, a weighted category average is heavily determined by the gross margins of the advertised brands. Accordingly, *a weighted BGMR would overestimate the difference between the advertised and unadvertised brands*.

Table 8.1 offers a hypothetical example comparing the three different measures. In both product categories the advertised brands have lower gross margins than the unadvertised brands: 5 percent versus 10 percent for applesauce, 40 percent versus 50 percent for frozen orange juice. Yet if we lumped all the unadvertised brands together, took a simple average, and then did the same for the advertised brands, the opposite would appear to be true: The average brand gross margin is 30 percent for unadvertised brands, but 31.25 percent for the advertised brands. What has happened is that there are more advertised brands in the higher-margin than in the lower-margin product category, and fewer unadvertised brands. If instead we gave an example with more advertised brands in the lower-margin category (applesauce), the expected relationship—unadvertised brands have lower gross margins than advertised brands—would occur. The measured advertising–gross margin relationship, therefore, is dependent on the number of advertised and unadvertised brands in the various product categories. Accordingly, using brand gross margins to estimate the advertising–gross margin relationship in any sample of more than one product category is risky and, for our purposes, unacceptable.

The more pertinent comparison in between the *weighted* BGMR (category gross margin as the denominator, which is computed by adding the brand gross margins weighted by their unit sales for all the brands in the product category) and the *unweighted* BGMR (the simple, unweighted average of the gross margins of the brands in the product category as the denominator). Looking at applesauce in Table 8.1, we can see the difference in the two computations. The category gross margin (always weighted) is: (60% × 5%) + (40% × 10%) = 7%; the average brand gross margin in the category, however, is: (5% + 10%)/2 = 7.5%, as relative sales shares of brands are irrelevant since all brands are treated as having equal sales shares. The difference in the two BGMRs is, therefore, that as long as advertised brands have lower gross margins and higher sales shares than the unadvertised brands (as is common), the category gross margin will be lower than the simple average of the brand gross margins, since the advertised brands are given more weight in the computation of category gross margin than the unadvertised brands.

The most important result of these computational differences is that the weighted BGMR will underestimate the difference between the advertised brands and the unweighted average brand gross margin in the product category and *overestimate the difference between the advertised and unadvertised brands*. This occurs because the category gross margin is heavily determined by the gross margins on the advertised brands, and the smaller denominator of the weighted BGMR—that is, 7 percent versus 7.5 percent for applesauce, 41 percent versus 42.5 percent for frozen orange juice—produces a larger measured size differential than if the unweighted BGMR is used—that is, (132.5 − 91.25) = 41.25 versus (125.5 − 87.25) = 38.25. Because we wish to compare the gross margins

Table 8.1 Different Specifications of Brand Gross Margins

Product Category	Brand	Sales Share	Brand Gross Margin	Weighted Category Gross Margin	Weighted Brand Gross Margin Ratio	Average Brand Gross Margin in Category	Unweighted Brand Gross Margin Ratio
Applesauce							
	Advertised A	60%	5%	7%	71	7.5%	67
	Unadvertised B	40%	10%	7%	143	7.5%	133
					(average:107)		(average:100)
Frozen Orange Juice							
	Advertised A	30%	40%	41%	98	42.5%	94
	Advertised B	30%	40%	41%	98	42.5%	94
	Advertised C	30%	40%	41%	98	42.5%	94
	Unadvertised D	10%	50%	41%	122	42.5%	118
					(average:104)		(average:100)
					(total average:105)		(total average:100)

BRAND GROSS MARGINS

Unadvertised Brands: $\left(\dfrac{50\% + 10\%}{2}\right) =$ ⟦30%⟧

Advertised Brands: $\left(\dfrac{40\% + 40\% + 40\% + 5\%}{4}\right) =$ ⟦31.25%⟧

WEIGHTED BRAND GROSS MARGIN RATIOS

Unadvertised Brands: $\left(\dfrac{143 + 122}{2}\right) =$ ⟦132.5⟧

Advertised Brands: $\dfrac{98 + 98 + 98 + 71}{4} =$ ⟦91.25⟧

UNWEIGHTED BRAND GROSS MARGIN RATIOS

Unadvertised Brands: $\left(\dfrac{133 + 118}{2}\right) =$ ⟦125.5⟧

Advertised Brands: $\left(\dfrac{94 + 94 + 94 + 67}{4}\right) =$ ⟦87.25⟧

of advertised and unadvertised brands unadulterated by unit sales (which we can include in the analysis later as a separate variable), the unweighted BGMR—the brand gross margin as a percentage of the average brand gross margin in that category—is the proper specification.

Finally, there is another property of the BGMR that we require: The average BGMR for a product category and the entire sample should be 1 (100 through multiplication). As shown in Table 8.1, the weighted BGMR produces an average greater than 100: 107 for applesauce, 104 for frozen orange juice, and 105 for the two product categories combined. For our sample of 488 brands, the average is 111.2 This occurs because advertised brands tend to have greater sales shares and lower gross margins than unadvertised brands. Note that the unweighted BGMR always produces an average of 100, as would be expected. This is therefore not only a more sensible formulation, but also a more useful one: a BGMR of 91 means that the brand gross margin is 9 percent less than the average brand gross margin in the product category, whereas a BGMR of 120 indicates that the brand gross margin is 20 percent higher than the average brand gross margin in that category.

Having decided that an unweighted average for the BGMR should be used to specify brand gross margin in our statistical analysis,[2] we are left to consider the specification of brand advertising. The question here is not one of weighting, but rather whether to specify brand advertising as a *share* of total category advertising or as a *ratio*, like BGMR, of the average level of brand advertising in the product category. There is no one answer to this question. *The choice of specification depends on how the results are to be used.* Accordingly, we will use the brand advertising share for the most part, but we will use the brand advertising ratio at times as well, depending on the question addressed.

Simply put, the statistically "cleaner" specification of brand advertising is the brand advertising ratio, since it transforms advertising into the same units as BGMR. The R^2s are higher for the linear BGMR regressions using the advertising ratio (and thereby unit sales ratio) than the BGMR regressions using the advertising share (and thereby unit sales share). Moreover, this specification has to be used when attempting to quantify the savings in gross margin dollars from brand advertising, because both variables must be in the same units. This specification, therefore, is used in Chapter 10 when we quantify these savings, and it is shown at different points in this chapter for comparative purposes.

On the other hand, an advertising ratio in not considered by most managers and has little practical meaning. Whereas the BGMR

makes sense to retailers, indicating the percentage difference between a brand's gross margin and the average brand in that category,
advertisers less often think of their expenditures in terms of the
deviation of their advertising from the average brand in that product
market. Instead, advertisers often think in terms of their advertising-
to-sales ratio (and its deviation from the norm in their market) or,
it is held, their share of total category advertising. In addition, many
brand managers like to know their advertising share in relation to
their sales share for the brand: Is it greater or less than one? Accordingly, advertising share (and unit sales share) is the more sensible
specification. Although it is not measured comparably to BGMR and
therefore does not produce the R^2s of the advertising ratio, advertising share does produce results that are *managerially useful*. For
these reasons, *the primary statistical relationship examined will be
between BGMR and the advertising share*.

Overview of the Effect of Advertising on Gross Margin

Table 8.2 and Figures 8.1 and 8.2 offer an overview of the results.
Table 8.2 indicates that of the 48 product categories with at least
one advertised and one unadvertised brand (no unadvertised brands
in canned dog food, cottage cheese, and baby foods), in 33 the
advertised brands have a lower gross margin than the unadvertised
brands. In 15 other product categories, however, the unadvertised
brands have lower gross margins. But in these 15 categories where
the expected relationship does not occur, just four product categories
have significantly lower gross margins on the unadvertised brands,
and in all instances, each category has only one unadvertised brand
to compare with the advertised brands of that category. Accordingly,
we can safely say that as a group, there is a general trend toward
lower gross margins on the advertised brands, particularly in the
nonfood product categories. However, we must also note that this
general trend is much stronger in some product categories than in
others; in the next chapter we will show that this variation can be
accounted for systematically, on the basis of certain category
characteristics.

Figure 8.1 is constructed for the entire sample of 488 brands. The
brands have been divided into three classifications based on their
respective levels of advertising share. A 4 percent cutoff point was
chosen to divide the 377 advertised brands into two groups, less
advertised and highly advertised, each with approximately the same
number of brands (182 versus 195). Advertising share is measured

Table 8.2   Difference in Gross Margins for Advertised and Unadvertised Brands in Each Product Category

Advertised Brands with Lower Gross Margins	Unadvertised Brands with Lower Gross Margins
FOODS	FOODS
*Breakfast cereals (RTE)	*Canned fruits
*Cake mixes	Canned soups (condensed)
Candy bars	*Cat food (canned)
Canned baked beans	Coffee (instant/freeze-dried)
*Canned fruit juices	Coffee (regular)
*Canned tuna	Cooking oil
Canned vegetables	Evaporated canned milk
Cat food (dry)	Frozen orange juice
Cheese	Frozen vegetables
Dog food (dry)	*Italian box dinners/noodles
*Flour	Margarine
Frozen dinners/entrees	Pasta products
Frozen seafood	Pickles
Granulated cane sugar	Powdered soft drink mixes
*Mayonnaise	*Spaghetti sauces
Milk additives	
*Nuts	
Peanut butter	
*Plain canned meats	
Ready-to-serve fruit juices	
Salad dressings	
Shortening	
*Tea bags	
NONFOODS	
*Bar soap	
*Cigarettes	
Disposable diapers	
*Fabric softeners	
Facial tissues	
*Hand dishwashing liquids	
*Laundry detergents	
*Paper towels	
Plastic garbage bags	
*Toilet tissues	

* The difference in gross margins between the advertised and unadvertised brands is significant, as assessed by a two-tail t test.

as the four-year total of a brand's advertising dollars divided by the four-year total of all advertising expenditures in that product category, multiplied by 100. The results show that, on average, the highly

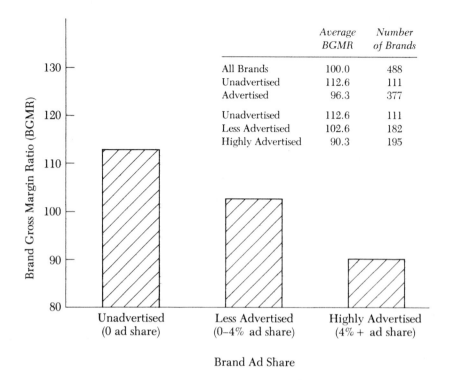

Figure 8.1 Total Effect of Advertising on Brand Gross Margin.

advertised brands sell for gross margins that are 22 percentage points lower than the unadvertised brands and 12 percentage points lower than the less advertised brands. These differences are statistically significant at the 99 percent level (Chi-square test). Thus *our basic proposition is confirmed*. Moreover, the magnitude of the difference between advertised and unadvertised brands is large enough to warrant a more detailed investigation of the phenomenon.

Figure 8.2 is similar to Figure 8.1, except that the effect of advertising on retail gross margins is diagrammed for brands with "high" unit sales shares and for those with "low" unit sales shares— in effect, roughly isolating the effect of advertising on gross margin independent of its effect on gross margin through unit sales. In other words, advertising can lead to high unit sales and thereby lower gross margins; that process of advertising affecting gross margin has been removed from the two dashed lines depicted in the figure. It should also be noted that, as with all cutoff points used in the statistical analyses to divide a sample (except the unadvertised–advertised cutoff), the value of the cutoff point is se-

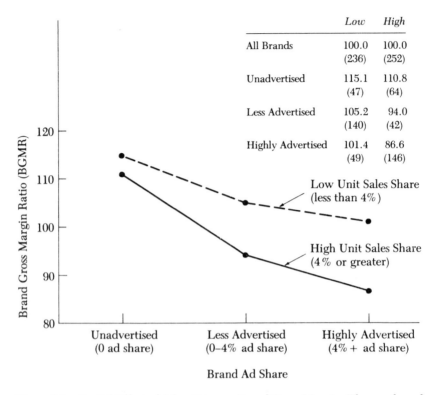

	Low	High
All Brands	100.0 (236)	100.0 (252)
Unadvertised	115.1 (47)	110.8 (64)
Less Advertised	105.2 (140)	94.0 (42)
Highly Advertised	101.4 (49)	86.6 (146)

Figure 8.2 Partial Effect of Advertising on Brand Gross Margin. The number of brands in each cell is given in parentheses underneath the unweighted average BGMR for the group of brands in that cell.

lected to equalize as much as possible the number of observations in the subsamples. For Figure 8.2, the cutoff point is a 4 percent unit sales share, which divides the sample into 236 and 252 brands. Unit sales share is measured as the brand's unit sales divided by the total unit sales for the product category, multiplied by 100. Moreover, throughout the analysis *the results using brand unit sales share or dollar sales share are very similar*. As such, brand unit sales share (or ratio, when appropriate) is used in Chapters 8 and 9.

The results show that independent of advertising's effect on gross margin through unit sales, advertised brands have lower gross margins than unadvertised brands. For brands with a high unit sales share, the effect is greater: a 24 percentage point difference between highly advertised and unadvertised brands versus a 14 percentage point difference for the low unit sales share brands. This difference between the two groups (24 versus 14) occurs because highly advertised brands generally have high unit sales (.6 correlation between advertising share and unit sales share in our sample), and unit sales has its own, independent effect on gross margin. Still, the consistently lower gross margins of the advertised brands in both groups indicate that these differences in gross margins between advertised and unadvertised brands—statistically significant at the 99 percent level—for both the high and low unit sales brands remain prominent *above and beyond advertising's effect on gross margin through unit sales*. Before further investigation of this relationship, however, the question of causality must be addressed.

Simultaneity of the Advertising–Gross Margin Relationship[3]

We have already mentioned the possibility of what we called the *feedback effect* of gross margin on advertising: Whereas advertising may lead to lower gross margins, these lower margins may in turn translate into lower retail prices, higher unit sales, and a further increase in manufacturers' advertising expenditures. This possibility is particularly important if advertisers keep a fixed advertising-to-sales ratio. With more sales dollars from higher unit sales—and the same factory price even though the retail price has declined—advertisers may increase their outlays. Accordingly, any regression analysis would need to analyze the advertising–gross margin relationship using simultaneous equation estimation rather than the simple OLS (ordinary least squares) method shown in the last chapter. More important, any implications drawn from the results would have to recognize that whereas an inverse advertising–gross margin reltionship may exist, *it may be lower retail gross margins leading to higher levels of manufacturers' advertising, not necessarily advertising leading to lower gross margins*.

Because of this potential problem, we have looked at the bias *for this particular data base* that occurs when we use OLS instead of simultaneous equation estimation. Two methods were used to compute the bias: the Griliches and Ringstad (1971) formulation that allows us to estimate the simultaneity bias directly and two-stage least squares. The critical relationship for a feedback effect to occur turns out to be between the retail price ratio and BGMR: Whereas we proposed in Chapter 6 that gross margin is a function of retail price (negative relationship), retail price is also a function of the gross margin (positive relationship). Single-equation estimation, therefore, will not separate out these two relationships, resulting in an upward bias (toward zero) of the retail price ratio coefficient in our basic brand equation: BGMR regressed on advertising share, unit sales share, and the retail price ratio.

In computing the biases, we used brand unit size (.8 correlation with the retail price ratio), advertising share, and unit sales share as the second-stage equation (explains 60 percent of the variation in the retail price ratio among 488 brands) in the simultaneous equation system. The results indicate that with linear specifications of all variables, the bias of single-equation estimation of the total effect of advertising on gross margin is on the order of only 3 percent; a bias of similar magnitude (always less than 5 percent) was estimated for the partial, indirect effect of advertising on gross margin. As such, single-equation estimation can be used without much loss in precision, and *a causal effect of advertising on gross margin maintained*. This finding is compatible with the one other study that examined the direction of this relationship (Reekie, 1979, discussed in Chapter 3).

One final note on the retail price ratio variable is necessary before we continue the empirical analysis. The simultaneous equation estimation measured the bias in the coefficient of this variable in single-equation estimation of BGMR on advertising share, unit sales share, and the retail price ratio to be on the order of nearly 50 percent, that is, an underestimation of the effect of retail price (reflecting brand contribution and salience) on gross margin independent of the identity that a higher gross margin, all other factors equal, translates into a higher retail price. Still, Albion (1981) showed that this factor remains a significant explanatory variable of the BGMR in all regression analyses, no matter what other independent variables are used in the estimation and regardless of functional form. But for our purposes, we will not use this independent variable in our analyses, but will limit ourselves to advertising share and unit sales share. The reader should be aware, however, that the effect of leaving out this variable is mostly lower R^2s, as the strength and significance of the BGMR-advertising share and even the BGMR-unit sales share relationships are not significantly altered.[4]

The Margin Elasticity of Advertising

In Chapter 6 we introduced three measures of the effect of advertising on retail gross margins. These are: the *total* effect of advertising on gross margins (the total margin elasticity); the *indirect* effect from the greater salience and increased retail price competition of advertised brands (the partial margin elasticity); and the *direct* effect from higher sales of advertised brands (the sales partial margin elasticity). Table 8.3 shows the linear estimates of these margin elasticities of advertising for both advertising share and advertising ratio. The advertising ratio is measured as the advertising share times the

Table 8.3 Regression Equations Explaining Brand Gross Margins (n = 488)

Intercept	Ad Share	Unit Sales Share	Ad Ratio	Unit Sales Ratio	R^2
103.8[a]	−.4322[a]				.043[a]
(1.6)	(.0926)				
106.2[a]		−.5921[a]			.071[a]
(1.7)		(.0969)			
106.6[a]	−.1707[c]	−.4893[a]			.076[a]
(1.7)	(.1106)	(.1175)			
107.4[a]			−.0823[a]		.077[a]
(1.8)			(.0129)		
108.8[a]				−.0859[a]	.085[a]
(1.8)				(.0120)	
110.5[a]			−.0458[a]	−.0619[a]	.112[a]
(1.9)			(.0152)	(.0143)	

NOTE: The dependent variable is expressed as the brand gross margin ratio (BGMR).

The significance of the regression coefficients is tested using a one-tail t test. The significance of the coefficients of multiple determination is tested using the F test. Standard errors are in parentheses.

[a] Coefficient is significant at the 99 percent level.
[b] Coefficient is significant at the 95 percent level.
[c] Coefficient is significant at the 90 percent level.

number of brands carried by the retailer in the product category: the four-year total of a brand's advertising dollars divided by the simple, unweighted average four-year total of brand advertising in that product category, multiplied by 100. It measures the difference between a brand's advertising share and the average brand advertising share in that product category. In this manner the specification of advertising is comparable to BGMR. The transformation from the unit sales share to the unit sales ratio is similar in kind.

With the BGMR regressed on advertising share and unit sales share, the total effect has a coefficient of .43, the partial effect .17, and the sales effect .26 (.43 − .17). On the basis of these estimates, and on the fact that the feedback effect is about 3 percent of the total effect, we can say that above and beyond advertising's ability to increase retail turnover and lower the gross margin, a substantial 38 percent (17/43 = 40 percent × 97 percent = 38 percent) of the total effect of advertising may be attributed to something else. This "something else"—the indirect effect—serves as our proxy for the ability of advertising to increase the salience of a brand to consumers and thereby the price competition among the retailers. We have proxied (and controlled for) a brand's total contribution by the unit sales share (or ratio); as mentioned, there is almost no change in the regression results if dollar, instead of unit, sales are used. Absent from the analysis, however, is some measure of brand retail handling expenses, which have been assumed to vary negligibly among brands in a product category. Even if other factors are included in this measurement, *there remains a significant effect of advertising on gross margin independent of its direct effect on a brand's total contribution*.

The first three regressions in Table 8.3 use advertising share, the second three use the advertising ratio. The R^2s are low, due to the large degrees of freedom, few independent variables, and the dependent variable expressed not as a level (that is, brand gross margin) but rather as a ratio—a deviation from a level (Farris and Buzzell, 1980). Two further points are noteworthy in this regard. First, our objective in the brand analysis is not to explain the variation in brand gross margins within a product category (as it was for category gross margins in the product category analysis), but rather *to establish and isolate the effect of advertising alone on brand gross margins*. Therefore, only factors that directly affect this relationship between advertising and retail gross margins are included. Second, explaining about 10 percent of the interbrand variation in gross margins (R^2 of .100) in this manner is an important finding for such a low-margin business as supermarket retailing. In addition, we will show in the next section that the cross-sectional relationship may not be linear, thereby limiting the explanatory power of linear regressions.

To put the advertising coefficients of Table 8.3 into practical, useful terms is not as simple as it may appear. Given a margin elasticity of about .4 in the first regression, this means that a 5 percentage-point increase in advertising share results in a 2 percentage-point decrease in BGMR. *To translate any change in the advertising share into a change in the brand gross margin, however, is not simply formulated*. The change in brand gross margin depends upon the brand's sales share in the product category—the greater the share, the greater the difference between the change in the brand gross margin and the change in the BGMR. In addition, the units of measurement of the two variables must be the same, as they are for BGMR and the advertising ratio. We will show how to use these coefficients in Chapter 10, when we estimate the savings to consumers in lower retail gross margins from $1 million of brand advertising. Otherwise, managers can use advertising share coefficients to indicate how an increase in their advertising share affects the retail gross margins of their brands relative to the average brand in that product category.

In summation, the analyses indicate that advertising has a strong effect on gross margin, and that the effect remains strong, independent of advertising's effect on gross margin through its effect on unit sales. Using linear estimation, this indirect effect of advertising accounts for 38 percent of the total effect, with the direct effect of advertising (through unit sales) accounting for 59 percent; 3 percent is the feedback effect found through simultaneous equation estimation. This indirect effect serves as our proxy for the effect of advertising on gross margin due to advertising's ability to increase the salience of a brand to consumers and thereby the price competition among retailers selling the brand.

Nonlinear Specifications

It was suggested in the last section that the relationship between BGMR and advertising share may not be linear. A key question, therefore, is "Over what ranges of advertising share does the relationship appear to be most pronounced?" Figure 8.3 shows a plot of six groups of brands according to the average BGMR and advertising share of each group. Groupings of 0, <1, 1–3, 3–8, 8–20, and ≥20 percent advertising shares provided an approximately equal number of brands in each group and covered the extreme values of advertising share insofar as was practical. From this graph it is apparent that the relationship between BGMR and advertising share is not linear. Although the BGMR declines continually as advertising share increases, the most rapid decline occurs from 0 to 5 percent advertising shares.

To determine the exact specification of advertising that best fits this relationship, we analyzed the residuals of the regressions. The residuals were plotted against the regression fit and the individual variables to test for possible nonlinearities. The residuals do show a distinct pattern when plotted against advertising share: large residuals at higher levels of advertising share, as the regression tries to "fit" the BGMRs of the 111 unadvertised brands. As such, since it may be argued that unadvertised brands are under different competitive forces than the other brands and therefore should be considered separately, we removed the unadvertised brands from the sample. However, the basic nonlinearity in the BGMR-advertising share relationship remains.

A number of nonlinear specifications can be tried, since there is no theoretical mandate at this time for one specification over another. Albion (1981) used polynomial terms (advertising share squared, advertising share cubed) to capture the curvilinearity and test for two BGMR–advertising share response functions: "S"-shaped with a threshold level, increasing returns, and then decreasing returns, or just constantly decreasing returns throughout. He found constantly declining returns as advertising share increases across the 488 brands,

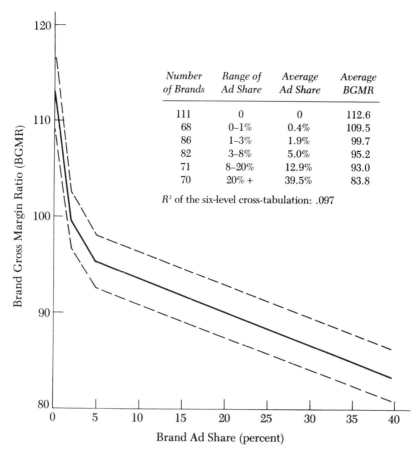

Number of Brands	Range of Ad Share	Average Ad Share	Average BGMR
111	0	0	112.6
68	0–1%	0.4%	109.5
86	1–3%	1.9%	99.7
82	3–8%	5.0%	95.2
71	8–20%	12.9%	93.0
70	20% +	39.5%	83.8

R^2 of the six-level cross-tabulation: .097

Figure 8.3   General Relationship between the Brand Gross Margin Ratio and Ad Share. The area enclosed by the broken lines illustrates the standard error of estimates.

that is, a negative linear coefficient, a positive square coefficient, and a negative cubed coefficient—all significant at the 99 percent level. Polynomial terms are generally superior to other nonlinear specifications for purposes of testing the shape of a function. In our case if the signs of the coefficients had been the reverse—positive linear coefficient, negative squared coefficient, positive cubed coefficient—an "S"-shaped function would have been warranted. However, given these research results and others by Albion,[5] as well as Figure 8.3, we can safely say that a logarithmic specification of advertising share is most appropriate. In other words, *the relationship between BGMR and advertising share appears to be log linear.*

Figure 8.4 diagrams the linear and log-linear regressions of BGMR

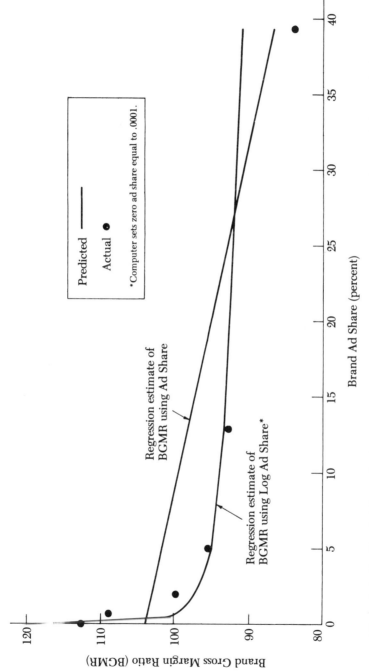

Figure 8.4 Predicted Relationship between the Brand Cross Margin Ratio and Ad Share, Log Ad Share. The figure is constructed for ease of reading. The difference between actual and predicted values and total explanatory power of the model are accurately reflected by R^2s.

on advertising share, the log of advertising share, with the actual, average values of BGMR for each of our six groups of brands indicated by X's. It is apparent that the log-linear regression "fits" our data better, but this equation still tends to underestimate BGMR for brands with relatively low advertising shares and overestimate BGMR for those with high advertising shares. This can be due to an improper model or the failure to account for some other variable, such as unit sales.

Table 8.4 shows regressions comparable to those in Table 8.3, except that advertising share (and advertising ratio) is expressed logarithmically; that is, a semi-log relationship between gross margin and advertising is being "fit" on our sample of 488 brands. The first regressions of the two tables are the ones diagrammed in Figure 8.4. Whereas the logarithmic specification of advertising share improves significantly its ability to predict variations in BGMR, a logarithmic specification of the advertising ratio has little effect on its significance. The inclusion of a measure of unit sales increases the predictive power of the model greatly for either advertising specification. In addition, the basic advertising–gross margin relationship is essentially unchanged. These results indicate that *linear estimation of the partial margin elasticity (the indirect effect) may underestimate its significance*. Recall from Chapter 7, however, that we cannot compare directly the magnitude of the coefficients of, for example, the log of advertising share (such as, -1.910) with the coefficients of advertising share in Table 8.3 ($-.4322$). Once transformed for comparability, this coefficient of the log of advertising share is approximately $-.2715$. We can, however, compare the R^2s, as the dependent variable (BGMR) is expressed similarly throughout.

Table 8.4   Regression Equations Explaining Brand Gross Margins with Log of Advertising (n = 488)

Intercept	Ad Share (log)	Unit Sales Share	Ad Ratio (log)	Unit Sales Ratio	R^2
98.0[a]	-1.910[a]				.079[a]
(1.4)	(0.295)				
103.7[a]	-1.705[a]	$-.5203$[a]			.134[a]
(1.7)	(0.289)	(.0944)			
102.9[a]			-1.829[a]		.076[a]
(1.5)			(0.288)		
109.7[a]			-1.450[a]	$-.0724$[a]	.141[a]
(1.9)			(0.286)	(.0120)	

NOTE: The dependent variable is expressed as the brand gross margin ratio (BGMR).

The significance of the regression coefficients is tested using a one-tail t test. The significance of the coefficients of multiple determination is tested using the F test. Standard errors are in parentheses.

[a] Coefficient is significant at the 99 percent level.

A more direct comparison of the linear and log-linear estimates using advertising share is shown in Table 8.5. The table contains the numbers used to diagram Figures 8.3 and 8.4., as well as BGMR estimates for the second regression in Table 8.4: BGMR regressed on the log of advertising share, unit sales share. By examining the residuals shown in parentheses in Table 8.5, we can see how unit sales share improves the regression fit, particularly by not over-estimating BGMR for brands with relatively high advertising shares. On average, the log advertising share estimate is off by 3.8 BGMR points per brand group, whereas including unit sales share reduces this difference to 1.8 BGMR points.

In summation, the BGMR–advertising share relationship appears to be log linear, with the larger decrease in BGMR occurring at relatively low levels of advertising share. *It is important not to misinterpret why this result may have occurred or what this finding means.* As the analysis is cross-sectional (a comparison of different brands with different levels of advertising share) and not time-series (a comparison of the same brand with different levels of advertising share over time), we must be careful in drawing implications from these statistical results. What the findings do show is that the incremental (and average) effect of advertising on gross margin is less for brands with high advertising shares than for brands with low advertising shares. This does *not* mean that there are constantly

Table 8.5 Linearity of the Advertising—Gross Margin Relationship

Number of Brands	Range of Ad Share	Average Ad Share	Average Unit Sales Share	Average BGMR	BGMR Estimates Ad Share	BGMR Estimates Log Ad Share	BGMR Estimates Log Ad Share, Unit Sales Share
111	0	0	11.1%	112.6	103.8 (−8.8)	116.0* (+3.4)	113.8* (+1.2)
68	0–1%	0.4%	3.4%	109.5	103.6 (−5.9)	100.6 (−8.9)	104.3 (−5.2)
86	1–3%	1.9%	3.5%	99.7	103.0 (+3.3)	96.8 (−2.9)	100.8 (+1.1)
82	3–8%	5.0%	6.4%	95.2	101.6 (+6.4)	94.9 (−0.3)	97.6 (+2.4)
71	8–20%	12.9%	12.1%	93.0	98.2 (+5.2)	93.1 (+0.1)	93.0 (0.0)
70	20% +	39.5%	27.9%	83.8	86.7 (+2.9)	91.0 (+7.2)	82.9 (−0.9)

NOTE: Numbers in parentheses are the residuals (the difference between the actual, average, BGMR and the estimated BGMR).

* Computer sets zero ad share equal to .0001.

declining returns (in terms of decrease in retail gross margin) to increases in advertising *dollars* (and thereby advertising share) for a particular brand's manufacturer. Since nationally advertised brands with high advertising shares are commonly in less heavily advertised categories than national brands with low advertising shares ($-.4$ correlation), advertising dollars and advertising share measure different relationships in a cross-sectional analysis of this type. As such, declining returns with respect to advertising share in a sample of many brands does not eliminate the possibility of a threshold effect for any particular brand, which in a cross-sectional sample can also be assessed by examining the absolute advertising dollar expenditure.

Advertising Dollars versus Advertising Share

Low advertising share brands are often in product categories with high levels of category advertising. Most nationally advertised brands of laundry detergents and cereals, for example, hold only a 2 to 3 percent ad share, but represent three times the advertising dollars of Domino sugar, which for 1975–78 had a 40 percent advertising share. Indeed, a 2 percent advertising share in cereals represents more advertising dollars than a 100 percent advertising share in sugar. Recognizing this fact, we are faced with two questions: (1) Is it advertising share or advertising dollars that has an important effect on retail gross margins? and (2) Is there a threshold effect in terms of advertising dollars or the same declining returns as found for advertising share? The answers to these questions are of great importance to both marketing managers and policymakers.

The first issue concerns whether it is a brand's share of advertising messages in the market—that is, its *relative* impact in the market—or its own "volume" of messages—its *absolute* impact—that is more important. In the first instance, $2 million of brand advertising in a product market with $10 million in total advertising, for example, would have roughly the same effect as $1 million in a market with $5 million in total advertising; in each case the brand holds a 20 percent advertising share. But if instead it is the absolute impact of brand advertising dollars that is important, then $2 million of advertising is equivalent only to $2 million in advertising—no matter what the total level of advertising is in the market(s).

Table 8.6 was constructed to address this issue in a very general manner. The results of the regressions indicate that *both advertising dollars and advertising share may be important determinants of the level of retail gross margins*. Whereas Figure 8.3 showed a generally declining response of gross margins to advertising share, implying

Table 8.6 Regression Equations Explaining Brand Gross Margins with Advertising Dollars, Advertising Share (n = 488)

Intercept	Ad Share	Ad Dollars	Ad Share × Ad Dollars	Unit Sales Share	R^2
107.1[a]	−.4465[a]	−.433E-8[a]	.723E-10[b]		.070[a]
(1.8)	(.1302)	(.115E-8)	(.371E-10)		
111.4[a]	−.2648[b]	−.511E-8[a]	.132E-09[a]	−.6040[a]	.115[a]
(2.0)	(.1322)	(.113E-8)	(.381E-10)	(.1214)	

NOTES: The dependent variable is expressed as the brand gross margin ratio (BGMR).
  The significance of the regression coefficients is tested using a one-tail *t* test. The significance of the coefficients of multiple determination is tested using the *F* test. Standard errors are in parentheses.
[a] Coefficient is significant at the 99 percent level.
[b] Coefficient is significant at the 95 percent level.

that the BGMR–advertising share relationship is log linear, it indeed seems true that this observed relationship is caused, at least in part, by the fact that the low advertising share brands are in more highly advertised product categories than the high advertising share brands. These low advertising share brands, therefore, may represent more advertising dollars than the high advertising share brands—implying that there could be a threshold effect in terms of advertising dollars in the effect of advertising on gross margin. If this is so, advertisers may have an additional consideration (to a threshold level of the advertising–sales response function) in their budgeting: reaching a critical mass of advertising dollars to increase consumer demand for the brand to the point that retailers begin to compete intensively on the price of the brand by lowering their gross margin.

Figure 8.5 illustrates the relationship between advertising dollars and BGMR; the figure is comparable to Figure 8.3 for advertising share. In fact, the shape of the relationship is somewhat similar to the BGMR–advertising share relationship, or at the very best, the BGMR–advertising dollars relationship is linear. Whereas the level of advertising dollars may also be important in determining the level of brand gross margin, *the figure offers no evidence that there is a threshold effect in terms of advertising dollars*. We conclude, therefore, that this cross-sectional evidence does not support a threshold effect. Time-series or cross-national data for individual brands are needed to test this threshold effect more precisely. Still, a threshold effect may exist for some product categories, but not others. Both the shape and strength of the effect of advertising on brand gross margins may differ among product categories. This is the topic of the next chapter.

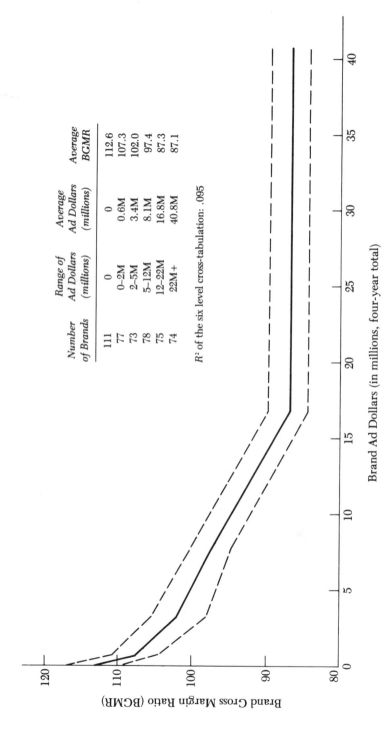

Figure 8.5 General Relationship between the Brand Gross Margin Ratio and Ad Dollars. The area enclosed by the broken lines illustrates the standard error of estimates.

Summary

In this chapter we demonstrated that the effect of advertising on brand gross margins is robust, and the indirect effect of advertising on gross margin—our measure of the increased retail competition on advertised brands—is significant as well. It does appear from our results that the retailer is pricing as if advertising has increased the one-way cross-elasticity of advertised brands with the rest of the products in the store. In other words, the results show that *there is a significant, measurable difference in the pricing of advertised and unadvertised brands that is not the result of differences in the brands' total contributions, but rather, we infer, of differences in the traffic–building potential of the brands*. Since advertised brands are better traffic builders on average than unadvertised brands, lower gross margins result in part from reduced retail prices and price promotions.

The statistical analysis of 488 brands in 51 product categories required that we specify the brand gross margins and brand advertising as percentages of their respective product category levels. Accordingly, we examined the relationship between the brand gross margin ratio and the brand advertising share. We found the relationship to be *causal*—that is, advertising leads to lower gross margins—and *nonlinear*—the effect is the greatest for brands with low advertising shares (from about 0 to 5 percent advertising shares), tapering off for brands with high advertising shares. In cross-sectional analysis a linear specification of the impact of advertising on brand gross margins, therefore, can underestimate the significance of advertising. We argued from this and other evidence that a possible reason for this finding is that national brands with low advertising shares are commonly in highly advertised product categories (detergents, cereals) and, concomitantly, high advertising share brands (Domino) are often in lightly advertised categories (sugar). It was suggested that the statistical result is caused by the importance of advertising dollars as well as advertising share, and possibly the existence of a threshold effect in terms of advertising dollars: Some critical mass of advertising expenditures is needed before they have an appreciable effect on sales and retail gross margins. However, analysis of the entire sample found no evidence of a threshold effect.

Overall, the effect of advertising on gross margin—even independent of advertising's effect on unit sales—was shown to be an important marketing reality. The statistical evidence of this simple marketing relationship implies that advertising budgeters may be underestimating the returns of successful advertising by not considering how advertising increases the retail competition on their brands. The market outcome may be a retail price much closer to the factory price than it would be with less advertising. In other words, the manufacturer captures a larger percentage of the retail price to consumers or, said otherwise, with a particular factory price, the retail price is competed downward over time, thereby further increasing the manufacturer's sales. In the next chapter, we will examine how and why this effect of advertising on brand gross margins may differ in importance among various product categories. In so doing, we will also investigate further the possibility of a threshold effect for certain groups of product categories in our analysis of the relationship between different category characteristics and the margin elasticity of advertising.

Endnotes

1. I am indebted to discussions with Paul Farris for the point of why the average brand gross margin in a category is a superior formulation for our purposes to the weighted average category gross margin. He is also responsible for parts of Table 8.1.
2. The reader should be aware that using either a weighted or an unweighted average in the formulation does not make a significant difference in the statistical results. For similar analyses using the weighted average, see M. S. Albion, *The Effect of Manufacturer's Advertising on Retail Gross Margins in Supermarket Retailing* (unpublished Ph.D. dissertation, Harvard University, May 1981), Chapter 8.
3. For a detailed look at this problem with empirical estimations of the bias, see Albion, *op. cit.*, pp. 203–210. The bias has also been re-estimated using different specifications of gross margin and/or advertising; the results show the bias to be never greater than 4.8 percent.
4. For these analyses using the retail price ratio and for all the analyses done on just the food and/or household product categories, see Albion, *op. cit.*, Chapter 8.
5. Albion, *op. cit.*, Chapter 8 contains results using the polynomial terms as well as other multiplicative terms: advertising share times unit sales share and advertising share times retail price ratio. These findings uncover some other relationships concerning unit sales and retail price that are not of primary concern for the arguments of this book.

Chapter 9

EMPIRICAL ANALYSIS OF DIFFERENT PRODUCT CATEGORIES

That the effectiveness of advertising varies among product categories has been established in much of the literature on the effect of advertising on sales and the determinants of the level of advertising expenditures. Similarly, the margin elasticity of advertising—our measure for the effect of advertising on retail brand gross margins—may also differ among product categories. As indicated by Table 8.2 of the last chapter, even within our fairly homogeneous sample of supermarket products, the magnitude of the margin elasticity can differ significantly from one product category to another.

Having shown that there is a strong effect of advertising on retail brand margins and that the effect is nonlinear, we examine in this chapter how the strength of this advertising–gross margin relationship differs among product categories. To do so, we use statistical analysis on groups of product categories, grouped by certain category characteristics, and look at individual product categories of particular public policy concern. The reasons for these variations in the margin elasticity among product categories are established by combining the category and brand analyses of gross margin.

Once we have reviewed why the margin elasticity of advertising differs among product categories, we examine the total effect of advertising on gross margin with cross-tabulations and graphs. Regression analysis is used next to analyze variations in the indirect effect of advertising on gross margin (the effect from increased retail price competition). Advertising is specified logarithmically in keeping with our analysis in the last chapter. These analyses provide evidence for our central proposition that *product categories with character-*

*istics reflecting relatively high (low) category gross margins have
relative low (high) margin elasticities of advertising.*

The chapter concludes with a look at some individual product
categories of interest to policymakers, such as cereals, laundry detergents, and candy bars, and four groups of product categories—
what are traditionally thought of as "traffic builders," "sweets,"
"soaps," and pet foods and baby products. These analyses allow us
to see, at another level of inspection, how the effect of advertising
on brand gross margins varies in strength and significance among
product categories. Acknowledging this variation has strong managerial implications as well, for both advertisers and retailers.

Variations in the Margin Elasticity of Advertising

The central proposition that explains how the magnitude of the effect
of advertising on brand gross margins differs among product categories serves to connect the category and brand models of Chapters
5 and 6 and the statistical analyses of the past two chapters. The
proposition is, holding all other factors constant:

> *Product category characteristics that are directly (inversely) related
> to category gross margins are inversely (directly) related to the strength
> and significance of the margin elasticity of advertising.*

For example, product categories with a large number of different
package sizes should have higher category gross margins and lower
margin elasticities than categories with a smaller number of sizes.
In this regard, the effect of advertising on brand gross margins should
be relatively stronger for mayonnaise (4 package sizes) than for soft
drink mixes (22 package sizes).

At the start of Chapter 7 we discussed the logic behind this proposition. To reiterate, we argued that the more the retailer "adds
value" to the final product sold to consumers, the greater the retailer's bilateral market power and/or the less consumers care about,
or are able to find out about, any interstore price differentials on
a brand, the weaker should be the margin elasticity of advertising
and the greater the category gross margin. Our empirical analysis
of the independent category variables that explain variations in the
level of category gross margins supported one part of this proposition.
If the entire proposition is sound, these same category characteristics
should be essential in isolating how the margin elasticity of advertising varies among product categories.

Before we proceed with the results, a more intuitive explanation
of this proposition is useful. First of all, the proposition can be more

simply stated as: *Product categories with high gross margins have low margin elasticities of advertising*. To illustrate—if, as has been shown, advertising does lead to a lower gross margin for the advertised brand, the lower brand gross margin will lead to a lower average brand gross margin in the product category—the amount to which this will occur depending on the size of the decline in brand gross margin and the number of other brands carried in the category by the retailer. As long as the brand is not the only one carried by the retailer in the product category, the brand gross margin ratio (BGMR) will decline as well.[1]

The amount of the decline in the BGMR will depend on the strength of the product category factors reflecting the level of category gross margin. The stronger the category characteristics reflecting low category gross margins, the less the category gross margin (or average brand gross margin in the category—the denominator of BGMR) can decline. Accordingly, the measured decline in the BGMR is greater and the margin elasticity of advertising is estimated to be greater.[2]

In addition, there are reasons that high or low category gross margins exist, as discussed and demonstrated in Chapters 5 and 7, respectively. Given these reasons, advertising should be (and may have already been) more effective in product categories that for one reason or another are more responsive to advertising. These product categories typically have low gross margins. The margin elasticity of advertising, therefore, should be greater in these product categories. This contention for a narrow range of supermarket products is similar to Porter's (1976) reasoning for convenience (low retail gross margins) and nonconvenience (high retail gross margins) product classes: Advertising is more effective in low retail gross margin (convenience goods) product categories.

Figure 9.1 shows the relationship between the level of the category gross margin and the effect of advertising on brand gross margins. The graph is nearly identical if we use the average brand gross margin in a product category instead of the category gross margin. As in all our analyses, wherever possible the division of "high" and "low" (here at 15.1 percent) is picked to divide the sample as equally as possible. The graph shows that the spread in average BGMRs between highly advertised and unadvertised brands is indeed significantly greater (99 percent level, Chi-square test) in the low than the high category gross margin group: 46 percentage points versus less than 6 percentage points. Though there is a strong correlation between category gross margin and brand gross margin ($-.76$), the use of ratios in the construction of the BGMR should take care of any possibility that the results are a statistical artifact; that is, all

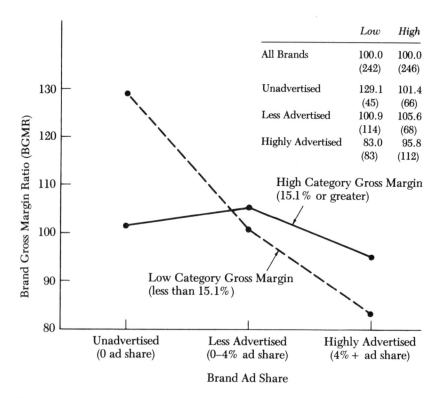

	Low	High
All Brands	100.0	100.0
	(242)	(246)
Unadvertised	129.1	101.4
	(45)	(66)
Less Advertised	100.9	105.6
	(114)	(68)
Highly Advertised	83.0	95.8
	(83)	(112)

Figure 9.1   Product Category Gross Margin and the Margin Elasticity of Advertising. The number of brands in each cell is given in parentheses underneath the unweighted average BGMR for the group of brands in that cell.

product categories have an average BGMR of 100. Moreover, the category gross margin (or again, the average brand gross margin in the category) has no correlation with the BGMR (−.00) and little with advertising share (−.06). *What we are observing, therefore, seems to be a real phenomenon, not a statistical creation.*

Beyond the use of ratios, one further point should be made about the margin elasticity proposition. If the use of ratios is still felt to be an insufficient control, then the product category characteristics (and the gross margin) should be inversely related not only to the margin elasticity of advertising, but also to a margin elasticity of unit sales. Our model, however, does not predict this to be the case, nor do our statistical results support this contention. This independent variable (brand unit sales) *directly* affects the brand's total contribution, and thereby its gross margin, regardless of the characteristics of the product category. Advertising, on the other hand, must work *through* these other variables to affect the retailer's total contribution (and gross margin) on the brand. It is in this process of advertising's effect on brand salience and sales that the inverse relationship between product category characteristics and the margin elasticity of advertising occurs.

Cross-Tabulation Analysis of the Total Margin Elasticity

Using cross-tabulations first, we will analyze how the total margin elasticity of advertising, with advertising specified linearly (ad share), varies among product categories grouped by certain category characteristics. As a group, *those category characteristics that were strong explanatory variables of the category gross margin in Chapter 7 are also strong category criterion variables in this analysis*. All of the product category characteristics, including household penetration, are examined in Figures 9.2–9.6 and Table 9.1. The figures have been diagrammed not necessarily for the most statistically significant results, but rather for those characteristics with the most interesting implications for management and policy. The remaining cross-tabulations are presented in the table. The interaction terms (category advertising times number of brands, number of items times number of sizes) are not shown because these results offer no new information.

The format selected to display the results does not allow us to use more than one category characteristic at a time to divide the sample (three-dimensional graphs are often very confusing). The use of graphs does, however, allow us to see clearly the relationship being tested. Still, the results do generate some carefully drawn implications that will be re-examined for validity in the multiple regression analysis. It should be reiterated that no result is presented that was not validated by the 1978 data without "outlying" product categories, such as cigarettes (very high advertising, little price variation), and without unadvertised brands, and on the 1977 data.

Food and Nonfood Product Categories

Figure 9.2 diagrams the difference in the impact of advertising on retail brand gross margins for the 363 food brands and 125 nonfood brands. The figure indicates that there is a significant difference in the margin elasticities of the food and nonfood product categories. Recall that the nonfood brands in this sample are selected from only ten product categories, essentially household products, which include laundry detergents, soap, dishwashing liquids, facial and toilet

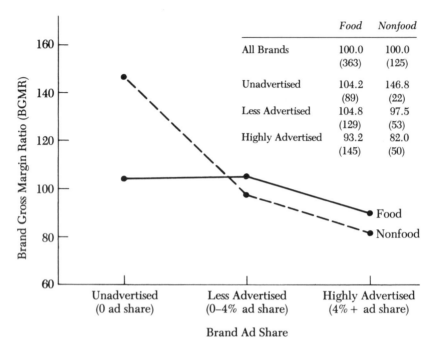

	Food	Nonfood
All Brands	100.0	100.0
	(363)	(125)
Unadvertised	104.2	146.8
	(89)	(22)
Less Advertised	104.8	97.5
	(129)	(53)
Highly Advertised	93.2	82.0
	(145)	(50)

Figure 9.2   Margin Elasticity of Advertising for Food and Nonfood Categories. The number of brands in each cell is given in parentheses underneath the unweighted average BGMR for the group of brands in that cell.

tissues, paper towels, and the like. Although we expect that a more general selection of food and nonfood product categories would show food categories to be more salient and have lower gross margins (and accordingly, higher margin elasticities) than the nonfood categories, that is not the case here. As we discussed in Chapter 7, the sample selection method (store sales-share minimum) resulted in a sample that includes a group of highly salient, highly advertised nonfood categories with lower gross margins than the food product categories in the sample. Indeed, the nonfood categories average $262 million for their four-year total of advertising expenditures and have an 11.7 percent average category gross margin; the food categories average only $74 million and 16.6 percent. We see a much greater margin elasticity of advertising, therefore, for the 125 nonfood brands (10 product categories) than for the 363 food brands (41 categories) that, given this explanation, would be expected. In fact, there is a 65 percentage-point difference in average BGMRs between the unadvertised and highly advertised brands in the nonfood product categories, but only a 11 percentage-point difference in the food categories (significant difference, Chi-square test).

We still must caution against generalizing from these results. Whereas the level of category advertising is one reason for the difference between the two types of product categories, a closer look at Figure 9.2 indicates another essential difference: *the pricing of unadvertised brands* (by volume, 98 percent of which are private labels). First, it should be recognized that only 22 unadvertised brands in nonfood product categories partially determine the large differences observed. Discounting these brands, there is less difference between the food and nonfood product categories: a difference in average BGMRs between the less advertised and highly advertised brands of 15.5 percentage points for the nonfood categories and an 11.6 percentage-point difference for food categories. This differential—15.5 versus 11.6—is not significant (Chi-square test). There appear to be, therefore, two essential differences between the food and nonfood subsamples.

The difference in the pricing of unadvertised brands (essentially private labels) between the two types of product categories is worthy of further attention. As already discussed in the summary and implications of Chapter 7, whereas private labels hold a lower share in the nonfood than in the food product categories (8.7 percent versus 13.6 percent), they are priced to effectively raise the average category gross margin by a greater amount (13.2 percentage points in nonfood versus 0.7 percentage points in food). One reason for this pricing difference could be that in more salient, highly advertised product categories (nonfood), private labels are less salient to consumers, and the retailer—competing fiercely on the heavily advertised brands—tries to compensate for the very low margins with relatively very high margins on the private labels.

However, further data analysis shows that the difference in pricing private labels between the two types of product categories is more than just a difference in category salience, as proxied by category advertising (measured over four years). For example, with our sample divided into product categories with low and high levels of advertising, an increase of 10 percentage points in private label sales results in an increase in the average category gross margin of 1.0 versus 3.8 percentage-points for the less advertised versus the more highly advertised product categories, respectively—a difference of 2.8. A similar 10 percentage-point increase in private label sales produces an increase in the average category gross margin of 0.55 versus 8.19 percentage points for food versus nonfood categories, respectively—a difference of 7.64. This differential (2.8 versus 7.64) is significant at the 99 percent level (Chi-square test). In other words, the results of this analysis suggest that the private label pricing differences between these two types of product categories are more than just a function of category salience, as proxied by category advertising.

One explanation for this finding concerns the economics of the two different product markets. We may argue that part of the pricing difference between the food and nonfood product categories is allowed because of a possibly larger profit margin to be divided between manufacturer and retailer in the nonfood categories. In food markets, manufacturers as well as retailers may be under greater competitive pressures (and may have less excess capacity). The retailer may therefore be able to extract larger price concessions from the private label manufacturer(s) in nonfood than in food markets. On the other hand, the results could be caused by consumer behavior (private labels in nonfood categories less salient for reasons other than those measured by category advertising) or the retailer's contribution objectives (need for high-margin private labels in these nonfood categories to compensate for the very low margins on the advertised brands). In any case, the implication is that *the retailer has more latitude in the pricing of private labels (unadvertised brands) in these more highly salient nonfood categories than in the food product categories*.

Moreover, Figure 9.2 indicates that retail gross margins are very responsive to low levels of manufacturers' advertising in nonfood product categories. This statistical result could occur for one or both of two reasons: (1) A 1 percent advertising share for the nonfood subsample is equivalent to a 3 percent advertising share in the food subsample, and (2) there may be a threshold effect of advertising on gross margin for certain product categories, particularly those with relatively low levels of category advertising.

Product Category Advertising

Figure 9.3 depicts the difference between product categories with high category advertising ($125 million or greater for a four-year total; $262 million average) and those with low category advertising (less than $125 million for a four-year total; $74 million average). The results are similar in some respects to those diagrammed in Figure 9.2 for food–nonfood categories: a strong margin elasticity for product categories with high category advertising at all levels of advertising share, with a strong margin elasticity for categories with low category advertising between only the less advertised and highly advertised brands. Whereas highly advertised brands have an average BGMR 31 percentage points lower than the unadvertised brands in the high category advertising subsample (includes cereals, candy bars, cigarettes, laundry detergents, bar soaps, and the like), there is less than a 19 percentage-point difference in the low category

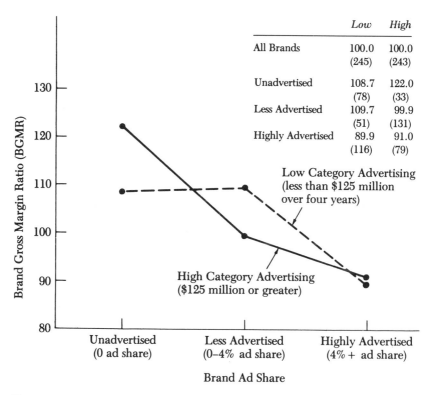

	Low	High
All Brands	100.0	100.0
	(245)	(243)
Unadvertised	108.7	122.0
	(78)	(33)
Less Advertised	109.7	99.9
	(51)	(131)
Highly Advertised	89.9	91.0
	(116)	(79)

Low Category Advertising (less than $125 million over four years)

High Category Advertising ($125 million or greater)

Figure 9.3   Product Category Advertising and the Margin Elasticity of Advertising. The number of brands in each cell is given in parentheses underneath the unweighted average BGMR for the group of brands in that cell.

advertising subsample. On the other hand, the differences between the less and highly advertised brands in the low (19.8 percentage points) versus the high (8.9 percentage points) subsamples reveal the opposite relationship.[3]

More important, there is a difference in the *shape* of the BGMR-advertising share relationship between the high and low subsamples. This difference reinforces our contentions in the last chapter about the importance of advertising *dollars* as well as advertising share. On average, three times the advertising share is required in the low category advertising subsample as for the product categories in the high category advertising subsample to obtain equivalent levels of advertising dollars. In the low advertising categories, the BGMR begins to decline only for brands with a relatively high advertising share; however, in the high advertising categories, the advertising share needed is much less. Accordingly, the largest differences in

BGMRs should appear for brands in high advertising product categories for two reasons: (1) It is in these categories that the difference among brands in both relative and absolute advertising "weight" is the greatest, and (2) it is in these highly advertised product categories that advertising has been found to be most effective—for whatever reasons.

Figure 9.3, therefore, offers the one piece of empirical evidence for a threshold level, in terms of advertising dollars, in the effect of advertising on brand gross margin. Although we saw in the last chapter (Figure 8.5) that the BGMR-advertising dollars relationship maintained declining returns for the entire sample, the relationship may still contain a threshold effect for some of the product categories in the sample. More specifically, these would be the product categories with low category advertising. Moreover, as the low advertising categories in our sample have an average annual advertising expenditure of $18.5 million, *less heavily advertised product categories not in this sample may be even more subject to a threshold effect of advertising on brand gross margin*. In any case, time-series analysis is required to measure directly for whether a threshold level does exist and for which product categories, if any. What we can say is that advertising dollars as well as advertising share are important determinants of the level of brand gross margins, and a threshold level—some critical mass of advertising expenditures—may have to be reached, at least for some product categories, before this effect of advertising on brand gross margins is realized.

Household Penetration and Product Category Sales

In Chapter 5 we discussed how a product category's unit sales can be separated into two distinct components: the frequency of purchase and the number of purchasers. It was held that the number of purchasers, otherwise called household penetration (measured as a percentage of the total number of purchasers in a product category), should affect the aggregate salience of a product category for the retailers. Product categories with high household penetration lend themselves to promotion as traffic builders. Further, advertising is more effective as a mass communication vehicle the greater the number of consumers that are interested in the product.

Figure 9.4 shows the difference in the BGMR–advertising share relationship for high versus low household penetration categories, with a cutoff point of 70.4 percent used to divide the sample into two groups (245 and 243 brands). The results indicate that the margin elasticity of advertising is very strong for high household penetration

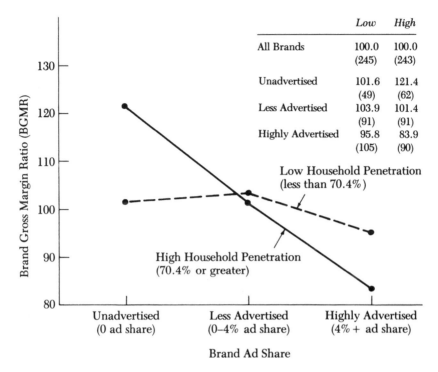

	Low	High
All Brands	100.0	100.0
	(245)	(243)
Unadvertised	101.6	121.4
	(49)	(62)
Less Advertised	103.9	101.4
	(91)	(91)
Highly Advertised	95.8	83.9
	(105)	(90)

Low Household Penetration
(less than 70.4%)

High Household Penetration
(70.4% or greater)

Unadvertised
(0 ad share)
Less Advertised
(0–4% ad share)
Highly Advertised
(4% + ad share)

Brand Ad Share

Figure 9.4   Household Penetration and the Margin Elasticity of Advertising.
The number of brands in each cell is given in parentheses underneath the
unweighted average BGMR for the group of brands in that cell.

categories, such as laundry detergents, sugar, flour, mayonnaise,
cereals, and canned tuna. For these product categories, the difference
in the BGMR between the highly advertised and unadvertised brands
approaches 40 percentage points. In the product categories with low
household penetration, such as ready-to-serve juices, canned meats,
pet and baby foods, the difference is less than 6 percentage points.
This differential (40 versus 6) is significant at the 99 percent level
(Chi-square test).

Along with the food-nonfood division, *the level of household penetration is the most significant category characteristic that reflects
the strength of advertising's effect on brand gross margins*. In multiple
regression analyses of the BGMR-advertising share relationship run
on all the product category variables at one time (to be discussed
in more detail shortly), the household penetration variable was continually significant at the 99 percent level. Only the food-nonfood
division was similarly significant. This finding raises an important
question: Is the effect of household penetration merely a result of
category sales levels rather than a separate proxy of product category

salience? In other words, since product category sales is a function of how many people buy the products and how often, is household penetration per se related to the margin elasticity of advertising?

Figure 9.5 answers our questions, demonstrating that there is no appreciable difference between product categories with high category sales and those with low category sales ($642 million cutoff based on national, not chain, data). The results show a 12 percentage-point and 12.5 percentage-point difference between unadvertised and highly advertised brands in the two groups. This finding further strengthens our contention that the level of household penetration is strongly related to the magnitude of advertising's margin elasticity.

Private Label Penetration

Figure 9.6 diagrams the relationship of private label penetration with the margin elasticity of advertising.[4] The Steiner model predicts that

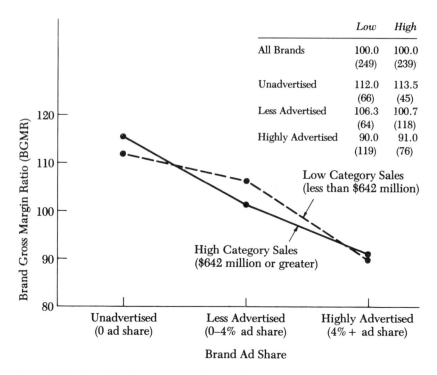

	Low	High
All Brands	100.0	100.0
	(249)	(239)
Unadvertised	112.0	113.5
	(66)	(45)
Less Advertised	106.3	100.7
	(64)	(118)
Highly Advertised	90.0	91.0
	(119)	(76)

Low Category Sales
(less than $642 million)

High Category Sales
($642 million or greater)

Brand Gross Margin Ratio (BGMR)

Unadvertised   Less Advertised   Highly Advertised
(0 ad share)   (0–4% ad share)   (4% + ad share)

Brand Ad Share

Figure 9.5   Total Product Category Sales and the Margin Elasticity of Advertising. The number of brands in each cell is given in parentheses underneath the unweighted average BGMR of brands in that cell.

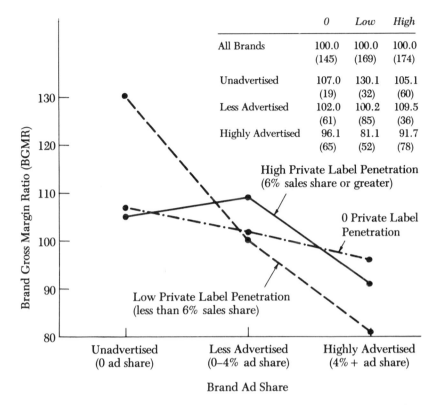

	0	Low	High
All Brands	100.0	100.0	100.0
	(145)	(169)	(174)
Unadvertised	107.0	130.1	105.1
	(19)	(32)	(60)
Less Advertised	102.0	100.2	109.5
	(61)	(85)	(36)
Highly Advertised	96.1	81.1	91.7
	(65)	(52)	(78)

Figure 9.6   Private Label Penetration and the Margin Elasticity of Advertising. The number of brands in each cell is given in parentheses underneath the unweighted average BGMR for the group of brands in that cell.

advertising's effects should be the strongest when there is some private label competition for the manufacturers ("mixed regimen"), with neither manufacturers' brands or private label brands dominating ("manufacturers' brand domination" and "private label domination," respectively). He maintains that retail prices are lowest in the "mixed regimen."

The results of Figure 9.6 indicate that for our sample, the margin elasticity of advertising is strongest when there is a low degree of private label penetration (up to 6 percent). The difference in average BGMRs between the unadvertised and highly advertised brands is nearly 50 percentage points, whereas this difference is only 11 and 13 percentage points for the product categories with no private label penetration and high (6 percent and over in this case) private label penetration, respectively. This differential (60 versus 11 or 13) is significant at the 99 percent level (Chi-square test). The difference in average BGMRs between the less advertised and highly advertised brands is negligible, however, in the low than in the high private label penetration subsamples (19.1 percentage points versus 17.8 percentage points, respectively). For brands with high advertising

Table 9.1 Product Category Criterion Variables and the Margin Elasticity of Advertising

	Retail Expenses (Dummy)		Item Size (Dummy)	
	Low	High	Small	Large
All brands	100.0	100.0	100.0	100.0
	(444)	(44)	(422)	(66)
Unadvertised	114.8	100.4	107.9	142.8
	(94)	(17)	(96)	(15)
Less advertised	102.5	107.3	103.4	98.0
	(176)	(6)	(158)	(24)
Highly advertised	89.5	97.6	92.3	78.0
	(174)	(21)	(168)	(27)
	Number of Sizes (11 cutoff point)		Preshopping Decisions* (32.4% cutoff point)	
	Small	Large	Low	High
All brands	100.0	100.0	100.0	100.0
	(233)	(255)	(176)	(219)
Unadvertised	116.8	108.1	102.4	107.8
	(58)	(53)	(54)	(35)
Less advertised	107.5	99.6	107.0	102.8
	(70)	(112)	(49)	(107)
Highly advertised	85.7	95.7	93.5	92.6
	(105)	(90)	(73)	(77)
	Number of Brands (10 cutoff point)		Number of Items (72 cutoff point)	
	Small	Large	Small	Large
All brands	100.0	100.0	100.0	100.0
	(238)	(250)	(241)	(247)
Unadvertised	109.2	120.8	115.3	108.7
	(78)	(33)	(66)	(45)
Less advertised	110.4	99.9	105.8	101.2
	(48)	(134)	(59)	(123)
Highly advertised	89.1	92.0	88.4	93.2
	(112)	(83)	(116)	(79)

NOTE: The number of observations (brands) in each cell is in parentheses, below the unweighted average brand gross margin ratio (BGMR) for the group of brands in that cell. The less advertised–highly advertised cutoff point is 4 percent.
* 395, not 488, observations (brands).

share levels, therefore, the impact of advertising on brand gross margins may not be related to the level of private label penetration. Product categories in the zero private label group include candy bars, cottage cheese, soaps, cigarettes, and pet foods; the 6 percent and over group has peanut butter, mayonnaise, frozen vegetables, frozen orange juice, canned fruits and canned vegetables, sugar, cooking oil, shortening, pasta products, and plastic garbage bags, among others; the 0 to 6 percent group contains product categories such as cake mixes, salad dressings, margarine, cereals, toilet tissues, paper towels, and laundry detergents.

Other Product Category Characteristics

Other category criterion variables not discussed are included in Table 9.1. All significant characteristics of product categories have the expected relationship with the margin elasticity of advertising. As such, the margin elasticity is stronger for categories with: low retail expenses (significant); large item sizes (significant); small number of sizes (significant); high percentage of preshopping decisions, large number of brands, and small number of items (significant). All but the number of brands has the expected relationship with the margin elasticity, and the result for the number of brands is not significant. As we discovered earlier in the chapter, this characteristic is meaningful only when the level of product category advertising is also considered.

In summation, the margin elasticity proposition has been confirmed in terms of the total effect of advertising on gross margin, with advertising specified linearly. Manufacturers, retailers, and policymakers should recognize that *advertising's ability to lead to lower retail prices (through a reduction in the gross margin) is limited in high gross margin product categories*. The more retailers find themselves in, or can create, a situation in which they do not need to respond to manufacturers' advertising, the higher should be their gross margin, all other factors being equal. In addition, policymakers are cautioned that if any restructuring of the manufacturing stage of a product market leads to changes in absolute brand advertising expenditures, this change may lead to higher retail gross margins, depending on, among other things, the operant range of the advertising–gross margin response function.

Multiple Regression Analysis of the Partial Margin Elasticity

In the cross-tabulation analysis we examined the *total* effect of advertising on gross margin, generally confirming our contention that product categories with high gross margins (and characteristics reflecting those high gross margins) have low margin elasticities of advertising. Using multiple regression analysis, we can look at the *indirect* effect of advertising on gross margin, otherwise called the partial margin elasticity of advertising. This is our measure for what we have inferred to be the effect of advertising on the salience of a brand and thereby the retail price competition on that brand. In addition, we specify advertising logarithmically in keeping with our findings of the last chapter.

Sample Splits versus Dummy Variables

Before we examine the regression results, it is important to know why we chose to "split" the sample rather than use dummy variables or some other method. The usual reason for splitting a sample is that it is believed that the variance of the error term is not the same for all observations in the data set. Furthermore, it is assumed that the model itself is different in the two or more subsamples—for example, brands in product categories with a large number of package sizes are different from brands in categories with a small number of sizes. At this time, however, our model is not refined to the point of making such assertions, although it should be mentioned that the variance of the residuals does differ within most sample splits. As a group, the residuals are consistently larger for the levels of category characteristics related to lower gross margins, but the difference is generally not significant. The essential reason for splitting the sample of 488 brands is that, most important, *it allows us to test the change in coefficients among the subsamples,* particularly changes in the partial margin elasticity of advertising.

Because there is no underlying theoretical mandate for the use of sample splits instead of dummy variables, it is instructive to mention what the results are using dummy variables. A two-part transformation of the data is required. The product category characteristics are first transformed into dummy variables—for example, household penetration of 70.4 percent and above is given a value of 1, and penetration below 70.4 percent is given a value of 0. The log of advertising share is then multiplied by the dummy value of the category characteristic for each characteristic. The use of multiplicative instead of additive terms—the log of advertising share times the household penetration dummy as an explanatory variable rather than the log of advertising share and the household penetration dummy as two separate explanatory variables of BGMR—is based on the theoretical model. Category characteristics are held to affect primarily the *slope* of the margin elasticity of advertising. Additive terms imply that the characteristics affect the *intercept*, not necessarily the margin elasticity. Sample splits allow both the slope and intercept to vary with the level of the category characteristic being analyzed.

On the other hand, multiplicative terms allow us to look at the relationships of more than one category characteristic with the margin elasticity of advertising at one time. As such, we can determine directly which characteristics have the most significant relationships with the margin elasticity. The results of these regressions are not significantly different from any inferences drawn from the sample splits in Table 9.2. Whereas a regression of BGMR on the log of advertising share and unit sales share results in an R^2 of .134 (Table 8.5), the R^2s of these regressions with the most significant characteristics included are around .250. The most important product category characteristics are continually shown to be the *food-nonfood classification* and *the level of household penetration*. The level of category advertising and the number of items in a category are also important, followed by the item size dummy, which serves as a proxy for product category salience. (Of the eight categories considered to have large items, flour, sugar, dry pet foods, disposable diapers, and laundry detergents are included—all quite often used as traffic builders.) A continuous measure of item size is never significantly related to the margin elasticity.

Regressions on Subsamples

Table 9.2 contains the sample splits for those category characteristics graphed in Figures 9.1–9.6 and the number of sizes and retail expenses dummy. For the characteristics not shown, the partial margin elasticity of advertising is stronger for product categories with a small number of items and large item size (dummy measure only). The results are not significant using the number of brands or the percentage of preshopping decisions. *All results are as expected and reinforce the cross-tabulation findings.* It should be mentioned, furthermore, that all results were checked in a number of ways: eliminating cigarettes from the sample; examining the product categories contained in a number of the subsamples to see whether the elimination of some large category(ies) (in terms of number of brands) affects the results; and changing cutoff points. At no time do these changes significantly affect the margin elasticity of advertising regression coefficient (excepting the category retail price, which is not discussed for that reason). Other than category advertising and category sales, the difference in the coefficients between the regressions on the subsamples for each product category criterion variable in Table 9.2 is significant (Chow test).

Table 9.2 Multiple Regression Equations Explaining Brand Gross Margins for Various Subsamples

Product Category Criterion Variable	Level	Intercept	Ad Share (log)	Unit Sales Share	R^2	Number of Observations (Brands)
Category Gross Margin [15.1%]	Low	103.2[a] (2.7)	-3.547[a] (0.510)	-.6005[a] (.1555)	.236[a]	242
	High	104.0[a] (1.9)	-0.359 (0.290)	-.4111[a] (.1001)	.075[a]	246
Food versus Nonfood [Dummy]	Food	104.8[a] (1.8)	-0.812[a] (0.287)	-.5091[a] (1.0909)	.108[a]	363
	Nonfood	101.0[a] (3.9)	-5.172[a] (0.761)	-.4481[c] (.2902)	.319[a]	125
Category Advertising [$125 million]	Low	108.1[a] (3.0)	-1.270[a] (0.383)	-.6376[a] (.1259)	.152[a]	245
	High	100.6[a] (2.0)	-2.469[a] (0.482)	-.4532[b] (.2035)	.135[a]	243
Household Penetration [70.4%]	Low	104.4[a] (1.9)	-0.357 (0.340)	-.4532[a] (.1012)	.088[a]	245
	High	103.2[a] (2.9)	-2.879[a] (0.447)	-.6546[a] (.1610)	.208[a]	243

Category Sales [$642 million]	Low	104.6[a] (2.5)	−1.494[a] (0.365)	−.4928[a] (.1170)	.144[a]	247
	High	103.2[a] (2.4)	−1.981[a] (0.472)	−.6276[a] (.1688)	.130[a]	241
Private Label Penetration [6%]	0	103.6[a] (2.1)	−0.377 (0.495)	−.4778[a] (.1488)	.089[a]	145
	Low	100.2[a] (3.3)	−3.810[a] (0.644)	−.4855[a] (.2239)	.228[a]	169
	High	107.0[a] (3.2)	−0.968[a] (0.396)	−.5730[a] (.1356)	.130[a]	174
Retail Expenses [Dummy]	Low	103.9[a] (1.8)	−1.953[a] (0.319)	−.5809[a] (.1046)	.152[a]	444
	High	102.4[a] (4.0)	−0.088 (.4916)	−.1645 (.1614)	.028	44
Number of Sizes [11]	Small	106.1[a] (2.8)	−2.363[a] (0.423)	−.6965[a] (.1407)	.211[a]	233
	Large	102.2[a] (2.1)	−0.991[a] (0.389)	−.3670[a] (.1270)	.066[a]	255

NOTE: The dependent variable is expressed as the brand gross margin ratio (BGMR). Cutoff points used to divide sample are in brackets. The significance of the regression coefficients is tested using a one-tail t test. The significance of the coefficients of multiple determination is tested using the F test. Standard errors are in parentheses.

[a] Coefficient is significant at the 99 percent level.
[b] Coefficient is significant at the 95 percent level.
[c] Coefficient is significant at the 90 percent level.

For seven of the eight characteristics, two-way sample splits are presented in Table 9.2. A three-way split was used for private label penetration, as it was in Figure 9.6. Three-way sample splits for the other characteristics yield results similar to those shown. The results are also similar for linear specifications of advertising and for simple regressions without unit sales share to measure the total margin elasticity. The unit sales share is strongly correlated with advertising share (.57), but not with the log of advertising share (.13), even if unit sales share is also specified logarithmically (.13). Moreover, it is important to note that, *whereas the partial margin elasticity of advertising is consistently related to the category characteristics (and category gross margin) as was proposed, the unit sales share regression coefficients are not.* In other words, the direction of change in the unit sales coefficients is not consistent with the direction of change in the advertising coefficient. For instance, although the partial margin elasticity is significantly stronger for nonfood categories and product categories with high household penetration, the unit sales share coefficient is not. As previously discussed, this is because advertising must work through other brand factors, that is, unit sales, and retail price, to affect the brand's total contribution and gross margin; unit sales need not, since it affects total contribution directly. It is in this working through other brand factors that advertising's effect on brand gross margin is influenced by the category characteristics that reflect the level of category gross margins.

Upon closer examination of Table 9.2, we find that we often need to use t statistics (value of coefficient divided by its standard error, that is, for the log of advertising share in low category gross margin, $3.547/0.510 = 6.95$) to compare some of the log of advertising share coefficients, since the coefficient is significant at the 99 percent level for both levels of a category characteristic. This is not the case, however, for *household penetration* and the *retail expenses dummy*. The partial margin elasticity of advertising is much stronger and more significant for high levels of household penetration and low retail expenses—the former, primarily a measure of product category salience, whereas the latter reflects only direct contribution. In fact, the importance of household penetration is even more manifest in a three-way sample split, with the highest level including product categories with over an 88.6 percent level of household penetration. The sample split using category (national *or* chain) sales, on the other hand, shows no significant variation in the partial margin elasticity.

Although the importance of category advertising is less than expected, the other characteristics of product categories show the partial margin elasticity of advertising to be decidedly more important in nonfood categories, and categories with a small number of sizes and low level of private label penetration. In summation, therefore, the results are as expected, reinforcing the cross-tabulation analysis and the margin elasticity proposition: Product categories with high gross margins (and characteristics reflecting the high level of those margins) have low margin elasticities of advertising. The type of product category (nonfood), the level of household penetration (high), and the retail expenses associated with the category (low) appear to be strongly related to the magnitude of the partial margin elasticity of advertising.

These findings indicate that any discussion of the importance of the effects of advertising on gross margin and retail price, more specifically advertising's effect on brand salience and retail price competition, must consider the characteristics of the product categories under discussion before any conclusions can be drawn. Whereas the margin elasticity of advertising appears to be robust under most circumstances, *it may not be a significant fact for certain product categories, particularly high gross margin categories*. A closer examination of some of the categories in our sample, previewed in Table 8.2, provides further insights.

Product Categories

Table 8.2 indicated that in 33 of 48 categories (no unadvertised brands in canned dog food, baby foods, and cottage cheese), the advertised brands have lower gross margins than the unadvertised brands. Analysis of the 1977 data shows the same general trend, as does regression analysis performed on each product category whenever possible.[5] Of additional interest is an examination of the margin elasticity of advertising for particular product categories and groups of categories. With the limited number of brands in many of the product categories, it is nearly impossible to analyze all the categories individually. However, we will look at four groups of product categories and a handful of individual categories with enough brands to facilitate this type of analysis. These four groups and the individual product categories selected are of particular concern to policymakers and managers alike.

Four Product Category Groups

Four groups of product categories were selected to analyze the effect of advertising on brand gross margins in four different product market situations. Each group contains relatively similar product categories. These four groups cover 219 of the 488 brands in the sample. The four groups selected are:

1. *Traffic Builders* (29 total brands)
   These product categories are purchased by nearly every household. Included are: canned tuna (6 brands), peanut butter (6), mayonnaise (6), flour (5), sugar (3), and shortening (3).
2. *Pet Foods and Baby Products* (44 total brands)
   These product categories are purchased very frequently by a small number of shoppers. Included are: canned dog food (13 brands), canned cat food (11), dry dog food (8), dry cat food (5), disposable diapers (5), and baby foods (2).
3. *Sweets* (102 total brands)
   These product categories are used primarily by children. Included are: ready-to-eat cereals (56 brands), candy bars (37), and soft drink mixes (9).
4. *Soaps* (44 total brands)
   These product categories are heavily advertised, high in hidden qualities and product externalities. Included are: laundry detergents (24 brands), hand dishwashing liquids (10), and fabric softeners (10).

A word of caution is necessary before examining the results. First of all, these four groups could obviously contain other product categories, such as toilet and facial tissues as traffic builders, or bar soaps in the soaps group. On the other hand, the four category groups may not be considered homogeneous enough. For example, in pet foods and baby products, it may be felt that the pet and baby products should be separated, or canned pet food and dry pet foods should be separated because of different item sizes and retail handling expenses. Moreover, in the soaps classification, laundry detergents and dishwashing liquids suffer from the same problem. What has been done is that in all cases the results have been checked by removing and adding individual product categories. Any results sensitive to such changes will be noted.

Table 9.3 shows the cross-tabulation results for the four category groups. The results indicate that, as expected, the traffic builders have the most consistently strong total effect of advertising on gross margin, with a 62 percentage-point difference in average BGMRs between the unadvertised and highly advertised brands. Pet foods and baby products demonstrate a consistent but quantitatively questionable total margin elasticity, whereas both sweets and soaps have inconsistent relationships. Soaps do not show a negative margin elasticity for advertised brands; sweets do, but may have slightly higher margins on the less advertised brands than on the unadvertised brands. Before we draw any conclusions from the results, however, it is worthwhile to examine these relationships with regression analysis.

Table 9.3 Brand Gross Margins for Four Product Category Groups

	Traffic Builders	Pet Foods and Baby Products	Sweets	Soaps
Unadvertised	130.1	107.9	105.1	163.4
	(11)	(6)	(14)	(9)
Less advertised	95.1	103.4	106.8	82.6
	(9)	(19)	(43)	(18)
Highly advertised	68.1	94.1	92.0	84.9
	(9)	(19)	(45)	(17)
Total number of brands	29	44	102	44
Low-high cutoff point*	29%	7%	2%	5%

NOTE: The number of observations (brands) in each cell is in parentheses, below the unweighted average brand gross margin ratio (BGMR) for the group of brands in that cell.

* Advertising share cutoff points were selected for each product category group so as to equalize the number of observations (brands) between the less advertised and highly advertised cells.

Tables 9.4 and 9.5 present the regression results for the four category groups. Both linear and logarithmic specifications of advertising are shown since it is not obvious which specification is more appropriate for these small subsamples. Moreover, regressions were run on each of the groups without the unadvertised brands. As might be predicted from the results of Table 9.3, excluding the unadvertised brands affects considerably the results for the sweets and soaps. On the whole, the analysis indicates that our measure of advertising's ability to increase retail price competition, the partial margin elasticity, is important for *traffic builders, advertised sweets,* and *low advertising share soaps.*

Table 9.4 contains a category group with a significant margin elasticity of advertising (traffic builders) and one with an insignificant margin elasticity (pet foods and baby products). These two groups allow us to contrast the importance of the two components of a category's unit sales: the number of purchasers and the frequency of purchase. The comparison reaffirms the point made earlier: *The retailer's pricing is affected by the number of purchasers more than by the frequency of purchase.* Product categories with a large number of potential purchasers (traffic builders) make excellent loss leaders for the retailer because of the opportunity to affect more consumers; categories with few but frequent purchasers are very salient only to those few.

The results of Table 9.5 are fairly complicated when variations of retail price within each group are also examined: In both groups, the effect of advertising on gross margins is to a large extent through retail price (mostly due to soft drink mixes in sweets and laundry detergents in soaps).[6] In sweets, we see that the linear specification

Table 9.4 **Regression Equations Explaining Brand Gross Margins for Traffic Builders and Pet Foods and Baby Products**

Product Category Group	Intercept	Ad Share	Ad Share (log)	Unit Sales Share	R^2	Number of Observations (Brands)
Traffic Builders	113.2[a] (10.3)	−.8095[b] (.3768)			.146[b]	29
	127.8[a] (12.6)	−.5448[c] (.3884)		−.9139[b] (.4947)	.245[b]	29
	90.6[a] (7.9)		−4.401[a] (1.266)		.309[a]	29
	113.9[a] (10.6)		−4.275[a] (1.121)	−1.114[a] (0.382)	.479[a]	29
Pet Foods and Baby Products	103.6[a] (5.4)	−.2816 (.2393)			.032	44
	108.9[a] (4.6)	1.460[a] (0.420)		−2.014[a] (0.430)	.369[a]	44
	100.3[a] (4.5)		−1.053 (1.108)		.021	44
	109.6[a] (5.3)		0.170 (1.109)	−.7058[a] (.2466)	.184[b]	44

NOTES: The dependent variable is expressed as the brand gross margin ratio (BGMR).

The significance of the regression coefficients is tested using a one-tail t test. The significance of the coefficients of multiple determination is tested using the F test. Standard errors are in parentheses.

[a] Coefficient is significant at the 99 percent level.
[b] Coefficient is significant at the 95 percent level.
[c] Coefficient is significant at the 90 percent level.

of the total margin elasticity is weaker than that of the partial margin elasticity. This too is mostly the result of advertising's effect on gross margin through retail price, and because many of the higher sales share brands have higher gross margins. The point to be made from these results is that for sweets, there is a strong margin elasticity among the advertised brands; for soaps, the strong margin elasticity indicated by the table is unstable and disappears once the unadvertised brands are eliminated from the sample and retail price variations are accounted for. But before we draw any hasty conclusions, it is useful to look at some of the individual product categories in these two groups and a few other categories.

Selected Product Categories

To examine the effect of advertising on brand gross margins in individual categories, a cross-tabulation analysis was performed on all

Table 9.5 Regression Equations Explaining Brand Gross Margins for Sweets and Soaps

Product Category Group	Intercept	Ad Share	Ad Share (log)	Unit Sales Share	R^2	Number of Observations (Brands)
Sweets	101.7[a] (2.1)	− .6240[c] (.3870)			.025	102
	102.3[a] (2.2)	− 1.395[b] (0.723)		.5157 (.4088)	.041	102
	99.0[a] (1.9)		− 1.144[b] (0.519)		.046[b]	102
	99.2[a] (2.0)		− 1.116[b] (0.532)	− .0579 (.2221)	.047[c]	102
Soaps	112.8[a] (9.2)	− 2.006[b] (0.883)			.108[b]	44
	111.0[a] (9.5)	− 3.246[b] (1.696)		1.417 (1.654)	.125[c]	44
	94.5[a] (6.0)		− 7.305[a] (1.329)		.418[a]	44
	94.4[a] (8.2)		− 7.310[a] (1.429)	.0076 (.7477)	.418[a]	44

NOTE: The dependent variable is expressed as the brand gross margin ratio (BGMR).

The significance of the regression coefficients is tested using a one-tail t test. The significance of the coefficients of multiple determination is tested using the F test. Standard errors are in parentheses.

[a] Coefficient is significant at the 99 percent level.
[b] Coefficient is significant at the 95 percent level.
[c] Coefficient is significant at the 90 percent level.

product categories that fulfill two requirements: a minimum of ten brands and the same sign (negative or positive) total margin elasticity of advertising in the 1978 data and, as a check, the 1977 data. Eight product categories meet these criteria and are exhibited in Table 9.6 for 1978. All but two of the product categories, cigarettes and instant/freeze-dried coffee, were contained in the category groups just discussed.

Reading from left to right, the first five product categories, grouped in our soaps and sweets classifications, show a generally negative margin elasticity. For the soaps, there is a large decline in gross margin between the unadvertised and less advertised brands, characteristic of the nonfood, household product categories in our sample. The decline continues, albeit to a far lesser extent, for two of the soaps, but not for fabric softeners. For the sweets, ready-to-eat ce-

Table 9.6 Brand Gross Margins for Selected Product Categories

	Hand Dishwashing Liquids	Laundry Detergents	Fabric Softeners	Ready-to-Eat Cereals	Candy Bars	Cigarettes	Instant/ Freeze-Dried Coffee	Canned Cat Food
Unadvertised	28.75 (3)	19.20 (4)	28.01 (2)	18.44 (4)	31.46 (8)	9.63 (1)	15.78 (2)	12.84 (1)
Less advertised	10.72 (3)	10.73 (9)	18.20 (4)	16.49 (29)	31.92 (15)	9.22 (17)	16.77 (5)	20.97 (5)
Highly advertised	9.79 (4)	10.03 (11)	19.00 (4)	13.27 (23)	28.43 (14)	9.43 (17)	15.44 (5)	18.44 (5)
Total number of brands	10	24	10	56	37	35	12	11
Cutoff point*	8%	3.5%	8%	2%	2.5%	2.5%	8%	7.5%

NOTE: The number of observations (brands) in each cell is in parentheses, underneath the unweighted average brand gross margin for the group of brands in that cell. All gross margins are percentages.

* Ad share cutoff points were selected for each product category so as to equalize the number of observations (brands) between the less advertised and highly advertised cells.

reals show a continued decline in gross margin associated with in-creased advertising, whereas candy bars do so only among the ad-vertised brands.

These five highly advertised categories are very representative of supermarket product categories most commonly under attack by advertising critics, charging that advertising leads to higher prices. The evidence offered here, that retailers price the advertised brands in these product categories so as to take a lower gross margin, mitigates—or at the very least questions—the claims of advertising critics. Furthermore, the lack of such a relationship in some other product categories, represented in Table 9.6 by instant/freeze-dried coffee and particularly canned cat food, re-emphasizes that although a negative margin elasticity may be the general rule, it certainly does not apply at all times to all product categories. This evidence, however, is still not conclusive, as it deals only with the *retailer's* economic price (the retail gross margin), not the manufacturer's fac-tory price (or gross profit margin) and the absolute price level of a product category.

A closer look at three product categories of high public policy concern, under the most recent pressing attack by advertising critics, is warranted. These categories are laundry detergents, candy bars, and ready-to-eat cereals. Attacks have been made that advertising to children can be deceptive and unfair, and can create too easily strong brand loyalties based on advertising, not satisfaction with the product (candy bars and ready-to-eat cereals); that advertising of products with high externalities and hidden qualities raises retail prices to near monopolistic levels (laundry detergents); and that collusion among competitors can create a "shared monopoly" market situation in which prices are raised unfairly and competitors kept out, with the result of billions of dollars in unnecessary costs to consumers (ready-to-eat cereals).

Tables 9.7 and 9.8 provide the results of regressions run on each of the three product categories separately. It should be noted that, whereas the ratio (BGMR) and share (advertising share, unit sales share) formulations were used, this was done so for comparability of these coefficients with those in other tables. Since the analysis is performed on one product category at a time, absolute levels can be used (that is, brand gross margin, advertising dollars, and unit sales, similar to Table 9.6). Either way, the results will have the same R^2s, levels of significance (and t statistics), and coefficient signs, but different levels of magnitude for each coefficient and, of course, for the intercept. Analysis was performed on all the brands in each product category and on just the advertised brands, although the latter analysis is reported for ready-to-eat cereals only.

Table 9.7 contains the regression analysis of candy bars and laundry detergents. For candy bars, the margin elasticity appears to be linear; for laundry detergents, the margin elasticity seems to be stronger for the relatively low advertising dollar outlays, decreasing with additional dollar outlays (semi-log). Analysis of only advertised brands reinforces this point: The margin elasticity is even stronger and more significant with 50 percent higher R^2s for candy bars, but positive and insignificant for laundry detergents. For both product categories and in all instances, unit sales share is insignificant. These findings imply that the effect of advertising on retail brand gross margins is a very important consideration in any policy discussions about candy bars and their retail prices; on the other hand, the same cannot be said about laundry detergents. In this sample, excepting brands with a relatively low level of advertising share and dollars—found to be 2 percent or about $2 million annual expenditures—no significant effect of advertising on retail gross margins appears in the market.

Table 9.7 Regression Equations Explaining Brand Gross Margins for Candy Bars and Laundry Detergents

Product Category	Intercept	Ad Share	Ad Share (log)	Unit Sales Share	R^2	Number of Observations (Brands)
Candy bars	107.3[a]	−3.029[a]			.222[a]	37
	(3.3)	(0.959)				
	107.2[a]	−3.168[a]		.1756	.223[b]	37
	(3.4)	(1.172)		(.8230)		
	99.0[a]		−.7012		.035	37
	(2.8)		(.6251)			
	101.7[a]		−.4355	−.8755	.067	37
	(3.7)		(.6694)	(.8034)		
Laundry detergents	111.6[a]	−3.157			.059	24
	(14.3)	(2.684)				
	111.4[a]	−2.096		−0.879	.063	24
	(14.7)	(4.692)		(3.152)		
	94.5[a]		−7.072[a]		.314[a]	24
	(9.0)		(2.227)			
	95.5[a]		−6.950[a]	−0.226	.315[b]	24
	(12.1)		(2.457)	(1.699)		

NOTE: The dependent variable is expressed as the brand gross margin ratio (BGMR).

The significance of the regression coefficients is tested using a one-tail t test. The significance of the coefficients of multiple determination is tested using the F test. Standard errors are in parentheses.

[a] Coefficient is significant at the 99 percent level.
[b] Coefficient is significant at the 95 percent level.

Because of the recent antitrust case on the ready-to-eat cereal industry (which the cereal companies eventually won), a separate table for cereals has been constructed. Table 9.8 indicates that *the ready-to-eat cereal industry is the classic textbook example of our proposed relationships of advertising and unit sales with gross margin*. The margin elasticity of advertising is *in all situations* highly significant and strong—the largest advertising coefficient on average of any of the 51 product categories in our sample. All the explanatory variables (including retail price, if used) always have the predicted signs and significant coefficients. These results are further support for Brian Harris's analysis of the industry (Chapter 3) and his contention that trademark licensing and a concomitant rearrangement in market shares (quite possibly causing changes in advertising shares and total category advertising dollars as a result) may lead to higher retail gross margins in the industry. If the rise in retail gross margins more than compensates for the expected (or hoped for) decline in

Table 9.8 Regression Equations Explaining Brand Gross Margins for Ready-to-Eat Cereals

Intercept	Ad Share	Ad Share (log)	Unit Sales Share	R^2	Number of Observations (Brands)
115.4[a] (3.0)	−8.947[a] (1.360)			.445[a]	56
117.8[a] (2.9)	−5.993[a] (1.528)		−4.193[a] (1.253)	.542[a]	56
98.2[a] (2.3)		−3.415[a] (0.843)		.233[a]	56
110.0[a] (2.5)		−2.893[a] (0.640)	−6.467[a] (0.995)	.573[a]	56
114.3[a] (3.1)	−8.569[a] (1.358)			.443[a]	52*
115.1[a] (2.9)	−4.620[a] (1.765)		−4.668[a] (1.474)	.538[a]	52*
99.5[a] (2.1)		−7.643[a] (1.711)		.285[a]	52*
109.4[a] (2.8)		−3.239[b] (1.708)	−6.069[a] (1.283)	.509[a]	52*

NOTE: The dependent variable is expressed as the brand gross margin ratio (BGMR).

The significance of the regression coefficients is tested using a one-tail *t* test. The significance of the coefficients of multiple determination is tested using the *F* test. Standard errors are in parentheses.

[a] Coefficient is significant at the 99 percent level.

[b] Coefficient is significant at the 95 percent level.

* These regressions include only advertised brands.

factory prices, there may be no decline in retail prices. However, as we have seen, these same contentions may not be true for some other supermarket product markets as well.

In summation, we have looked at four product category groups covering nearly one half of our entire sample—traffic builders, pet foods and baby products, sweets, and soaps—and eight individual product categories, most prominently candy bars, laundry detergents, and ready-to-eat cereals. We have found that, whereas the margin elasticity of advertising is essentially robust, it is not necessarily significant for all the product categories in our sample. In this regard, it is the large number of potential purchasers (traffic builders), not the frequency of purchase (pet foods and baby products) that is strongly related to advertising's effect on brand gross margins. Moreover, we saw that the sweets, candy bars, and especially ready-to-eat cereals product markets have significant margin elasticities of advertising, whereas this effect of advertising may be much less important in laundry detergents for brands with more than a relatively low level of advertising expenditures. As a group, therefore, the findings indicate that for some of the product categories in which policymakers are most worried about the effects of advertising on retail price, *these effects may be overestimated if the impact of advertising on retail gross margins is not considered.* In addition, these findings have strong implications for advertisers and retail managers, the subject of the next chapter.

Summary

We found in the last chapter that the effect of advertising on retail brand gross margins is characteristically a consistent, important economic reality of most of the supermarket product markets studied. On the other hand, we were quick to point out that proof of the existence of this marketing relationship could not necessarily be generalized to all supermarket product markets. As Harold Demsetz (1974) has pointedly observed, "Casual generalization and uninformed opinions come easily in such a situation. Academics are no exception; indeed, sensitive scholars are expert in nothing if not generalization." In this spirit, we felt that the most productive research direction was to specify carefully under what conditions and in which product markets advertising is most likely to have this role. As such, in this chapter we have looked at why the margin elasticity of advertising should vary among product markets, and offered statistical evidence of how this effect does in fact differ for different product categories and groups of categories.

The investigation of variations in the effect of advertising on gross margins was carried out for three levels of analysis: groups of product categories based on certain category characteristics established in Chapters 5 and 7; four groups of product categories of particular interest for comparative purposes; and individual product categories of public policy concern. First we developed intuitively the essential proposition that relates the category characteristics to the margin elasticity of advertising: *product categories with high gross margins (and characteristics reflecting these high margins) have low margin elasticities of advertising.* The statistical analysis that followed confirmed this proposition. Advertising's potential to lead to lower prices is limited in high gross margin product categories. Most interestingly, we found that it is the number of potential purchasers of a product (household penetration), not the frequency of purchase, that is significantly related to the magnitude of the margin elasticity (stronger in product categories with high household penetration). In addition, advertising is more effective in highly advertised categories, such as the household product categories in our sample (facial and toilet tissues, paper towels, laundry detergents, fabric softeners, hand dishwashing liquids, and so on).

Other category characteristics, such as the number of different package sizes carried in a product category and the level of retail handling expenses, which were significant predictors of the level of category gross margins (Chapter 7), were also significantly related to the strength of the margin elasticity. The percentage of private label sales showed a nonlinear relationship with the margin elasticity, implying that the effect of advertising on gross margin is potentially strongest in product categories with some private label competition for manufacturers' brands, but not too much. Similarly, this effect of advertising was found to be negligible in some product categories until a certain "threshold level" is reached. As always, however, we must be careful in drawing "causal" implications from cross-sectional analysis.

Four groups of product categories were also selected to test for variations in the margin elasticity of advertising: traffic builders (high household penetration), pet foods and baby products (high purchase frequency with low household penetration), sweets (advertising directed at children), and soaps (high externalities and hidden qualities). The first two groups were selected to test further the importance of household penetration; the other two groups represented heavily advertised categories under pressing attacks by advertising critics. The results indicated that, indeed, it is household penetration, not frequency of purchase, that reflects a strong margin elasticity, and these heavily criticized categories do show, at least for certain ranges of advertising, a significant tendency for advertising to lead to lower retail gross margins. Further investigation of eight individual product categories was carried out. Three were examined in detail because of high policy interest in advertising's effect on retail prices: ready-to-eat cereals, candy bars, and laundry detergents. Whereas advertising's ability to lead to lower gross margins was questioned for laundry detergents above approximately $2 million in annual advertising outlays, *a strong effect appeared consistently for cereals and advertised candy bars*. The subject of a recent antitrust case, ready-to-eat cereals seem to be the textbook case of increased levels of advertising and unit sales leading to lower retail gross margins—with the margin elasticity of advertising the strongest of any one of the 51 product categories in our sample.

These findings imply that even with an effect that is comparatively pervasive, we must be careful in extrapolating the overall results to each and every product category. Still, the effect of advertising on retail brand gross margins is evident in many of the product markets, indicating that manufacturers who do not consider this effect of their advertising may be underestimating their incentives to advertise. On the other hand, these variations in the margin elasticity give retailers additional reasons to monitor carefully those factors under their control, such as the number of package sizes and items carried and the percentage of private label sales. More specific implications of all these results will be the subject of the next chapter.

Endnotes

1. The average brand gross margin in a product category, used as the denominator in computing the brand gross margin ratio (BGMR), has a .95 correlation with the category gross margin. The difference, it will be recalled, is that the average brand gross margin is an unweighted, simple average, whereas the category gross margin is a weighted average, with brand unit sales as weights. Because of the very high correlation between these two measures, they are considered nearly identical for discussion purposes.

2. Brand gross margins are not under the same limitations as are category gross margins, or similarly, the average brand gross margin in a category. Although product categories can be loss leaders just as brands can, not every category can be a loss leader, but every category can have at least one brand that is a loss leader. As a rule, the retailer competes on the prices of brands to attract shoppers, not the prices of product categories. Exceptions are fresh meat and produce, which are not part of our data base.

3. If all unadvertised brands are removed from the sample, the results of Figure 9.3 are qualitatively the same: BGMRs only begin to drop for brands with a 4 percent advertising share or more in the low category advertising subsample, whereas the decline begins for much lower advertising shares in the high category advertising subsample.

4. See Chapter 7, endnote 2 for explanation of the measure of private label penetration.
5. For a more detailed analysis of cross-tabulations and regressions run on individual product categories, see M. S. Albion, *The Effect of Manufacturer's Advertising on Retail Gross Margins in Supermarket Retailing* (unpublished Ph.D. dissertation, Harvard University, May 1981), pp. 327–330.
6. For a regression analysis of these and other product categories with retail price (ratio) as an independent variable and unadvertised brands eliminated from the sample, see Albion, *op. cit.*, pp. 334–339.

Chapter 10

CONCLUSIONS AND IMPLICATIONS

The past two decades have been marked by renewed interest in the economic effects of advertising. In particular, managers and policymakers have been more keenly aware of the effect of advertising on the prices and profits of the individual firm and for the industry as a whole. In the economic boom of the sixties, advertising outlays skyrocketed, only to be questioned and often curtailed by many firms during the recessions of the seventies. Public opinion against advertising rose in the seventies, resulting in the cereal antitrust case and the Federal Trade Commission (FTC) charges against advertising directed toward children. Within this context, in which many of the effects of advertising on the public were being questioned, managerial and policy decisions had to be made. Too often managers overlooked all the potential beneficial effects of their advertising on the sale of their products. Too often retailers were unaware of some of the hidden contributions of advertised brands to store profits—particularly in inflationary periods—as discovered regretfully by the Great Atlantic and Pacific Tea Company's supermarkets. And too often policymaking with regard to advertising was colored by political and socioeconomic values that were frequently drawn from the *apparent* effects of advertising in a few highly visible product categories—categories that were then held as the model for *all* consumer products.

Marketing and economic researchers collectively were aware of two possible roles of advertising in the economy—as an instrument of market power, advertising may lead to higher consumer prices; as a tool of market competition, advertising may lead to lower consumer prices. Unfortunately the result of this controversy over whether advertising is more a persuasive or an informative communications tool was an ongoing two-decade debate. Neither side seemed to learn much from or listen much to the other point of view.

Even more grievous, researchers forgot an important lesson of the earlier stream of advertising research, which began with the work of the great British economist Alfred Marshall (1919), and effectively ended with Neil Borden's landmark book (1942), *The Economic Effects of Advertising*. Both men realized the important effects of manufacturers' advertising on the resellers of the manufacturers' brands. As stated expertly by Borden, commenting on the struggle for brand control, which began in the 1880s:[1]

> *Experience has shown then that the handling of well-known manufacturer's brands has often led to keen price competition upon these brands within the trade, with the resultant reduction of trade margins.*

Moreover, as this effect of advertising on price competition among resellers may decrease a brand's contribution, the resellers (essentially, the retailers) still find it necessary to carry these brands because of their importance to store traffic. As noted by Marshall:[2]

> *They [the retailers] had little defense against the selling cheaply of those few branded goods, which had already so strong a hold on the public, that a refusal to handle them would simply drive away customers.*

Finally, with the competitive pressure on retail prices and the high merchandise costs of the advertised brands depressing their contribution, the high turnover of these brands helps increase the retailer's total contribution on advertised brands—especially important in inflationary times when the carrying costs of inventory are high. These are the *hidden effects of advertising*.

In this book we examined the economics of the mass retailer and, within this context, the effect of the manufacturer's advertising on the retail profits and pricing. The hidden effects of advertising are all reflected in the *retail gross margin*. Accordingly, in granting the retail stage of a market importance equal to that of the manufacturing stage, we have focused on the relationship of manufacturers' advertising to retail brand gross margins. After a brief summary of the study, we will discuss the implications of our findings for managers, policymakers, and researchers, and suggest some future avenues of research.

Summary of the Study

This study began with the basic premise that manufacturers' advertising causes retailers to take a lower gross margin on an advertised brand than on an identical, unadvertised (or less advertised) brand in that product category. We posited that there are two reasons why advertised brands should be sold by the mass retailer at lower gross margins than unadvertised brands: faster turnover and greater brand salience to consumers. The faster turnover of the advertised brands leads to lower retail unit costs; the greater salience of these brands results in higher factory prices and increased retail price competition. In addition, we argued that the importance of this relationship between advertising and retail pricing may differ among product categories, and that these differences are observable, measurable, and "systematic." In other words, we can predict how and explain why these differences should occur on the basis of certain characteristics of the product categories. It was proposed that product categories with high gross margins (and characteristics directly reflecting the level of those margins) should have a weaker advertising–gross margin relationship among brands. Similarly, product categories with low gross margins (and characteristics directly reflecting the level of those margins) should have a stronger advertising–gross margin relationship among brands.

These two premises led to a review of the literature on the relationship of advertising and prices in general and, more specifically, advertising and retail gross margins (Chapters 2 and 3). The review indicated that empirical evidence and a descriptive model of mass retailers are needed to provide further insights into the effects of manufacturers' advertising on retail pricing. As food is of great importance to most consumers and the economy, the empirical testing was performed on a sample of supermarket products. Accordingly, the model of the mass retailer was developed with supermarket retailing in mind.

The theoretical model was presented in Chapters 4, 5, and 6. The general purpose of the model is to answer the question: Why do retail brand gross margins differ among product categories? We approached this question by separating it into two parts: Why do product category gross margins differ (Chapter 5)? Why do brand gross margins differ within a product category (Chapter 6)? For example, in comparing the retail gross margin on a can of private label tuna with the margin on a box of Kleenex tissues, we want to know first why canned tuna has a lower gross margin than facial tissues, and second, why private label canned tuna has a higher gross margin than Bumble Bee tuna (or similarly, why Kleenex has a lower gross margin than private label tissues). If the analysis of any sample of product categories does not separate the relevant dimensions in this manner, reasons for differences in the level of product category gross margins may be confounded with reasons for differences in the level of brand gross margins within a product category. In our empirical analysis of the variation in gross margins among brands, therefore, we decided to specify brand gross margins, and brand advertising and unit sales, as percentages of their product category levels, that is, the ratio of a brand's gross margin to its unweighted average product category gross margin. It is within this context that we investigated the role of manufacturers' advertising.

The mass retailer's economic environment was described in Chapter 4. It was maintained that the retailer can maximize store profits by maximizing the total contribution to profits and overhead for the entire group of products in the store. We then considered what this means for individual products, recognizing that the retailer operates in a monopolistically competitive environment. This framework allowed us to examine how the retailer should allocate shelf space among product categories (Chapter 5) and set prices on brands within a product category (Chapter 6) so as to maximize the store's total contribution. Accordingly, the book's central theoretical concept, drawn from consumer behavior, was introduced: the *salience* of a product to consumers, which is comparable in economic terms to what we called the *one-way cross-elasticity* of a product. The notion is that the more salient a "product"—a generic term used throughout the book to refer to an entire product category (such as canned tuna), a single brand (such as Bumble Bee canned tuna), and/or an item (6½ ounce can of Bumble Bee tuna)—the more likely it is that this product affects the sales of the rest of the products in the store. In other words, the greater the degree to which consumers notice and care about the terms of sale of a product (salience), the more likely it is that a low price on that product can build store traffic. The economic effect on the retailer of these traffic builders is "one-way," since these products may affect the sales of other products in the store, even though the other products may not have that same ability. It was argued that this economic effect is essential to explaining the level of both product category and brand gross margins, as well as the magnitude of the effect of advertising on brand gross margins.

This traffic-building effect of certain products was incorporated into our understanding of how the retailer should allocate shelf space among product categories and set prices on brands within a product category. We maintained that the retailer must consider not only the *direct* total contribution attributable to a product, but also the *indirect* contribution from this traffic-building effect of certain products in order to maximize the store's total contribution. As such, in Chapter 5 we derived a number of category characteristics that should be related to the direct and/or indirect total contribution per square foot of a product category, and thereby the equilibrium gross margin of that product category. In Chapter 6 we concentrated on how advertising may affect brand salience and how it can, therefore, lead to lower brand gross margins in equilibrium. Other factors that may affect this relationship between advertising and retail brand margins, such as brand unit sales, were also discussed. Furthermore, it was maintained that this ability of advertising to lead to lower gross margins on advertised brands varies among product categories, with the strength of the effect reflected in those product category characteristics most strongly related to the level of category gross margins.

Derived from a 1978 data base assembled on an item-by-item basis for 51 fast-moving, highly salient product categories with 488 brands, the empirical analysis confirmed both premises. The analysis of product category gross margins (Chapter 7) indicated that a number of category characteristics are important predictors of the level of category gross margins and the magnitude of the effect of advertising on brand gross margins—referred to as the margin elasticity of advertising. The level of retail expenses in a product category and the number of different package sizes in a category were presented as prominent explanatory factors, along with other characteristics under particular circumstances.

Nearly 70 percent of the variation in product category gross margins was accounted for by the model. The level of category advertising was found to be an important secondary determinant of the level of product category gross margins. Advertising seems to work mostly at the brand level and through other variables, such as brand sales and out-of-store, preshopping decisions, resulting in a weaker, but evident, impact on category gross margins. Moreover a significant disparity between the 41 food and 10 household product categories in the sample became prominent in the analysis: The sample selection method resulted in a highly salient, highly advertised subset of nonfood product categories with lower gross margins than the food product categories in the sample. In this regard, it was pointed out that conclusions drawn on these nonfood product categories should not necessarily be extrapolated to other nonfood categories.

The statistical analysis of the effect of advertising on retail brand gross margins was carried out in Chapters 8 and 9. Here advertising was found to be an important determinant of the variation in gross margins among brands. Simultaneous-equation estimation indicated that causality is essentially in one direction, except that the gross margin–retail price relationship is indeed two way. Accordingly, retail price was dropped as an explanatory variable, leaving brand advertising and unit sales (comparable to dollar sales in all estimations) as the primary predictors of the level of brand gross margins.

As diagrammed in Figure 10.1, we considered three effects of advertising on gross margin: (1) the *indirect* effect of advertising on gross margin, (2) the *direct* effect of advertising on gross margin through its effect on sales, and (3) the *feedback* effect on advertising from gross margin through sales (basically through retail price, as dollar sales is the product of unit sales and retail price). Effect (1) was technically referred to as the partial margin elasticity of advertising, (2) the *sales* margin elasticity of advertising, and (1)+(2) the *total* margin elasticity of advertising—the total effect of advertising on gross margin. It was held that the direct effect captures the impact of advertising on a brand's total contribution, since we assumed that interbrand differences in retail handling expenses should be negligible, such as in the handling expenses of Green Giant canned peas versus Libby's canned peas. The indirect effect of advertising on gross margin was maintained, therefore, to proxy the ability of advertising to increase retail price competition on an advertised brand, leading to a lower gross margin. In short, the empirical analysis demonstrated that the total effect is robust, and this indirect "competitive" effect is evident as well.

Subsequently we investigated the shape of the margin elasticity of advertising over ranges of advertising shares and dollars for the entire sample of 488 brands. We found that in both cases the measured cross-sectional relationship is log linear, implying constantly declining returns. For advertising share, the impact on retail gross margin appeared to be greatest among brands with relatively low levels (0 to 5 percent). However, since the evidence supported the importance of advertising dollars and share, and because many brands with small advertising shares represent large advertising dollar outlays (cereals, laundry detergents), it was not clear whether certain brands or product categories are subject to a threshold level, that is, whether increased declines in gross margin occur after a

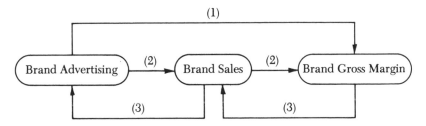

Figure 10.1 System of Effects in the Advertising–Gross Margin Relationship. All variables are expressed as percentages of their category levels in analyzing more than one product category: Ad Share, Sales Share, and Brand Gross Margin Ratio. (1) = indirect effect; (2) = direct effect; and (3) = feedback effect.

certain level of advertising expenditures. Time-series analysis is required for this assessment. But in cross-section, the analysis of the entire sample did demonstrate that the margin elasticity of advertising does vary among brands with different levels of advertising outlays, with no indication that the magnitude of advertising's effect may be greater for brands with high advertising shares or high advertising dollars.

The empirical analysis of Chapter 9 examined how the strength of the effect of advertising on brand gross margins differs among product categories. Per our original premise, the margin elasticity was found to vary systematically among product categories, based on the level of certain category characteristics that reflect the magnitude of the category gross margins. As a group, the variations were most significant for those characteristics shown in Chapter 7 to be the most significant explanatory variables of product category gross margins.

Evidence of a possible threshold level for advertising's impact on gross margin was found among brands in product categories with low or moderate levels of advertising expenditures (less than $30 million per annum). Two other findings were particularly interesting, one dealing with the household penetration of a product category, the other involving the type of product category and level of advertising in the category. We concluded first that it is the number of people who buy items in a product category, not the frequency of purchase, that is related to the strength of the margin elasticity of advertising. Second, we saw that, whereas the food and nonfood (household products) categories in our sample differ in levels of product category advertising, not only the level of category advertising is associated with the magnitude of the margin elasticity but also the *type* of product category: Retailers have much more latitude (or at least, they price as if they do) in pricing private labels in these nonfood product categories than they do for food categories sold in supermarkets.

We completed our analysis of the margin elasticity of advertising by examining four groups of product categories and some individual product categories of public policy interest as well. The results reinforced our proposition that the number of people who buy items in a product category is strongly related to the effect of advertising on retail brand gross margins. Further investigation of product categories in which advertising's ability to raise prices is often cited— ready-to-eat cereals and candy bars—showed a strong margin elasticity of advertising, that is, evidence of some of the beneficial effects of advertising for consumers in these product categories. On the other hand, similar effects for laundry detergents did not appear among brands above a relatively low level of annual brand advertising expenditures (approximately $2 million).

Implications for Advertising Budgeting[3]

Since the turn of the century, the advertising budgeting decision has been based almost solely on the ability of advertising to affect sales by increasing consumer demand for the brand. Although statistical techniques and managerial know-how have become more sophisticated since that time, there has been little change in the basic philosophy. As expressed by Aaker and Myers:[4]

> *The theoretical underpinning of an advertising budget is based on marginal analysis and easily expressed. A firm should continue to add to the advertising budget as long as the incremental expenditures are exceeded by the marginal revenue they generate.*

Rarely has the retailer's gross margin been included by advertisers in any assessment of the marginal revenue generated by their advertising, or even been an implicit consideration in advertising budgeting decisions.

The thrust of this research, however, has been to demonstrate why *traditional budgeting methods still used by most manufacturers may be underestimating the long-term contributions of advertising to sales (and thereby profit) goals*, particularly for manufacturers of heavily advertised, leading national brands. Using incremental sales, priced at the manufacturer's factory price, as the only criterion for evaluating advertising budgets may lead manufacturers to seriously underestimate their incentives to advertise. Although manufacturers realize the need to advertise to obtain shelf space, dealer support, and retail penetration when introducing a new brand, once the brand is established, most manufacturers neglect the retailer's everyday pricing and focus only on promotional pricing. The everyday retail price, as well as the factory price, is critical to the manufacturer's long-term sales goals. Any long-term advertising policy therefore must consider the effect of the advertising on probable retail pricing policies. Advertising budgeting should *explicitly* recognize the impact of advertising on everyday, average, retail gross margins.

Why should the manufacturer be concerned with the gross margin taken by retailers on the sales of the manufacturer's brand? The research has shown a strong impact of manufacturers' advertising on retail brand gross margins. This fact is well known to retailers but, as just mentioned, not explicitly recognized by most manufacturers, who consider an advertising budget only in terms of its effect on sales volume and the factory price, not on the retail price. Two reasons for manufacturers to consider the effect of advertising on brand gross margins in their budgeting decisions are (1) the percentage of the retail price captured by the manufacturer and (2) the potential barrier to growth of small, unadvertised brands created by this effect. This potential barrier to entry is dealt with in the section on public policy implications.

The Multiplier Effect of Advertising

In general, the ability of advertising to decrease manufacturers' competition *and* simultaneously increase retail price competition should come as welcome news to marketers. Depicted in Figure 10.1 and measured by the sales and partial margin elasticities, advertising has been shown to affect retail brand gross margins in two ways: directly by stimulating sales and indirectly by affecting the salience and thereby retail price competition on an advertised brand. The strength of these (and the total) effects of advertising indicates that advertising leads to increases not only in the retail productivity—particularly turnover—of a brand, but also in the one-way cross-elasticity of a brand, that is, the brand's potential to draw store traffic.

These effects of advertising have important implications for manufacturers' long-term budgeting policies. They indicate that as advertising leads to lower retail gross margins, manufacturers of leading advertised brands should find that not only can their advertising stimulate sales volume, but it also may allow them to capture an increased percentage of the retail price. In other words, advertising may lead to greater sales volume *and* a higher factory price for the manufacturer with little or no increase in the retail (consumer) price. Or, advertising may lead to an even *greater* increase in sales volume with lower retail prices and little or no change in the factory price.

In this regard, this simple marketing relationship between manufacturers' advertising and retail gross margins creates a *delayed* advertising effect—what we may call a "multiplier effect." Over time, advertising may have two effects: first, a stimulation of consumer demand; and second, a decrease in retail gross margins and prices, and thus *another* stimulation of demand. On the other hand, the second delayed effect could be a decrease in retail gross margins from an increase in factory price, with retailers maintaining the same price and thereby no second stimulation of demand. Still, the manufacturer realizes greater sales volume *and* a higher (factory) price. In either case, the manufacturer obtains a larger increase in sales revenue than is recognized by only the first effect. And if advertising budgets do not include this second, perhaps longer-term effect, the total contribution of advertising to sales and profits may be underestimated.

In short, because advertised brands usually have lower retail gross margins (notwithstanding higher relative retail prices), the advertiser may command factory (wholesale) price premiums over less heavily advertised competitors that are even greater than the retail price premiums obtained. In addition, the advertiser receives a larger percentage of the retail price—a percentage that should increase in the long run as a result of either a rise in the factory (wholesale) price or a decline in the retail price (or, as always, some combination of the two). An illustration of these effects is given in Table 10.1.

Table 10.1 illustrates the two extreme possibilities with a hypothetical example (price elasticity assumed to be −4). The table shows a nationally advertised brand that sells for $1.00, of which the manufacturer receives 90¢ and the retailers 10¢ (10 percent retail gross margin). One million units of the brand are sold, which generates $200,000 ($0.20 × 1,000,000) for the manufacturer after production and distribution costs, and $100,000 ($0.10 × 1,000,000) for the retailers. Over time, after a long-run increase in advertising outlays, the manufacturer's brand franchise has grown. The manufacturer can now either raise the brand's factory price (second column) or keep it the same (third column); if the latter, the increased volume and

Table 10.1 Illustration of the Multiplier Effect of Advertising

	National Brand before Ad Increase	National Brand after Ad Increase (factory price change)	National Brand after Ad Increase (retail price change)
Average retail price	$1.00	$1.00	$.95
Retail gross margin	.10	.06	.05
Factory price (wholesale)	.90	.94	.90
Manufacturing and distribution cost	.70	.70	.70
Amount available to manufacturer per unit for advertising and profit	.20	.24	.20
Sales volume	1,000,000	1,500,000	1,800,000
Total amount available to manufacturer	$ 200,000	$ 360,000	$ 360,000
Total amount available to retailers	$ 100,000	$ 90,000	$ 90,000

NOTE: Retail prices and margins are assumed to reflect manufacturers' promotions and allowances to distributors.

salience of the brand to consumers will cause the average retail price to fall. The example was constructed so that there is no dollar difference for either manufacturer or retailer in these two outcomes. If the manufacturer decides to raise the factory price ($0.94), there is a one-shot increase in sales volume (up 500,000 units), with the manufacturer receiving $360,000 ($0.24 × 1,500,000) and the retailers $90,000 ($0.06 × 1,500,000). If the manufacturer less typically decides to maintain the same factory price, retailers will compete the price of the brand down to 95¢, so that there is a two-shot increase in sales volume (up 500,000 units plus 300,000 units). The manufacturer receives the same $360,000 ($0.20 × 1,800,000), and the retailers the same $90,000 ($0.05 × 1,800,000). Moreover, the manufacturer's percentage of the retail price is now 94 or 95 percent, instead of the original 90 percent.

It is important to realize that if we did not recognize this second, longer-term contribution of advertising to the manufacturer's profits, we would still estimate correctly the total amount of revenue available in the market after the advertising [($1.00 − 0.70) × 1,500,000 = $450,000], but not the distribution of this amount. Instead, we would estimate that $300,000 ($0.20 × 1,500,000) is received by the manufacturer with the remaining $150,000 going to the retailers. Accordingly, *the increase in total revenue available to the manufacturer would be underestimated by $60,000*. Of this amount, $50,000 accrues to the manufacturer (at the expense of the retailers) due to a decrease in the retail gross margin that is compensated for by an increase in the retailers' sales volume; the remaining $10,000 has been assumed here to accrue to the manufacturer (it could go to consumers) because of increased retail price competition. If the advertising increase had no effect on retail price competition, then the retailers would still make $100,000 after the advertising increase, maintaining a gross margin of almost 1¢ higher (manufacturer would get $350,000). But our model predicts and the statistical analysis confirmed that advertising can in fact increase retail price competition (proxied by the indirect effect), in which case the retailers will be willing to take a reduced gross (and quite possibly net) profit to maintain and attract store traffic.

Of course a decrease in advertising expenditures can reverse the entire cycle. A long-term cut in an advertising budget may lead to lower sales volume, which in turn means that retailers need to realize higher gross margins to cover the loss in sales. Either the manufacturer must then elect to lower factory (wholesale) prices and accept a lower profit margin or retailers will have to increase their prices, which *further* reduces sales volume. In addition, the retail price competition on the brand may be reduced. Retailers would then increase the price of the brand to consumers not just in reaction to lower sales volume, but also as a result of a decreased one-way cross-elasticity of this now less salient brand. The less retailers need to worry about customers using the brand as a price benchmark for a store's overall pricing policy, the less the retailers need to be concerned with the pricing of the brand to maintain store traffic. In short, a long-term reduction in advertising may be translated into an unfortunate sequence of events for the manufacturer, a direct result of the multiplier effect of advertising.

Advertising budgeting techniques, therefore, must be careful not to underestimate the long-term contributions of advertising by recognizing only advertising's initial effect on consumer demand and neglecting its subsequent effect on retail gross margins. This is especially true of budgeting techniques that assume fixed prices and market tests conducted over relatively short time periods. Similarly, estimates of the duration of advertising's effect on sales may be biased if advertising's effect on pricing is not explicitly acknowledged. It should be realized that it may not be possible to change advertising expenditures without also changing either factory (wholesale) or retail prices.

The results suggest that manufacturers carefully watch the response of retail gross margins to their advertising in different geographical areas for their product categories and distribution channels. Some product categories and, no doubt, some channels are more responsive to manufacturers' advertising than others. Our research showed that the effect of advertising on gross margin varies noticeably among the supermarket product categories in our sample. For instance, product categories with high household penetration have stronger margin elasticities of advertising than do those with low household penetration. This finding deals directly with a characteristic of product categories; indirectly, it implies that the margin elasticity of advertising should be stronger for densely distributed products and these types of distribution channels than for products that are exclusively distributed. And although this study looked at only convenience goods and one type of distribution channel, the results are complementary to Porter's findings (1976) on the difference in the effectiveness of advertising when convenience and non-convenience distribution outlets are compared. Porter's study showed that the more the retailer adds to the final product sold to consumers—that is, the greater the level of retail expenses—the less effective is advertising in leading to higher manufacturers' profit margins. Our study of a group of convenience products revealed that the greater the level of retail expenses, the less the effect of advertising in lowering retail gross profit margins.

Finally, we found that the magnitude of advertising's effect on gross margin may vary over ranges of advertising shares and advertising dollars. Due to the cross-sectional nature of the analysis, however, it was difficult to determine whether the shape of the advertising–gross margin response function is an additional consideration for the advertising–sales response function, that is, some threshold effect before advertising dollars translate into declining gross margins. In general, the shape of the margin elasticity of advertising appeared to be log linear (declining returns) or, at most, linear. The only direct evidence for increasing returns among brands was produced for certain groups of product categories, particularly those with relatively low levels of total category advertising. Evidence based on the entire sample did show, on the other hand, that managers of very highly advertised brands should realize that there are limits to how much advertising can induce retailers to cut gross margins and compete on the brand's retail price. These limits vary depending upon the amount of value-added that is contributed by the retailer to the sale of the manufacturer's brands, such as the amount of retail space required, retail handling expenses, and the like. Even so, *there remain substantial, heretofore hidden incentives for manufacturers to advertise, based on the effect of their advertising on the resellers of their brands.*

In short, manufacturers must be careful not to underestimate the long-term contributions of their advertising. These contributions are the result of the economic structure of the retailers who carry the manufacturers' brands. We have demonstrated how advertising can induce an increase in sales revenue from an initial and delayed stimulation of demand and a greater percentage of the retail price accruing to the manufacturer—all due to a reduced retail brand gross margin. In the policy section, we will show how, over time, this reduced retail margin can also be profitable for the advertiser in terms of an absolute cost entry barrier for other firms with less heavily advertised brands and for potential entrants.

Implications for Retail Management[5]

Supermarket retailers are finding their margins squeezed by increased competition from other supermarkets and other types of distributors and from rising costs, particularly energy and labor costs. The grocery market's real annual growth rate between 1975 and 1980 was a mere 0.3 percent, as net margins, which had consistently been above 1 percent in the 1960s, dropped below 1 percent for all but one year in the 1970s. Supermarket retailers need to know the most effective way to increase their gross profit margins and reduce costs without losing store traffic.

A retailer's gross profit margins can be raised by increasing the percentage of private labels and generics carried (and sold), and/or by shifting the store's product line toward higher-margin product categories whenever possible, such as household products and health and beauty aids. Costs can be reduced by decreasing brand selection; by using fewer personnel for item marking, displaying merchandise, checking, and bagging; and/or by minimizing high-expense items carried, such as frozen and chilled products. However, each of these strategies may result in a loss of store traffic.

1. An increase in private labels and generics, called "trading down," runs the risk of a possible loss of image and store traffic, discovered by A&P in the mid 1970s. Furthermore, warehouse stores have now entered this market, growing from 0 to 5 percent of grocery sales between 1977 and 1980. Price competition on generics has increased steadily in many markets.

2. A shift to more of the higher-margin, household product categories places the supermarket in direct competition with health and beauty aid discounters. These discounters sell only the higher-margin products and thus do not need the margins of these products to cross-subsidize the thin margins on other products that supermarkets must carry. If the supermarket's margins on these products are too high, some store traffic could be shifted to these discounters—many of which are located in the same shopping mall. Moreover, groceries may be bought by former customers at other stores, as the highly salient health and beauty aids are used by shoppers as a benchmark of the supermarket's average price level on all products. In addition, supermarkets with "all the frills" (lavish layout, additional services, and so forth) have entered the higher-margin market for food products and represent stiff competition in this market niche.

3. Reducing costs by strategies such as decreased brand selection also puts the supermarket in direct competition with the warehouse stores. This tactic runs the risk again of a possible loss of image and store traffic.

Faced with the fact that many of the comparative advantages that led to the rise of supermarkets are now gone, supermarkets are at a crossroads (see Bloom, 1978, and Bellenger and associates, 1977, for historical descriptions and predictions). Supermarkets can no longer compete successfully by trying to be all things to all shoppers. A weak economy and changing social mores have helped to bifurcate consumers into two groups: two-income families who are more time sensitive and convenience-oriented, and the more price-sensitive shoppers. As discussed, this market segmentation has led to the rise of convenience stores, "all-frills" stores, "super stores" (Stop & Shop in Pembroke, Mass.), and warehouse stores as alternatives to traditional supermarkets. Supermarkets must respond by carefully targeting their customers and assessing how to appeal successfully to them while maintaining margins and cutting costs. This analysis can then be translated into merchandising decisions for individual categories.

Certainly our research does not purport to address many of these problems and opportunities, such as how to improve a store's image or what to do about technological changes (automation, scanning systems). Still, in establishing the determinants of product category gross margins and how the margin elasticity of advertising varies over ranges of advertising dollars (and shares) and among product categories, the research indicates three general areas for possible profit improvement. These three areas are the number of brands and items the retailer carries in each product category, the amount of private label brands the retailer tries to sell in each category, and the retailer's response to manufacturers' advertising in terms of advertising dollars and advertising shares.[6]

Margins and the Number of Items Carried

This study found an overall weak relationship between the number of brands (and the number of items) carried in a product category and the level of category gross margins. We did find, however, that once the level of category advertising is accounted for (recall Figure 7.1), the number of brands does have a significant direct relationship with gross margin. Further analysis found that the relationship was significant only for product categories with "low" levels of category advertising—low for this sample, which means less than $125,000,000 in advertising over four years. On the other hand, the number of items was significantly related to gross margin only when an interaction term (number of items times number of different package sizes) was included in the multiple regression analysis. *The number of different package sizes* was the most important explanatory variable of category gross margins.

The evidence suggests that in heavily advertised categories, retailers cannot be effective in increasing their bilateral market power and their gross margins by carrying more brands. This tactic may only incur additional costs for the retailer and lower the total contribution per unit of shelf space in these categories. Moreover, the evidence suggests that in categories where carrying more items may be warranted, it is carrying more package sizes that allows retailers to increase their gross margin for a category, not merely carrying more items per se.

The evidence also suggests that in heavily advertised categories, the retailer should monitor whether the movement of less popular brands warrants carrying them. With decreased brand loyalty, less attention to advertising, and more attention to perceived price-value relationships for many consumers, today's shopper may be ready for a decreased choice of brands and items within some product categories. Similarly, the number of items carried may be larger than necessary and should be reevaluated, particularly for product categories with high retail expenses, such as frozen and chilled foods. At the very least, shelf space allocation (and reductions) should be seriously reconsidered.

However, remembering that maximizing total contribution per unit of shelf space, not gross margin, is the retailer's objective, we must consider a few other factors before recommending the selective addition or deletion of items or brands. Product categories may differ in the amount of shelf space used, unit handling and selling expenses, and turnover. Even though we have controlled for turnover in the analysis, these other two variables, critical to the total contribution per unit of shelf space for a category, have not been factored into the analysis.

What this means is that retailers must be sure that the extra gross margin earned by selectively carrying more items is not offset by higher handling expenses or lower space productivity. Conversely, they must be careful that the space released by carrying fewer items in highly advertised categories is not given to merchandise that generates even less contribution per unit of shelf space. Whereas the retailer may be acting optimally in our 1978 sample, the evidence here and the trends of the 1980s suggest a careful reassessment of the number of brands and items carried in different categories—at least at any one time on the shelves. Specific selections will depend in part on what type of shopper the retailer wishes to attract—the more "time" sensitive (upscale, two-income family) or the more "price" sensitive (one-income, large family).

Margins and Private Labels

The retailer always has the opportunity to increase the average category gross margin with more private label penetration. However, there is also always the concern of a loss of store traffic if, as was the case with A&P, shoppers see the increase in private labels as a signal of a decrease in desired assortment. But the consumer's perception of private labels, and generics as well, seems to have changed substantially in the years since the A&P attempt in the mid 1970s.

Recent literature has noted some interesting trends as consumers have become less brand loyal and less responsive to manufacturers' advertising (see Murphy and Laczniak, 1979). Private labels in many product categories are perceived to be of equal quality to the national brands and have been very successfully marketed with more attractive packaging; generics are seen by some consumers in certain instances as acceptable substitutes for national brands, with little cannibalization of private label sales. Some manufacturers (notably Procter & Gamble with Summit brand paper towels and toilet paper) are even producing brands without any advertising aimed at the non-nationally branded market. If implemented properly, the introduction of more private labels in certain product categories may be a profitable strategy for supermarket retailers.

Traditionally researchers have maintained that private labels can be most easily introduced into product categories where a substantial amount of consumer familiarity with the product has already taken place through advertising, prior purchases, or similar means. The private labels, therefore, can be "free riders" on the advertising of the manufacturers' brands. On the other hand, private labels may be limited to small shares in highly advertised, highly salient categories, if consumers are more "brand oriented." Brand orientation, however, may be becoming less important in many product categories, even to those traditionally considered "upscale shoppers."

We found that private label pricing allows the retailer a much higher gross margin in household product categories than in food categories. We reasoned that this might be because private labels are generally more salient to consumers in food than in nonfood product categories. Furthermore, we noted that there may be a greater total profit margin for the manufacturer and retailer to divide in these nonfood product categories. This would allow the retailer to offer the consumer a lower price on private label nonfood items, while still obtaining a higher gross margin than on private label food items. In either case, in view of the trends just cited, supermarket retailers are urged to watch carefully the sales of private labels (and generics). Given that the number three and four national brands are already in trouble, excess manufacturing capacity should increase. As this occurs, the bargaining power of the chains should increase as well. This greater bargaining power could reduce the purchase price to the chains of private labels, and make them even more profitable for the supermarket retailers.

Retailer Response to Manufacturers' Advertising

The main problem for retailers handling highly advertised brands was stated forty years ago by Borden, commenting on the struggle for brand control since the 1880s:[7]

> *The distributor is actuated also by a desire to be free from the direct price comparison upon merchandise that consumers know to be identical. The prices charged to the trade on well-established manufacturers' brands ordinarily . . . provide adequate recompense to distributors for their services; but for marked products which require dense distribution and hence stocking by directly competing distributors, the fierce price competition which is likely to occur in both wholesale and retail channels brings a shading of list prices and a consequent narrowing of trade margins.*

But most retailers still need these brands to maintain store image and attract customers who desire manufacturers' advertised brands. In addition, the manufacturers' advertising reduces the amount (and type) of advertising retailers have to do. And particularly in inflationary times, the high turnover and steady demand for these brands adds to retail profitability and reduces risk. In this regard, our brand analysis did provide one further important finding for retail pricing decisions on advertised brands.

Certainly it is important for the retailer not to underestimate the contribution of advertised brands to storewide profits. As mentioned, in inflationary times the carrying costs of inventory increase. Because of their higher turnover advertised brands may, at least to some extent, be a necessary antidote. On the other hand, on the basis of our linear measurements in cross-section, we found that nearly 40 percent of the total effect of advertising on gross margin may be attributed to its effect on retail price competition—the result of retailers responding to the perceived superiority of advertised brands as traffic builders. Given the nature of our analysis, the implication is that the retailer is pricing as if it is believed that advertising has increased the one-way cross-elasticity of an advertised brand with the rest of the products in the store.

But, even if the retailer feels this is the optimal, profit-maximizing response to advertising, the importance of all advertised brands to store traffic must be weighed carefully to judge whether the retailer is pricing these brands properly. For instance, it may be found that the *everyday* traffic-building abilities of many advertised brands has declined. This decline in some of the brand consumer franchises may be the result of a change in consumer preferences in the respective product categories or just generally less concern with the everyday pricing of advertised brands in the retailer's local market. In this instance the retailer may not be helping storewide profits by carrying these brands at all, or at the least, by not reducing the shelf space allocated to them. Or the retailer's prices may be too low. If the latter is true, the retailer should raise the average retail price by increasing everyday retail prices and then, if so desired, increasing (or maintaining) the number of temporary price cuts. In this way the brands can still serve to build traffic on the basis of *promotional* price, but can maintain higher everyday and average retail prices. On the other hand, if the reduced salience of the brands mitigates the effectiveness of price promotions as well, the average retail prices can be raised by either increasing the everyday prices or reducing the number (and magnitude) of price promotions.

This advice should be pertinent particularly for the merchandising of the less advertised brands—the number three and four brands in product categories dominated by one or two leading national brands. Our analysis found the margin elasticity of advertising to be log linear, with a smaller difference in margins realized between the less advertised and highly advertised brands than between the un-advertised and less advertised brands. At least in some product categories, retailers may be overreacting to the importance of the merchandising of these less advertised, national brands to store patronage.

Implications for Public Policy

At the outset, we phrased the central concern of the consumer as, "Does advertising make the things I buy more expensive?" We have argued that an important element in answering this question—an element far too often neglected in most economic theories and models— is the effect of manufacturers' advertising on retail brand gross margin. It was established that this relationship is indeed robust for our sample as a whole, although its magnitude can vary over levels of advertising, among product categories, and with the intensity of retail competition. We may conclude, therefore, that this ability of advertising to stimulate retail price competition and lead to lower retail gross margins cautions policymakers against making any conclusions about the effects of manufacturers' advertising in a product market without *explicitly* considering the role of retailers in the market. Estimates of the impact of advertising on consumer price that consider retailers as passive participants in the market may *overestimate* the effects of advertising on consumer prices. Many of the most beneficial effects of advertising may occur at the retail stage of the market.

Furthermore, although advertised brands typically maintain a higher relative price than unadvertised brands in a product category, the critical issue, it has been held, deals with advertising's relationship to the absolute market-price level for a product category, not to the relative brand retail prices. The existence of a significant impact of advertising on retail brands gross margins is essential evidence for the contention that advertising can lead to a reduction in absolute market prices. The retail prices of the other brands in the product category must respond to the increased competition on the advertised brand. Thus the advertising of one brand can increase the downward price pressure within each store on the other brands in the product category. As Reekie contends:[8]

> . . . *advertising, in addition to reducing retail markups by increasing the rate of turnover, had another effect. That was the creation of product recognition which also depresses margins. Thus advertised brands not only come under increased competitive pressure through improved product identification, they also bring pressure to bear on the prices of private brands or nonadvertised goods of the same type. This creates a price ceiling for nonadvertised brands which they cannot go above.*

Moreover, our finding that manufacturers' advertising may have a significant effect on the retail gross margins of entire product categories supports these conclusions.

Although we have shown no evidence to contradict the assertions of the last paragraph, we do not feel drawn to conclude that advertising leads to lower absolute market prices in supermarket retailing. With no evidence on manufacturers' profit margins (or manufacturers' costs), it is difficult to conclude anything about manufacturers' advertising and retail price levels, particularly from a cross-sectional study of this type. What we have done is provide evidence that the impact of advertising on retail price has been *overestimated* in many cases, predominantly by research that considers only manufacturers' factory prices or profit margins. This research suggests that retail margins must be included in most examinations of the effects of manufacturers' policies on retail prices.

Exempted from this consideration would be situations in which there is not a fair market transfer price, that is, vertical integration from manufacturing to retailing for all competitors, or exclusive distribution. If all competitors are not integrated, however (as is Xerox's situation), the nonintegrated firms can enforce a fair market transfer price through competition. Moreover, the recent outburst of price competition on selectively distributed Levi jeans suggests that the impact of brand salience on retail prices is not limited to intensively distributed types of merchandise.

Retail Cost Savings

In the literature review in Chapter 2, we maintained that the potential cost savings attributed to advertising is an important consideration in ascertaining the effect of advertising on the absolute market price level of a product category. If advertising can be shown to lower the costs of getting a product to the marketplace, these business cost savings could serve as evidence that advertising may indeed lead to lower market prices. Unfortunately, we concluded that although some strong arguments and indirect empirical evidence exist in some instances, the magnitude of these cost savings remains unclear and difficult to measure. The margin elasticity of advertising, however, provides us with a contribution of advertising to marketing efficiency that can be measured.

Based on our 1978 sample, some rough calculations, containing some assumptions, have been made. Since these numbers come from cross-sectional averages in one particular sample, the numbers are to be used as guidelines only—guidelines that do offer a general level of magnitude for this contribution to marketing efficiency. *The more important point of this exercise is to show that this cost savings can be measured, and to offer a methodology for doing so.* Precise estimation would require time-series analysis of an individual product category, as well as more national, and less chain, data.

The calculations are based on linear regressions with the advertising ratio and unit sales ratio (Table 8.3) as the explanatory variables of the brand gross margin ratio. Advertising and unit sales share are not used, so the units of measurement are the same for the independent and dependent variables; that is, all average 1 (or 100 percent). The partial margin elasticity of advertising—our measure of advertising's ability to increase retail price competition—is used instead of the total margin elasticity in order to retain a conservative estimate of retail cost savings. Moreover, unless brand advertising can be maintained to lead to an increase in category sales, a reduction in the space allocated to the category, a decrease in the number of brands carried in the category, or some combination of all these effects, the direct effect of advertising on gross margin through sales should not be included: Advertising then merely shifts sales among brands within the product category. Finally, as we are interested in the effect of a one-year increase in brand advertising, the partial margin elasticity estimate used ($-.0348$) is based on the advertising ratio measured for one year of advertising, not for four years ($-.0458$, Table 8.3).

Under these conditions, the calculations show that a $1 million increase in brand advertising translates approximately $100,000 of

savings from reduced retail gross margins that may go to the consumer in lower retail prices—a savings previously unrecognized by
policymakers, managers, and researchers. In other words, approximately *10 percent* of the effects of brand advertising have ostensibly
gone unnoticed. Table 10.2 provides the numbers and symbols required for this estimate. In nearly all cases, the numbers used are
conservative and, if anything, would underestimate the cost savings.

Given the numbers in Table 10.2, a $1 million increase in brand
advertising is comparable to about a 27 percentage-point increase
in the advertising ratio: an average of 10 brands per category, so
that the average brand advertising for one year is $32.5M × .1
= $3.25M; a $1 million increase becomes, therefore, a $4.25M/
$3.35M = 1.2687, or a 26.87 percentage-point increase ($3.25M
+ $1M = $4.25M; $3.25M + $1M/10 = $3.35M). Using the for-
mula to translate a change in the advertising ratio to a change in the
brand gross margin ratio in decimal terms, $R_{t+1} = R_t(1 + am)$, the
change in the brand gross margin ratio is $R_t \cdot am = 1 \times .2687 \times -.0348 = -.0094$.

Table 10.2   Variables Used to Compute the Cost Savings of Advertising

Variable	Symbol	Value
Average category advertising for one year	—	$32.5 M
The partial margin elasticity of advertising for one year	m	−.0348
Average number of brands per category at the chain	—	10
Unweighted brand share of average number of brands per category	s	10%
Average chain category sales	—	$1.2 M
Total chain sales (including nonwarehouse sales)	—	$300 M
National grocery sales	—	$130 B
Change in brand ad ratio	a	—
Current brand gross margin ratio (unweighted average)	R_t	100%
Current national brand and category gross margin (unweighted average)	B_t, C_t	19.2%
Change in brand gross margin	x	—
Change in category gross margin	sx	.1x
Brand gross margin ratio after change in ad ratio	R_{t+1}	$R_t(1 + am)$
National brand gross margin after change in ad ratio	B_{t+1}	$B_t + x$
National category gross margin after a change in ad ratio	C_{t+1}	$C_t + .1x$

To find the change in the brand gross margin, x, we have $B_{t+1}/C_{t+1} = R_{t+1}$ and, therefore, using substitution, $(B_t + x)/(C_t + sx) = R_t(1 + am)$, with s the unweighted brand share of the average number of brands in a category $(1/10 = .1)$. Numerically, this gives us $(.192 + x)/(.192 + .1x) = 1 - .0094 = .9906$. Solving for the change in brand gross margin, we calculate to four significant digits that $x = -.0020$, so the change in category gross margin, sx, is $.1 \times -.0020 = -.0002$.

To translate this number into dollar savings at the national level, we multiply the chain's average category sales level (for our sample) by the ratio of national to chain sales: $\$1.2M \times \$130B/\$300M = \$520M$. Then to calculate the savings, we multiply the change in category gross margin by the average national dollar sales for a category: $-.0002 \times \$520M = \$104,000$. This number means that approximately 10 percent of every advertising dollar spent *may* be saved by consumers through increased retail price competition caused by manufacturers' advertising. However, some important qualifying comments about the numbers used are necessary.

Because the brand gross margin ratio was calculated as an unweighted average, the national brand and category gross margins should be as well. Whereas the 51 category gross margins were simply summed and divided by 51, the national brand gross margins (for which no data were available) were weighted, by unit sales, to derive the category gross margins. If advertised brands have higher unit sales and lower gross margins than unadvertised brands on average (as we would expect), this means that both of these averages (19.2 percent), particularly the national brand gross margin, are biased downward. This would cause us to slightly underestimate the total cost savings. On the other hand, and more important, our average chain category sales level ($\$1.2M$) is most probably high; our selection criteria produced a sample of fast-moving, high-volume categories. Accordingly, the average for all the product categories carried by the chain is more likely to be only about half of the $\$1.2M$, *reducing our measure of cost savings by half to approximately $\$50,000$ (5 percent).* It is assumed in this analysis that this bias is offset by the average category advertising level, which is also very high and therefore leads to an underestimation of the cost savings.

We hope that future research will examine the margin elasticity for particular brands and categories and their actual, not average, advertising levels, sales levels, margins, and the like. At that time, more practically useful estimates can be made. In any case, whatever the assumptions, the point is that there seem to be sizable, *measurable* savings for the consumer from a marketing efficiency of advertising previously unrecognized by policymakers. *This is the magnitude of this hidden effect of advertising.*

This retail cost savings is illustrated in Figure 10.2, which indicates that two other considerations are necessary before concluding this discussion. First, we have not considered whether the advertising and margin reduction will affect other brands (resulting in lower gross margins?) and/or other product categories (resulting in higher gross margins?) The former adds to the savings; the latter reduces them. The question is therefore whether this declining margin in one product category from the direct impact of the advertised brand represents a net savings for consumers purchasing many goods at the supermarket. In other words, how will retailers respond to this squeeze on their margins? Will they increase their prices (and gross margins) on other products, change shelf space allocation, change the composition of the entire product line in the store, or do nothing?

In the short run, the quick answer is that retailers will not be able to recoup the lost margin on the advertised brand by increasing prices on others. They may, however, reallocate shelf space to a limited extent—an action that should still benefit consumers by increasing retail productivity. The appropriate answer comes directly from our model: The retailer cannot maximize profits on an item-by-item basis, but must take into account the one-way cross-elasticity of a product with the rest of the products in the store.

For example, let us assume that the increase in advertising has been for Land O Lakes butter. The gross margin of Land O Lakes may fall, but any attempt to raise the prices of other products would be nonoptimal for the retailer, unless those other products were either nonoptimally priced before, or are now nonoptimally priced because of the change in relative prices resulting from the advertising. Within the product category, the retailer may try to raise the gross margin of other brands of butter to compensate for this loss of margin. However, this tactic is limited; the decreased margin on the advertised brand puts a price (and thereby margin) ceiling on the other brands of butter (Reekie, 1979). The other, less advertised brands need to keep a relative retail price advantage over Land O Lakes. As such, the decreased gross margin on Land O Lakes could lead to lower margins on the other brands as well, or at the least, no change in their margins. Furthermore, our statistical analysis confirmed that the effect of advertising on retail gross margins may indeed be significant for the entire product category. We can safely say, therefore, that in this regard, a substantial cost savings remains that may accrue to consumers.

On the other hand, there may be quite a different effect of the lower category gross margin of butter on other product categories carried by the retailer. If the advertising has now increased the demand for Land O Lakes, it may also have increased the demand for butter. If so, the price of margarine would have to fall (lower

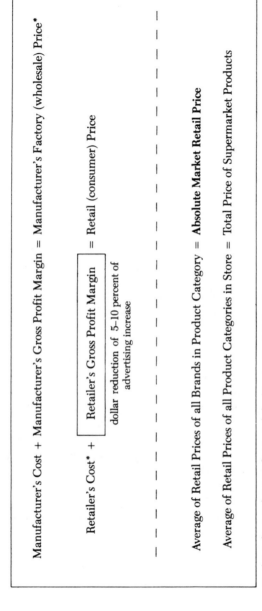

Figure 10.2   Retail Cost Savings from Advertising. (Figure suggested by Alden G. Clayton.)

gross margin) to compensate for the swing in volume to its substitute, but the price of bread (complement) would most probably rise. The net effect should remain: lower gross margins on average. Some shelf space reallocation may occur, but in the short run, if the product category is important to store traffic, and aggregate demand for the category has not declined, this tactic is also limited.

In the long run, however, the equilibrium must change. If profits were at a competitive level, this reduction in gross margin for Land O Lakes (and butter) must be compensated for, or retailers will leave the industry. The increased salience for Land O Lakes (and butter) may be at the expense of other brands and product categories carried by the retailer. As such, the benefits in the long run to consumers of this decreased retail gross margin are determined by *productivity:* If there are constant returns in distribution, there will be no benefit. But if the reduced gross margin from the advertising stimulates more efficient forms of retailing (neighborhood stores to supermarkets, warehouse stores?), techniques (automation, scanning systems, and so on), or management (reallocations of shelf space), then the net result for consumers, even in the long run, should be positive.

The second consideration is *the gross profit margins of the manufacturers.* Our analysis presented a *retail* cost savings for consumers. Advertising has been shown in other research to lead to higher manufacturers' selling prices and gross profit margins. Furthermore, as shown in our illustration of the multiplier effect of advertising (Table 10.1), *the consumer savings from a lower retail gross margin may go to the manufacturers in their margins.* The net effect of advertising on consumer cost, therefore, cannot be answered without examining the manufacturers as well as the retailers in the market. The decreased retail gross margin from increased retail price competition (caused by advertising) may be totally offset by an increase in the manufacturer's gross profit margin. Moreover, if Land O Lakes advertises, what will be the response of the other manufacturers in the market? Could they not all advertise to obtain this reduction in retail gross margin, with the result that the advertising of each brand cancels out the advertising of the others?

Realistically, not all firms find that advertising is equally effective in maximizing their profits; brands fill different market niches, as the firms use different strategies. As will be discussed in the section to follow, changing strategies can be quite expensive—thus the appearance of different strategic groups, with strong "mobility barriers" to strategic changes (Caves and Porter, 1977). Still, the thrust of the argument remains intact: The decline in retail gross margins may be completely offset by an increase in manufacturers' gross profit margins, with no net consumer savings from the effect of advertising

on retail price competition. The evidence presented in Chapter 2
on advertising and retail price sensitivity (and absolute market prices)
questions, however, whether the offset is complete.

In summation, there remain cost savings for consumers from increased marketing efficiencies in distribution generated by advertising—an effect of advertising previously unrecognized by policymakers. This finding has important implications for antitrust policy.
Past policies have seriously overestimated the impact of advertising
on the total gross profit margin of a product market by neglecting
the effect of manufacturers' advertising on retail pricing behavior.
High manufacturers' gross profit margins may be mandated by the
type of product sold: The manufacturer contributes most of the value
added to the final product sold to consumers. For many of these
highly advertised product categories, retailers enjoy high turnover,
have little need for display space and product promotion, and can
help their average category gross margin with the introduction of
private labels. Thus lower retail markups are required on manufacturers'
advertised brands. High manufacturers' gross profit margins, therefore,
may be associated with low retail gross margins. Policies that reorganize
the economic environment of the manufacturers may lower their
profit margins, but may increase by an even greater extent the gross
margins of retailers. As such, *both* margins need to be considered
in any antitrust policymaking, for it is the total profit margin ap-
propriable to manufacturers and retailers combined that is a relevant
criterion of consumer welfare.

Barriers to Entry

Not all the implications of this marketing relationship suggest more
competitive prices and profits. Although advertising may serve to
increase retail competition, leading to reduced gross margins, this
effect can result in an absolute cost entry barrier to future competitors
in the market and a mobility barrier to the growth of small, unadvertised brands in a mature product category. Thus, over time competition among manufacturers may be limited. An example, similar
to Tables 1.1 and 10.1, is useful to illustrate this situation.

For simplicity, we assume a situation in which a large, nationally
advertised brand has a dominant share of the market, two or three
less advertised brands have somewhat smaller shares, and the remainder of the market is represented by private labels and unadvertised brands. Furthermore, it is assumed that retailers earn gross
margins of 5 percent on the leading brand, 15 percent on the less
advertised brands, and 25 percent on the unadvertised "price" brands
and private labels. With equivalent manufacturing and distribution
costs, the price and cost structure might appear as in Table 10.3.

Table 10.3 Retail Gross Margins as an Entry Barrier

	Leading Advertised Brand	Less Advertised Brands	Unadvertised Brands and Private Labels
Average retail price	$1.00	$0.90	$0.80
Retail gross margin	5%	15%	25%
Factory price (wholesale)	$0.95	$0.765	$0.60
Manufacturing and distribution cost	$0.55	$0.55	$0.55
Amount available to manufacturer per unit for advertising and profit	$0.40	$0.115	$0.05

NOTE: Retail prices and margins are assumed to reflect manufacturers' promotions and allowances to distributors.

The less advertised brands, in order to achieve a shelf price of 10 percent under the leading brand, must discount their factory price by 20 percent. The unadvertised brands, to sell at a 20 percent discount to the consumer, must cut their factory price by 37 percent. The result is that the leading brand accrues 70 percent more contribution per unit for advertising and profit than the less advertised brands and nearly 90 percent more than the unadvertised brands. With differences in unit sales volumes, the disparity between the leading brand and the other brands in funds for advertising and profit is even greater. Therefore, a substantial, absolute cost entry barrier may exist.

Under this scenario, brands with less consumer goodwill may have a hard time challenging the leading advertised brand. By giving a larger gross margin to retailers to obtain shelf space and by taking a smaller profit margin to be competitive with the leading brand, the other brands may find it difficult to generate enough funds from their narrower profit margins. In addition, if the manufacturer of the leading national brand needs extra funds and can get them by raising factory price, this increase in factory price will cause a smaller change in demand for this brand than it would if done by the manufacturers of the other brands for two reasons: the retail gross margin and the consumers' price elasticity of market demand. The lower retail gross margin on the leading brand means that any increase in its factory price leads to a smaller increase in retail price than it would for the other brands. Moreover, as explained in Chapter 6, advertising causes the market demand curve for the brand to be more inelastic to price increases (above the average market retail price), though more elastic to price decreases (and more elastic for the entire store demand curve). Any increases in retail price, therefore, have less effect on market demand for the leading brand than for the others.

In conclusion, there may be more *inertia* in the structure of the
manufacturing stage of the market when the retail stage is included
in the ultimate chain of effects than when the market is analyzed
only in terms of the competitive structure of the manufacturers.
Whereas all firms may wish to advertise and reap the benefits of
lower retail margins, the ability of the leading brand to counteract
these advertising increases with increases of its own may make that
strategy unwise for its competitors. As such, *the ability of advertising
to lead to lower retail gross margins may be a double-edged sword*.
On the one hand, it helps to induce lower retail prices through a
reduced retail gross margin. On the other hand it may act as a
barrier to growth for small, unadvertised brands, and a barrier to
entry for the new brands of other manufacturers, reducing competition among manufacturers over time. Manufacturers' gross profit
margins, therefore, may be even higher in the long run.

Category Characteristics

Since the analysis is cross-sectional, time-series analysis is required
before we can be certain that the descriptive statistics of cross-section
have provided the correct normative implications. With this caveat
in mind, the number of different package sizes in a product category
has important implications for policymakers. Our results reiterate
the pleas consumer groups have voiced for nearly twenty years.

The number of different package sizes in a product category was
at all times the most important explanatory variable of the level of
category gross margins. This direct relationship dominated all others,
including those of gross margin with the number of items or brands
in a product category. For consumerists, the marketing practice
known as "packaging to price" is brought up again. Since the lengthy
congressional debate preceding the passage of the Fair Packaging
and Labeling Act of 1966, packaging to price has been continually
accused of being a deceptive practice that tricks consumers into
accepting price increases (see Bloom and Greenberg, 1976).

The evidence here strongly advocates *standardization* of package
sizes within supermarket product categories. With the low involvement nature of the products, unit pricing does not seem to have
made a major difference in terms of consumer information.[9] Indeed,
this "noncomparability," affecting the ease with which the consumer
can make price comparisons in a product category both intrastore
and interstore (it is difficult to remember exact sizes), may be an
important source of monopolistic profits not only for manufacturers
(reduced direct competition among manufacturers, allowing higher
factory prices), but also for supermarket retailers (with a reduced

margin elasticity of advertising as well). However, until further time-series evidence is uncovered, that is, evidence that shows that over time, the gross margin of a product category increases with the influx of more package sizes in the category, the reasons for our findings must be considered tentative; a more complicated process actually may be taking place.

In the same spirit, policymakers need to consider the level of retail expenses associated with the handling of a product category. This category characteristic was the second most important explanatory variable of the level of product category gross margins. The relationship of retail expenses and category gross margins implies that policymakers, especially when concerned with the profit margins in the typically low retail-expense, convenience consumer products, must recognize that high manufacturers' profit margins may be mandated by the type of product being sold; that is, high manufacturer's profit margins are associated with low retail profit margins, since the manufacturer contributes most of the value added to the final product sold to consumers. As discussed, both margins need to be considered in any antitrust policymaking.

Implications for Economic Theory

A central concern of this research has been the economic analysis of consumer product markets. As Porter notes, analyses that effectively ignore the retail stage of a market implicitly assume independence between the manufacturing and retail stages:[10]

> *The criterion of allocative efficiency relevant for consumers' welfare is the total lump of excess profit that is appropriable by manufacturing and retail stages together. Existing antitrust statutes implicitly assume that these are independent. . . . My theory clouds this interpretation. . . . A theory of the link between retail structure and retail performance and empirical verification of that theory are essential prerequisites for reaching a conclusion on this [welfare] question.*

In this research, we have examined the economic structure of mass retailing most generally (and supermarket retailing, more specifically) and improved upon the earlier British studies of distribution. These studies did not explicitly include either the retailer's cost-revenue structure and the various factors affecting the store's total contribution or the retailer's *interdependence* with the manufacturer. We have described theoretically and established empirically an important interdependence between a manufacturer's policy, advertising, and a measure of retail performance (gross margin).

Furthermore, the results imply that a marketing tool (advertising) that can lead to higher manufacturers' profit margins can also lead to lower retail gross profit margins. And if advertising does indeed lead to increased retail competition on an advertised brand, the result may be lower retail net margins as well. Combining this study with Porter's work, we have begun to build a framework for assessing that "total lump of excess profit" in a consumer product market.

Traditional models seem to assume implicitly that all distributors are passive participants in the market and a "derived demand" of consumers' wants satisfied by manufacturers' brands. This assumption and its implications for the advertising–gross margin relationship (and economic modeling) is well represented by Ferguson, who states:[11]

The theory of derived demand says that the more elastic the demand facing the retailers, the more elastic will be the retailers' demand for the manufacturers' brands. Retailers' demand for the producers' goods is derived from consumer demand for these goods at retail outlets.

This leads him to conclude:[12]

Thus, the margins and prices at the retail and producer levels should be positively related, not inversely related. . . . Thus, if producers' advertising increased consumer demand (and made it less elastic), the producers would also see retailers' derived demand increase (and become less elastic).

Ferguson's assertions (and the theory of derived demand) are correct if the relevant model is that of single-product competition, or if we can assume no interdependencies (zero cross-elasticities) among products sold by the retailer. His model is valid also only in a short-run partial equilibrium context, as competition (for our purposes, retail competition) must be assumed fixed. In other words, it is a theory of perfect competition, which does not apply to mass retailing.

Instead, in constructing a model of the multiproduct retailer, we have demonstrated the importance of one-way cross-elasticities in mass retailing. Traffic-building products are sold at margins lower than the optimal gross margins predicted by a single-product model—shown mathematically in Appendix 1, and demonstrated empirically by such variables as the percentage of consumer decisions in a product category decided upon prior to shopping (a direct proxy for the number of consumers who are very aware of the attributes of the different brands in a product category). Moreover, as illustrated in Chapter 5, some supermarket product categories (loss leaders) sell at lower gross margins than their handling expenses. This serves as further inferential evidence that interdependencies in the sale of the store's products directly affect the gross margins realized by retailers on many of these products. By increasing the salience of a brand to consumers, advertising can not only force a retailer to continue carrying a brand (or risk a loss in store traffic), but can also cause additional retailers to stock the brand and thus increase retail price competition.

Consistent with the results of the studies presented in Chapters 2 and 3, our research provides evidence that the two sets of studies on advertising and price sensitivity are compatible: Whereas advertising can decrease the price elasticity of demand facing the manufacturer, by the same token it can increase the price elasticity of demand facing the multiproduct retailer.[13] Our empirical finding of a significant inverse relationship between advertising and retail brand gross margins substantiates this claim. The effect of advertising on the salience of a brand to consumers induces changes in both these elasticities. The factory price elasticity is decreased as retailers are forced to stock the brand—even with its high factory price—so that the number of retailers carrying the brand rises. The retail (consumer) price elasticity for the store is increased because of the increased likelihood that consumers will use the price of the brand as a benchmark for the store's overall pricing policy—with the result that the brand is more likely to have an effect on store traffic.

The price elasticity facing the multiproduct retailer, therefore, is a function not only of consumers' demand for the brand (and product category), but also of the consumers' demand for the retail outlet at which to buy this brand and other products carried by this type of store. The retailer's demand for a brand (and product category) is, of course, derived from the consumers' demand for the brand (and product category). *What has been omitted in the economic models of derived demand is the consumers' demand curve for a particular retail outlet.* And this demand curve must be accounted for in any realistic treatment of retail pricing. As such, traditional economic models have implicitly neglected the ability of advertising to increase retail price competition on an advertised brand; thus it remains a hidden effect of advertising.

Implications for Future Research

Infatuation with oversimple answers to complex problems is one of the earmarks of intellectual mediocrity.

THEODOSIUS DOBZHANSKY, GENETICIST

The study offers numerous suggestions for future research. First, the data base is limited for the most part to one retail supermarket chain and only fast-moving, highly salient product categories. More cross-sectional analysis of other supermarket product categories, including slower-moving categories, health and beauty aids, and generics, would be useful. In addition, although national data are not currently available on a brand basis, more proprietary data, particularly for large chains, convenience outlets, and warehouse outlets could be used to provide more comparisons with these results. Data on other outlet classes, including shopping goods as well as convenience goods, would be useful in the same regard. Furthermore, a comparison of the significance of the advertising–gross margin relationship among brands in inflationary versus stable price per periods would provide insight into how this relationship is affected by inflation—particularly if the data include shelf space allocations.

Second, the research demonstrates repeatedly the need for some time-series estimation of the impact of advertising on retail gross margins for further validation of the strength and shape of this relationship. Of particular interest might be situations in which manufacturers' advertised brands have entered a market previously dominated by private labels (Perdue chicken, for example); markets that had entry could be compared to markets that did not in examining changes in absolute price levels. Or markets dominated by manufacturers' brands now faced with private label competition (such as replacement tires or many supermarket product categories faced with penetration by generics in the 1980s) would provide further evidence on the validity of a dual-stage model.

Third, our finding that advertising may have a significant effect on retail gross margins for entire product categories has important research implications. This evidence suggests that we examine more extensively the effect of manufacturers' advertising of consumer products on retail institutions and operations. By increasing competition among retailers and easing their selling task, advertising may stimulate the development of more efficient retail operations and contribute to the productivity of our distribution systems. Time-series analysis could be used to analyze the change in retail margins and/or prices, as advertising stimulates a shift in the distribution channel or mix of outlets used to sell the product category. Cross-sectional analysis would be valuable as well to make cross-national comparisons—for example, to compare product categories that are at different stages in their life cycles and distributed differently among countries, such as calculators and wine.

Fourth, a critical economic effect said to exist in this study is the one-way cross-elasticity of a product for the mass retailer. Although we have not measured it directly, we have *inferred* a causal relationship between brand advertising and this cross-elasticity from the significance of the partial margin elasticity of advertising—the indirect effect of advertising on gross margin, independent of advertising's effect on gross margin through sales. In other words, the empirical results show that the retailer is pricing as if this cross-elasticity exists; otherwise the partial margin elasticity would be measured as zero. Assuming that the retailer is pricing optimally, we have been able to make this inference.

This one-way cross-elasticity is essential to demonstrating the need for dual-stage models when examining consumer product markets. Tests could be made cross-sectionally by using proxies for direct product profits, but this would be very difficult because of the nature of costs in retailing. Instead, simulation or laboratory experiments may be more productive in isolating the one-way cross-elasticity of a product. Further measures of this cross-elasticity—particularly for brands with different levels of advertising—could be used for more precise estimates of the potential cost savings to consumers from advertising's ability to increase retail price competition on the brand.

Fifth, this research indicates that advertising budgeting decisions and policymaking which attempts to measure the impact of advertising in a product market must consider the economic structure of the retailers. Whereas we have demonstrated that advertising leads to lower retail gross profit margins, advertising may also affect shelf space allocation and dealer support and promotions. These effects need to be measured. They can result in additional contributions of advertising for manufacturers and/or consumers that have been previously overlooked. In this regard, entry barriers may exist for manufacturers in the retail marketing of their brands. Just as a reduced retail gross margin was shown to create an absolute cost entry barrier, so may increased shelf space allocation—as was argued in the cereal antitrust case. Increased dealer support and promotions may lead to yet another entry barrier: scale economies in communication costs for leading national brands. Empirical research of various product markets is needed to analyze these differences in the retail marketing of heavily and less heavily advertised brands—differences that affect the competition among manufacturers.

Theoretically, we have tried to extend the model of the multiproduct retailer by focusing on the interdependencies between the manufacturer and retailer in different product markets. In so doing, we have constructed a complement to the Porter model (1976). Whereas Porter focused on the manufacturers' economic structure and performance and the influence of the retailer on the manufacturer, we did so for retailers. In this regard, it is suggested that future research link these two models of bilateral market power, using as its framework the economic structure of the multiproduct firm described in this book. A model of this type would allow us to measure the *net* effect of advertising on consumer welfare, combining our estimates of manufacturers' and retail gross profit margins. The suppliers in the market, moreover, could also be included in the analysis to examine manufacturers' merchandise costs, just as Porter (1980) has done descriptively to improve competitive strategies. Such a theoretical framework would be capable of assessing the structure-performance relationships for an entire economic market of multiproduct competitors.

Endnotes

1. N. H. Borden, *The Economic Effects of Advertising* (Chicago, Ill.: Richard D. Irwin, 1942), p. 35.
2. A. Marshall, *Industry and Trade* (London: The Macmillan Press, Ltd., 1919), pp. 301–302.
3. I am indebted to discussions with Paul Farris for clarification on many of the arguments in this section. In addition, for another discussion of the advertising budgeting implications, see P. W. Farris, "Advertising's Link with Retail Price Competition," *Harvard Business Review*, 59 (January/February 1981), pp. 40, 42, 44. The rationale behind Table 10.1 comes from Exhibit II in the article.
4. D. A. Aaker and J. G. Myers, *Advertising Management* (Englewood Cliffs, N.J.: Prentice-Hall, 1975), pp. 51–52.
5. Much of the evidence behind the current-day trends mentioned in this section on retail management are drawn from *Business Week*, March 23, 1981, pp. 70–73, 76, 80; August 17, 1981, p. 122.
6. As already mentioned, we must be cautious in drawing implications of this sort from cross-sectional research. Causality is not necessarily established, and all relevant explanatory variables may not be included in the analysis. In other words, the actual relationships involved may be much more complex and/or generated by a different process than we determined. Moreover, in cross-section we assume that the retailer is acting optimally, so that we can use the findings for normative implications. In all cases we have tried to draw the implications carefully. Still, it remains difficult to say that the retailer can increase profits in a certain manner, but we can report on the relationships that appear to exist at a certain point in time.
7. Borden, *op. cit.*, p. 39.
8. W. D. Reekie, *Advertising and Price* (London: The Advertising Association, 1979), p. 55.
9. There remains conflicting evidence on whether shoppers use unit pricing or even notice it. This is not hard to believe, given the inconsistency with which supermarkets display unit prices. Early research in the 1960s maintained that consumers hardly noticed unit pricing at all (see Carman, 1972–1973, for a review). More recent research, most notably by McElroy and Aaker, 1979, and Aaker and Ford, 1980, provides evidence that earlier studies may have underestimated consumers' use of unit pricing, particularly since consumers are now much more aware that it exists. McElroy and Aaker do find, however, a negative

correlation between the number of different package sizes in a product category and unit price usage.

10. M. E. Porter, *Interbrand Choice, Strategy, and Bilateral Market Power* (Cambridge, Mass.: Harvard University Press, 1976), p. 240.

11. J. M. Ferguson, "Comments on Farris and Albion, 'The Impact of Advertising on the Price of Consumer Products,' " *Journal of Marketing*, 46 (Winter 1982). p. 103.

12. *Ibid*.

13. It should be reiterated that this statement specifically applies to the brand demand curve at the store. We maintained that advertising increases the price elasticity of store demand at all levels of retail price. The brand demand curve for the entire market, on the other hand, should be "kinked": less elastic above (approximately) the average market retail price and more elastic below this market price. Accordingly, with respect to market demand, the theory of derived demand remains technically consistent in terms of "upside" elasticity (decreased factory and retail price sensitivity), but not in terms of "downside" elasticity (decreased factory and increased retail price sensitivity). Further, it is not consistent with the findings of Eskin (1975), Eskin and Baron (1977), and Wittink (1977) on advertising and retail price sensitivity, nor our empirical validation that advertising leads to lower retail brand gross margins. See Chapter 6 for a more detailed discussion of this point.

Appendix 1

MATHEMATICAL ANALYSIS OF TRAFFIC BUILDING EFFECTS

In this mathematical appendix, a partial equilibrium model is presented for a single-product and a multiproduct mass retailer. The purpose of this mathematical model is to show how interdependencies among products affect the optimal gross margin of a product. It is maintained that a product that through a reduction in its own price can induce the sales of other products at the store (called "complementary" relationship in microeconomics[1]) should have a lower gross margin than products that do not, *ceteris paribus*.

The model has two initial assumptions that simplify the proof:

1. Competitive responses, retail services and other fixed costs, and decisions other than the retail price of a product are ignored (assumed to be independent of the pricing decision).
2. Factory prices are already determined, so that by optimizing price, the retailer optimizes the gross margin as well.

The contribution function (π), therefore, given n demand equations, is:

$$\pi = \sum_{i=1}^{n} p_i q_i - C, \tag{1}$$

where p and q refer to the price and quantity (units sold) of products and C represents the retail cost function, which is of the form, $C = C(q_1, q_2, \ldots, q_n)$. For a representative product (product 1), the demand function is of the form, $q_1 = q_1(p_1, p_2, \ldots, p_n)$.

To maximize total contribution, the retailer should optimize over the vector of n prices. The first-order condition for the representative product is:

$$\partial \pi / \partial p_1 = q_1 + \sum_{i=1}^{n} (p_i - \partial C / \partial q_i) \cdot \partial q_i / \partial p_1 = 0. \tag{2}$$

There are n equations of (2), which can be thought of as the retailer's attempts to equate marginal costs with marginal revenues. Equation (2) can be arranged for examination of the single-product (2a and b) or multiproduct (2c and d) retailer. Terms are arranged so that the product's contribution (and gross margin) can be shown on one side of the equation.

In the single-product case, equation (2) becomes:

$$p - \partial C/\partial q = -q/(\partial q/\partial p) \equiv p/\eta, \tag{2a}$$

where $\eta = -(\partial q/\partial p) \cdot p/q$. Notice that if we divide by p, retail gross margin (GM) has a simple relationship with the price elasticity of demand,

$$GM = 1/\eta + v/p, \tag{2b}$$

where v is other variable costs (not including merchandise costs).

In the multiproduct case, equation (2) becomes:

$$p_1 - \partial C/\partial q_1 = -q_1/(\partial q_1/\partial p_1) - \sum_{i=2}^{n} (p_i$$
$$- \partial C/\partial q_i) \cdot (\partial q_i/\partial p_1)/(\partial q_1/\partial p_1). \tag{2c}$$

If the dominant relationship of product 1 with the rest of the product line is one of complementarity, then

$$\sum_{i=2}^{n} (p_i - \partial C/\partial q_i) \cdot (\partial q_i/\partial p_1) < 0,$$

and with $\partial q_1/\partial p_1 < 0$, the second term in (2c) is positive and subtracted from the first. The second term is zero only if the cross-partials with respect to price are zero.[2]

Equation (2c) can now be arranged to show the equilibrium condition for the multiproduct retailer optimizing the price of product 1 as:

$$GM_1 = \frac{1}{\eta_1}\left\{1 + \sum_{i=2}^{n} \eta_{i,1} \cdot \left(GM_i - \frac{v_i}{p_i}\right)\frac{p_i q_i}{p_1 q_1}\right\} + \frac{v_1}{p_1}, \tag{2d}$$

where the term $\eta_{i,1}$ is the cross-elasticity of product 1 with all the other products carried by the store. In this regard,

$$\eta_{i,1} = \sum_{i=2}^{n} (\partial q_i/\partial p_1) \cdot p_1/q_i,$$

and is positive if the cross-commodity relationship is one of substitution, negative if the relationship is one of complementarity, and zero for the single-product retailer (like equation 2b). In other words, if product 1's dominant relationship with the rest of the product line is one of complementarity—as it would be for a traffic-building product—the elasticity term just described is negative, and the optimal gross margin for product 1 is lower than in the single-product case where no product interdependencies can exist.

Endnotes

1. If two products have a complementary relationship, their cross-elasticity is negative, $\partial q_2/\partial p_1 < 0$. If instead of being complements (bread and butter), two products are substitutes (butter and margarine), their cross-elasticity is positive, $\partial q_2/\partial p_1 > 0$.

2. In the case where there is symmetry in the cross-partial relationships—that is, if $\partial q_i/\partial p_1 > 0$ implies that $\partial q_1/\partial p_i < 0$, and quantitatively these two sets of relationships are equal—the price level of product 1 should be unaffected by the cross-commodity relationships. However, as described in chapter 5, the nonsymmetry of these cross-partial derivatives—what was called the one-way cross-elasticities—is an essential verity of mass retailing.

Appendix 2

CONSTRUCTION AND REPRESENTATIVENESS OF THE DATA BASE

This technical appendix describes the data base used in the empirical analysis. The appendix itself is divided into two sections. The construction of the data base is the subject of the first section; the second section deals with how representative the data base is of retailing in general and of food retailing in particular. A more detailed discussion of the data base, including descriptive statistics of the more important variables used and documentation of the computer programs required, is provided by Albion (1981).

The Data Base

The search for a national data base on the retail gross margins of brands was not successful. None of the national marketing information systems, including SAMI and Nielsen, collect these data in a form useful for our purposes. We were, however, able to obtain access to the December 30, 1978, "Wholesale Sales Analysis Report" (WSAR) of a supermarket chain with over $300 million in annual sales. Because of the importance of food and food-related products to consumers, it was decided that this report would serve as the crux of the data base.

The WSAR includes 1977 and 1978 data on an item-by-item basis. The data reported are:

- number of cases sold (1978 only)
- total cost of cases sold (1978 only)
- unit size of item
- items per case
- total dollar sales

273

- promotional dollar sales
- regular gross margin (of sales not on promotion)
- promotional gross margin
- average gross margin (of total sales)

In addition, product category totals are given for the number of cases sold, total cost of cases sold, dollar sales, and average gross margin. Unit sales and prices can be computed only for 1978, so the 1977 data were used for comparative purposes only.[1]

The WSAR covers approximately one third of the chain's total sales for 1978. Products not kept in the chain's warehouses are not reported in the WSAR. Excluded are most brands of soft drinks, fresh meat and produce, and health and beauty aids (rack jobbers used). The number of product categories included in the WSAR, with "product category" defined at the level of aggregation used by *Leading National Advertisers* (LNA),[2] is around 200. Because of the typical research restrictions—time and money—it was necessary to select a sample from these 200 product categories. The following four category selection criteria were used:

1. A product category must have at least one brand appearing in LNA.
2. A minimum of two brands in the product category is required.
3. Any product categories termed "miscellaneous" in WSAR are automatically excluded.
4. A sales share (of the WSAR) of at least 0.5 percent in 1978, approximately $500,000 in annual sales (at the chain), is required.

The first two criteria were established so that some interbrand variation would be measurable. Eliminating "miscellaneous" product categories (only a few of which met criterion 4) avoided the problem of including "catch-all" categories, on which no data would appear in any other data sources. Essentially, it was the "store share" criterion 4 that created a sample of 52 product categories with 3,815 items. After butter was eliminated from the sample (unrepresentative of national data), we were left with a sample of 51 product categories, shown in Table A2.1.

Two options were considered for the fourth criterion: a minimum store-sales share and a random selection of product categories from groups with different store-sales shares ("stratification"). Both criteria are objective. Stratification should produce a sample more representative of supermarket retailing and with greater variation in advertising and gross margin levels than the store-sales criterion. A minimum store-sales criterion, however, produces a sample that covers a greater percentage of the store's sales (for a given number of product categories), with the faster-moving, more heavily advertised product categories included and more sample homogeneity.[3] Since sufficient variation in the data was not a problem, it was decided that it would be better to analyze the "big sellers," in which the effects of advertising are of greater public policy concern, although the results may not apply to slower-moving product categories.

Table A2.1 The 51 Product Categories

Food Category	Percent Store Sales Share	Nonfood Category	Percent Store Sales Share
1. Baby food	0.81	42. Bar soap	0.67
2. Breakfast cereals (RTE)	3.19	43. Cigarettes	7.64
3. Cake mixes	0.60	44. Disposable diapers	1.10
4. Candy bars	0.73	45. Fabric softeners	0.53
5. Canned baked beans	0.73	46. Facial tissues	0.51
6. Canned fruit juices	1.07	47. Hand dishwashing liquids	1.42
7. Canned fruits	1.41	48. Laundry detergents	1.41
8. Canned soups (condensed)	1.43	49. Paper towels	1.39
9. Canned tuna	1.88	50. Plastic garbage bags	0.73
10. Canned vegetables	3.07	51. Toilet tissues	<u>1.69</u>
11. Cat food (canned)	1.39		
12. Cat food (dry)	0.69	Subtotal	17.09
13. Cheese	3.82		
14. Coffee (instant/freeze-dried)	3.37		
15. Coffee (regular)	2.23		
16. Cooking oil	0.67		
17. Cottage cheese	0.60		
18. Dog food (canned)	0.98		
19. Dog food (dry)	1.48		
20. Evaporated canned milk	0.52		
21. Flour	0.65		
22. Frozen dinners/entrees	0.91		
23. Frozen orange juice	1.86		
24. Frozen seafood	0.61		
25. Frozen vegetables	1.08		
26. Granulated cane sugar	1.08		
27. Italian box dinners/noodles	0.51		
28. Margarine	2.51		
29. Mayonnaise	0.84		
30. Milk additives	0.90		
31. Nuts	0.80		
32. Pasta products	0.88		
33. Peanut butter	0.81		
34. Pickles	0.50		
35. Plain canned meats	1.10		
36. Powdered soft drink mixes	0.60		
37. Ready-to-serve fruit juices	0.74		
38. Salad dressings	0.50		
39. Shortening	0.52		
40. Spaghetti sauces	0.57		
41. Tea bags	<u>0.51</u>		
Subtotal	49.15		

The selection of brands within a product category was made using a cutoff of 1 percent of category sales to eliminate the possibility of brand data based on just a small amount of sales. Very few data were unrecorded because of this cutoff. All the brands for each product category are listed in Appendix 3, with the chain's average gross margin (national gross margin in parentheses) in 1978 given for each product category.

National data on other variables were collected from three main sources:

> 1. *Leading National Advertisers*
> Manufacturers' advertising data for brands and product categories, 1974–1978.
> 2. *Chain Store Age Supermarkets Sales Manual*
> 1978 and 1977 product category data on gross margins, sales, assortment, and unit movement. Also, the POPAI/DuPont Consumer Buying Habits Study, based on a survey of 8,000 shoppers at 200 nationally representative supermarkets, classified purchase decisions into: specifically planned (out-of-store brand decision), generally planned (out-of-store product category decision), substitute (decision instead of another brand or product category out-of-stock), and unplanned, 1977.
> 3. *Target Group Index*
> As these data are confidential, they were used only to cross-check certain results in the empirical work and, in one instance (household penetration), to split the sample. Consumer variables include household penetration and purchase frequency of a product category, brand loyalty and share of users for a brand; largely 1977 data.

Representativeness of the Data Base

A number of useful comparisons can be made to provide a sense of the representativeness of the data base with regard to retailing, food retailing, retail chains, and food product categories. The following three subsections offer data on some of the more important comparisons.

Retail Outlet Classes

In 1972 food stores accounted for over one fifth of all retail sales and over one seventh of all retail outlets. Chains represented over 57 percent of all food sales and more than one third of sales of all retail chains. Food retailing also had high dollar sales per square foot and investment per outlet with very low labor costs.[4]

Table A2.2 shows how food retailing compares with the other outlet classifications in the *Census of Business*—low net income, low net and gross margins, and little retail advertising with substantial manufacturers' advertising. The variation in the average level of retail gross margins among outlet classes can be explained by the amount of the retailer's value added in the final product sold to consumers. In simple regressions on the ten major outlet classes (listed in Table A2.2), for example, a labor ratio (measure of payroll expenses) explains 90 percent of the variation across classes in gross margins, an investment ratio 65 percent, the retail advertising-to-sales ratio 29 percent—all directly related to gross margin and significant; the manufacturers' advertising-to-sales ratio (inversely related) accounts for less than 2 percent of the variation in the retail gross margins among these different retail outlet classes (Albion, 1979).

Retail Food Chains

It is important to see how representative the financial ratios of the food chain used in the data base are of food chains in particular and retail chains in general. Table A2.3, derived from *Management Horizons, Inc.* data, presents such ratios for the chain and the 52 food and 327 retail (includes food) chains in the MHI data base. For the most part, the years 1974–1978 are covered, although the fiscal years used by the different firms do vary.

Two points should be drawn from Table A2.3:

1. The retail food chain used in the data base is representative of food chains in general. Its average net margin over the last five years, for example, is only 0.01 percentage points different from the food chain average.
2. Food chains are not particularly representative of retail chains in general. Net margins are lower, and asset turnover is higher. The financial ratios without assets or sales, however, are very comparable (see, as defined in the table, RONW, S/E, FG).

In short, the data base should produce results that may be extrapolated beyond one retail food chain to most food chains.

Product Categories

Two questions should be asked of the data on the 51 product categories used in the empirical analysis:

1. How representative are the 51 product categories of all the categories in the WSAR?
2. How does the WSAR compare with national data on the 51 product categories?

Since the most important retail variable in this research is gross margin, comparisons are made on that basis.

Table A2.2 Comparison of Food Stores to Other Retail Stores

	% of Firms Reporting*	NY/SE†	Gross Margin	Net Margin	Net/ Gross Margin	Manufacturer A/S	Retail A/S
Food stores‡	**13**	**8.3**	**21.0**	**0.7**	**3.3**	**2.50**	**1.0**
General merchandise stores	68	13.9	37.3	3.4	9.1	1.68	2.8
Drug and proprietary stores	48	14.7	29.1	2.2	7.6	6.79	1.2
Apparel and accessory stores	41	12.3	38.2	2.9	7.6	0.97	2.0
Automotive dealers	29	17.3	14.7	1.2	8.2	0.83	0.9
Gasoline service stations	6	15.8	22.8	1.7	7.5	0.59	0.4
Furniture stores	33	10.6	35.7	2.2	6.2	1.34	3.3
Eating and drinking places	23	11.7	56.0	2.0	3.6	2.57	1.6
Building materials and hardware stores	41	14.6	23.8	2.8	11.8	0.88	0.8
Miscellaneous retail stores§	20	13.1	30.3	2.4	7.9	2.47	1.2

NOTE: All numbers are percentages.

* Source of data is the Internal Revenue Service *Sourcebook* of the *Statistics of Income*, 1972. This data base covers only a certain percentage of the firms included in the *Census of Business, Retail Trade Summary Statistics*, 1972.

† Net Income (before taxes)/Stockholder's Equity.

‡ These ten outlet classes correspond to Census classification numbers 54, 53, 591, 56, 55 excluding 554, 57, 58, 52, and 59 excluding 591, respectively, which are the broadest classifications of retail outlets in the *Census of Business*.

§ "Miscellaneous retail stores" includes mostly shopping goods stores: liquor stores, nonstore retailers, fuel and ice dealers, florists, cigar stores and stands, sporting goods stores, book stores, stationery stores, jewelry stores, toy stores, camera stores, gift stores, and sewing stores.

Table A2.3 Comparison of Retail Chain to Other Food Chains

| | Last Five Fiscal Years | | | | | | Last Fiscal Year | | | | | | | | |
	% Sales Growth	Margin 90	AT	ROA 90	F/L	RONW 90	% Change Sales	Profit	Margin 90	AT	ROA 90	F/L	RONW 90	S/E	FG 90
Retail chain	**13.9**	**0.85**	**5.4**	**4.6**	**3.1**	**14.2**	**9.5**	**30.7**	**0.94**	**4.6**	**4.3**	**3.5**	**15.2**	**0.71**	**12.0**
Food chains* (52)	12.8	0.84	5.3	4.4	2.5	12.2	11.4	29.5	1.02	5.3	5.2	2.7	13.6	0.77	11.7
All retail chains* (327)	13.4	2.28	2.3	5.7	2.1	12.0	13.9	21.4	2.40	2.4	6.0	2.1	13.5	0.82	12.1

SOURCE: *Management Horizons, Inc., Retail Performance Update,* ending the second quarter of 1979. Fiscal year for the retail chain used in the data base of this research ends 12/78.

NOTE: M × AT = ROA; ROA × F/L = RONW; RONW × S/E = FG.

% Sales Growth Compound annual growth rate of sales in percent (sales = net consolidated sales)
Margin Net profit margin; profits divided by sales in percent (profits = net consolidated after-tax profits before extraordinary items)
AT Asset turnover; sales divided by assets
ROA Return on assets; profits divided by assets in percent (assets = year-end total assets)
F/L Financial leverage; assets divided by net worth (net worth = year-end net stockholders' equity)
RONW Return on net worth; profit divided by net worth in percent
S/E Surplus to earnings; profits less cash dividends, divided by profits
FG Financial growth; RONW × S/E

* The food chains in the *Management Horizons, Inc.* data base account for over $70 billion in sales; the 327 retail chains account for over $150 billion (annual, through last recorded fiscal year).

Table A2.4   Product Category Group Comparisons

Category Group	Dollar Sales (1978)	Dollar Sales (1977)	Gross Margins (1978)	Gross Margins (1977)
The "51"*	$ 65,032,441	$60,687,626	14.8%	16.5%
The Chain (WSAR)				
Total	100,280,479	89,894,077	15.3	16.7
Grocery	78,820,039	72,771,397	14.2	15.5
Gen. Mdse.†	1,978,186	1,551,341	29.8	34.2
Dairy	10,694,664	9,058,278	15.2	19.7
Frozen	8,787,590	6,513,061	21.5	21.5
"51" (National)‡	—	—	19.2	18.7

* The "51" refers to the 51 product categories taken from the WSAR and used as the data base. Gross margins listed are unweighted averages.
† Technically, general merchandise includes many miscellaneous product categories such as light bulbs, batteries, lawn chairs, charcoals, and so on, and should not be confused with health and beauty aids or household products (toilet tissues, scouring pads, and so on).
‡ Source of the national data is *Chain Store Age Supermarkets Sales Manual*, July 1978 and July 1979. Gross margins listed are unweighted averages.

Table A2.4 addresses these questions with some aggregated data. Individual product category comparisons are given in the listing of brands by category at the end of this appendix. The gross margins of the group of product categories in the data base (the "51") are slightly lower than those in the entire WSAR, possibly because of the higher level of unit sales than for the other categories in the WSAR. However, if general merchandise product categories (not in the "51") are eliminated from the WSAR total, the difference in gross margins between the "51" and the entire WSAR is even smaller: 14.8 to 15.0, 16.5 to 16.4. Comparisons with the national data do not fare as well. The gross margins of the product categories at the chain are consistently lower than national gross margins: for 48 of the 51 in 1978 and 41 of the 51 in 1977. Whatever the reasons—more likely the economics of the chain's market areas, such as less expensive overhead or the population's income, than intense competition—this divergence is not a problem as long as the *relative* levels of the product category gross margins in the data base are similar to the relative national levels. On the whole, they are very similar.

Endnotes

1. Additional entry into the market in 1978 increased competition for the chain. As such, 1977 results are reported when they substantially differ from 1978.
2. This level of aggregation was used so that retail data would be compatible with data on manufacturers' advertising. For example, "canned vegetables," not

"canned peas," is defined as a product category, since LNA data are collected for "Green Giant canned vegetables," not "Green Giant canned peas."
3. A heterogeneous sample, requiring a sample split or a dummy variable, is more likely for a sample of fast-moving and slow-moving product categories than for a sample of just the so-called "big sellers."
4. Data used here are from the IRS *Sourcebook* of the *Statistics of Income,* 1972 and the *Census of Business, Retail Trade Summary Statistics,* 1972. An index of value added, based on four measures of retail costs (investment, inventory, payroll, and retail advertising), shows food stores with the second lowest index of the ten Census outlet classifications (gasoline service stations lowest) in 1972 (Albion, 1979).

Appendix 3

LIST OF BRANDS COLLECTED FOR EACH PRODUCT CATEGORY*

1. Baby Food: 10.4† (11.5)‡
   Beech-Nut; Gerber
2. Breakfast Cereals (Ready-to-Eat): 13.6 (17.4)
   General Foods (Post)—Alpha-Bits, Family Style, Fortified Oat Flakes, 40% bran flakes, Grape-Nuts, Honeycomb, Pebbles (all kinds), raisin bran, Sugar Crisp, Teen, Toasties;
   General Mills—Big G Crazy Cow, Buc Wheats, Cheerios, Cocoa Puffs, Corn Kix, family pack, Golden Grahams, Lucky Charms, monster (all kinds); Nature Valley Granola, Total, Trix, Wheaties;
   Kellogg's—All-Bran, Apple Jacks, Cocoa Krispies, corn flakes, Corny-Snaps, Cracklin' Bran, Country Morning, 40% bran flakes, Froot Loops, Frosted Mini-Wheats, Frosted Rice, Product 19, raisin bran, Rice Krispies, Snack-Pak, Special K, Sugar Corn Pops, Sugar Frosted Flakes, Sugar Smacks, Toasted Mini-Wheats;
   Nabisco—100% bran, shredded wheat, Team;
   Quaker—Cap'n Crunch (all kinds), Life, 100% natural (all kinds), puffed wheat, puffed rice, Quisp, unprocessed bran;
   Ralston-Purina—Chex, Chocolate Chip, Freekies Presweetened Grins and Giggles (combined), Moonstones, Oatmeal Flake, Van Wafer
   Kretschmer's—private label
3. Cake Mixes: 9.5 (18.1)
   Betty Crocker; Duncan Hines; Jiffy; Pillsbury; private label

---

* The list includes 502 brands. 14 of these brands had some missing data for 1978 so that the 1978 sample was based on the remaining 488 brands.

† Chain's 1978 average product category gross margin as a percentage of sales.

‡ National 1978 average product category gross margin as a percentage of sales.

4. Candy Bars: 28.2 (26.8)

Almond Joy; Andes Petit chocolate bars; Baby Ruth; Bit-o-Honey; Bolster; Bounty coconut bar; Butterfinger; Cadbury bars (all kinds); Choc-o-Lite; Chunky; Clark bars; Combo Munch peanut brittle; Forever Yours; Heath; Hershey's chocolate bars; Hershey's special dark chocolate bars; Kit Kat; Krackel; Luden's 5th Avenue bars; M&M's plain candies; Mallo Cups; Marathon; Mars almond bar; Milky Way; Mounds; Mr. Goodbar; Nestlé Crunch; Nestlé milk bars; $100,000 bar; Pom Poms; Rally; Reese's peanut butter cups; Seavey's Needhams; Sky Bar; Snickers; Sugar Babies; Sugar Daddy; Super Skrunch; Toffifay; 3 Musketeers; Willy Wonka Peanut Butter Oompas; York Peppermint Pattie

5. Canned Baked Beans: 14.8 (20.1)

B&M; Campbell's; Friend's; Libby's; Stewart's; private label

6. Canned Fruit Juices: 15.1 (19.5)

Bess; Dole; Libby's; Lincoln; Ocean Spray; ReaLemon; Sunsweet; Welch's; private label

7. Canned Fruits: 15.3 (20.7)

Brookville; Del Monte; Dole; Glorietta; Libby's; private label

8. Canned Soups (Condensed): 13.3 (17.7)

Campbell's; Doxsee; Habitant; Snow's; private label

9. Canned Tuna: 7.4 (14.3)

Bumble Bee; Chicken of the Sea; Geisha; Star-Kist; 3 Diamonds; private label

10. Canned Vegetables: 16.0 (21.2)

B in B mushrooms; Brookville; Del Monte; Green Giant; Libby's; Stewart's; private label

11. Cat Food (Canned): 16.5 (21.4)

Bright Eyes; Calo; Friskies; Kal Kan; Kitty; Lovin' Spoonfuls; 9-Lives; Purina; Puss 'n' Boots; Tabby; Whisker Lickins

12. Cat Food (Dry): 17.0 (19.6)

Cadillac; Corky; Friskies; Purina; Puss 'n' Boots

13. Cheese: 16.5 (27.4)

Borden; Churny; Harvest Moon; Hood; Kraft; Weight Watchers; Wispride; private label

14. Coffee (Instant/Freeze-dried): 14.1 (11.9)

Brim; Chock full o' Nuts; Kava; Maxim; Maxwell House; Mellow Roast; Nescafé; Sanka; Savarin; Sunrise; Taster's Choice; private label

15. Coffee (Regular): 15.2 (8.1)

Brim; Chase & Sanborn; Chock full o' Nuts; Eight o' Clock; Folger's; High Yield; Hills Bros; Luzianne; Maxwell House; Mellow Roast; Sanka; Savarin; Yuban; private label

16. Cooking Oil: 16.0 (17.0)

Crisco; Hollywood; Mazola; Planters; Puritan; Wesson; private label

17. Cottage Cheese: 20.1 (24.9)

Breakstone; Hood; Sealtest and Sealtest Light 'n' Lively (combined)

18. Dog Food (Canned): 17.4 (20.5)
    Alpo; Cadillac; Calo; Cycle; Friskies; Kal Kan; Ken-L-Ration; Mighty Dog; Recipe; Rival; Skippy; Strongheart; Vets
19. Dog Food (Dry): 12.5 (17.8)
    Alpo; Cycle; Corky; Friskies; Gaines; Ken-L-Ration; Purina; Sunshine
20. Evaporated Canned Milk: 7.3 (12.0)
    Carnation; Pet; private label
21. Flour: 10.0 (16.0)
    Gold Medal; King Arthur; Pillsbury; Robin Hood; private label
22. Frozen Dinners/Entrees: 22.0 (27.7)
    Buitoni; Chun King; Green Giant; Howard Johnson's; Morton; Swanson; Stouffer's; Weight Watchers
23. Frozen Orange Juice: 15.8 (25.9)
    Birds Eye; Minuet; Minute Maid; Old South; Snow Crop; Treesweet; Tropicana; private label
24. Frozen Seafood: 23.1 (29.7)
    Gorton; High-Liner; Mrs. Paul's; Taste o' Sea; Van de Kamp's; Wakefield; private label
25. Frozen Vegetables: 23.2 (28.6)
    Birds Eye; Genesee Valley; Green Giant; Stokely; private label
26. Granulated Cane Sugar: 4.2 (8.1)
    Domino; private labels (two types)
27. Italian Box dinners/Noodles: 15.0 (20.0)
    Appian Way; Betty Crocker; Chef Boyardee; Kraft; Prince; Vimco; private label
28. Margarine: 15.2 (21.8)
    Blue Bonnet; Bonnie Maid; Chiffon; Fleischmann's; Imperial; Land O Lakes; Mazola; Mrs. Filbert's; Parkay; Promise; Sampson's; Shedds; private label
29. Mayonnaise: 5.5 (8.6)
    Cains; Hellmann's; Kraft; Miracle Whip; Weight Watchers; private label
30. Milk Additives: 18.8 (20.2)
    Carnation; Hershey's; Milk Mate; Nestle; Ovaltine; PDQ; Swiss Miss; private label
31. Nuts: 28.1 (26.0) ·
    Blue Diamond; Planters; River Queen; Skippy; Southern Belle; private label
32. Pasta Products: 15.5 (21.8)
    Mueller's; No Yolk; Prince; Vimco; Viva; private label
33. Peanut Butter: 9.2 (16.2)
    Jif; Peter Pan; Planters; Shedds; Skippy; private label
34. Pickles: 20.8 (25.5)
    Cains; Daily; Heinz; Oxford; Vlasic; private label

35. Plain Canned Meats: 10.8 (19.3)
    Armour; Beard's; Dinty Moore; Hormel; Libby's; Spam; Swanson; Underwood
36. Powdered Soft Drink Mixes: 25.1 (27.0)
    Country Time lemonade; Funny Face; Golden Crown; Hawaiian Punch; Hi-C mixes; Kool-Aid; Minute Maid lemonade; Wyler's; private label
37. Ready-to-Serve Fruit Juices: 16.7 (25.7)
    Hood; Kraft; Minute Maid; Tropicana; private label
38. Salad Dressings: 20.4 (23.1)
    Cains; Good Seasons; Henri's; Ken's Steak House; Kraft; Pfeiffer; Seven Seas; Wish-Bone; private label
39. Shortening: 5.4 (11.9)
    Crisco; Spry; private label
40. Spaghetti Sauces: 15.7 (19.6)
    Chef Boyardee; Durkee; French's; Prima Salsa; Prince; Progresso; Ragú, private label
41. Tea Bags: 11.2 (18.9)
    Lipton; Magic Mountain; Red Rose; Salada; Tetley; private label
42. Bar Soap: 15.3 (19.3)
    Camay; Caress; Coast; Dial; Dove; Gay Bouquet; Irish Spring; Ivory; Lava; Lifebuoy; Lux; Palmolive; Safeguard; Tone; Zest
43. Cigarettes: 9.5 (10.0)
    Alpine; Belair; Benson & Hedges; Camel; Carlton; Chesterfield; Decade; Doral; Eve; Fact; Kent; Kool; L&M; Lark; Lucky Strike; Marlboro; Merit; More; Newport; Now; Old Gold; Pall Mall; Parliament; Raleigh; Real; Salem; Saratoga; Silva Thins; Tall; Tareyton; True; Vantage; Viceroy; Virginia Slims; Winston
44. Disposable Diapers: 10.4 (13.2)
    Baby Fresh; Huggies; Johnson's; Pampers; private label
45. Fabric Softeners: 19.9 (20.3)
    Bounce; Cling Free; Downy; Final Touch; Free-n-Soft; Purex; Rain Barrel; StaPuf; Static Guard; private label
46. Facial Tissues: 12.3 (17.9)
    Blue Ribbon; Kleenex; Scott and Scotties (combined); Vanity Fair; private label
47. Hand Dishwashing Liquids: 12.3 (18.9)
    Ajax; Dawn; Dove; Ivory; Joy; Lux; Minuet; Octagon; Palmolive; private label
48. Laundry Detergents: 10.6 (14.0)
    All; Ajax; Arm & Hammer; Bold; Bonus; Breeze; Cheer; Cold Power; Dash; Dreft; Duz; Dynamo; Era; Fab; Gain; Ivory Snow; Oxydol; Punch; Purex; Rinso; Super Suds; Tide; Wisk; private label
49. Paper Towels: 9.3 (17.5)
    Bounty; Coronet; ScotTowels; Teri; Vanity Fair; Viva; private label

50. Plastic Garbage Bags: 19.8 (26.5)
    Baggies; Glad; Handi; Hefty; Webster; private label
51. Toilet Tissues: 5.8 (15.7)
    Charmin; Cottonelle; ScotTissue; Soft-Weve; Toft; Vanity Fair; Waldorf;
    White Cloud; private label

GLOSSARY

All of these terms are defined in the text. They are collected here for the reader's convenience.

Absolute Market Price   The average retail price of all brands in a product category, weighted by the market share of each brand; also referred to as the absolute (average) market-price level; to be distinguished from relative retail price.

Ad(vertising) Dollars   Dollar amount of advertising expenditures, which for this study is measured as a four-year total.

Ad(vertising) Ratio   A brand's advertising expenditures divided by the average brand advertising expenditures in the product category, multiplied by 100.

Ad(vertising) Share   A brand's advertising expenditures divided by the level of category advertising, multiplied by 100.

Advertising   Manufacturers' brand advertising; to be distinguished from category advertising.

Advertising-Gross Margin Relationship   The effect of advertising on retail brand gross margins; also referred to as the margin elasticity (of advertising).

Advertising Intensity   Advertising-to-sales ratio.

Aggregate Salience   Salience of a product in terms of the total number of purchasers of the product at a store.

Brand Gross Margin Ratio   A brand's gross margin divided by the unweighted, simple average of the brand gross margins in the product category, multiplied by 100; also referred to as BGMR.

Category Advertising   The total amount of advertising in a product category, which for this study is measured as a four-year total; also referred to as product category advertising or total category advertising.

Category Characteristics   All explanatory variables of the level of product category gross margins; also referred to as product category characteristics (factors) and independent (product) category variables.

Category Criterion Variables   Category characteristics used to divide a sample of product categories into two or three subsamples.

Contribution The retail price less variable costs (expenses) for one unit of sales; equivalent to direct product profit.

Contribution Percentage The contribution as a percentage of the retail price; equivalent to net margin.

Direct Effect The effect of advertising on retail brand gross margins through its effect on sales; also referred to as the sales margin elasticity (of advertising); to be distinguished from the indirect effect.

Direct Product Profit(ability) Equivalent to contribution.

Downside Elasticity The price elasticity of a demand curve below a certain point on that demand curve; in this study it is the retail price elasticity of a brand's market demand curve below (approximately) the average market price of the brand; to be distinguished from upside elasticity.

Factory Price The delivered manufacturer's price, which for this study is equivalent to the wholesale price and therefore the retailer's merchandise costs.

Feedback Effect The effect of retail brand gross margins on advertising.

Goodwill The patronage, or brand loyalty, of a product in consumers' minds; in this study it is a long-run measure of advertising expenditures (four-year total).

Gross Margin The retail price less the factory price as a percentage of the retail price; this is the average retail gross margin, which is normally a weighted average (unit sales as weights) of the regular gross margin and the promotional gross margin over the course of some time period; also referred to as the gross profit margin or retail markup; to be distinguished from the manufacturers' gross profit margin.

Indirect Effect A proxy for the effect of advertising on retail price competition; the effect of advertising on retail brand gross margins, independent of advertising's effect on gross margin through its effect on sales; also referred to as the partial margin elasticity (of advertising); to be distinguished from the direct effect.

Interbrand Among brands within the same product category; comparison is usually made within the same story (intrastore); also referred to for simplicity as among brands.

Interproduct Among product categories.

Intrabrand On the same brand; comparison normally made among stores (interstore) when referring to retail price competition on a brand or, in this study, when referring to the bargaining between manufacturer and retailer on the factory price of the brand.

Intrabrand Competition Competition on the same brand, of two types;

manufacturer-retailer intrabrand competition deals with the factory price of the brand; retail intrabrand competition concerns competition among retailers on the sale of a particular brand, and usually refers to retail price competition.

Item A particular size (or color, flavor, and so on) of a brand in a product category, such as a 14-ounce bottle of Heinz catsup; technically referred to as a stock-keeping unit (SKU).

Loss Leader A product sold at a loss by the retailer for the purpose of increasing (or maintaining) store traffic; similar to a traffic builder, with the restriction that a loss leader must be sold at a negative net margin.

Margin Elasticity (of Advertising) General term for the responsiveness of the retail brand gross margin to advertising, measured in percentage terms (percentage of product category levels); also the technical counterpart for the effect of advertising on gross margin.

Market Equilibrium Equilibrium for the retailer, including all competitive responses; to be distinguished from partial equilibrium.

(Average) Market (Retail) Price The average retail price of a brand in a retail geographical market; to be distinguished from the absolute market price, which applies to an entire product category.

Mean Gross Margin An unweighted average of the gross margins for a subsample of product categories.

Merchandising "Promoting the sale of": the pricing, space allocation, display, and so forth of products by the retailer.

Net Margin Equivalent to contribution percentage.

Net Opportunity Costs Opportunity costs less the total contribution from the current use of the fixed resource (shelf space); equivalent to opportunity loss.

One-Way Cross-Elasticity The ability of a product to affect the sales of another product (or group of products) without the ability of the other product to affect the sales of that product; in this study, the term is used to describe the traffic-building effect of certain products; the cross-elasticity is also referred to as product interdependence.

Operating Costs Equivalent to variable costs in the short run, but includes fixed costs in the long run.

Opportunity Costs Total contribution of the best alternative use of the fixed resource (shelf space), that is, the forgone income (total contribution) from a particular use of a fixed resource rather than the best alternative use; if the retailer uses the shelf space optimally, total contribution will equal opportunity costs, and the opportunity loss will be zero.

Opportunity Loss Equivalent to net opportunity costs.

Other Retail Variable Costs   Variable costs, excluding merchandise costs; more commonly referred to as retail (handling) expenses.

Partial Equilibrium   Equilibrium for the retailer with no competitive responses accounted for (that is, holding competition constant).

Partial Margin Elasticity (of Advertising)   The responsiveness of the retail brand gross margin to advertising, measured in percentage terms (percentage of product category levels), independent of advertising's effect on gross margin through its effect on sales; a proxy for the effect of advertising on retail price competition; also the technical counterpart for the indirect effect.

Product   A generic term for the economic unit of analysis; to be distinguished from the more specific terms "item," "brand," and "(product) category."

Product Interdependencies   The effect of the merchandising of one product on another; also referred to as cross-elasticities between products.

Rate of Movement   The unit sales (volume) per unit of time; equivalent to turnover.

Relative Retail Price   The retail price of a brand relative to the retail price of another brand in the same product category.

Retail Penetration   The average commodity volume, which is the weighted average of the number of outlets carrying the product times the number of units of the product each outlet carries.

Retail Price   A weighted average (unit sales as weights) of the regular "everyday" selling price and the promotion selling price of a product to consumers; equivalent to consumer price.

Retail Price Competition   The price competition among retailers on the same product (or group of products); most commonly used for brands and therefore equivalent to retail intrabrand competition.

Sales Margin Elasticity (of advertising)   The responsiveness of the retail brand gross margin to advertising, measured in percentage terms (percentage of product category levels), through advertising's effect on sales; also the technical counterpart of the direct effect.

Salience   The ability of a product to attract consumer recognition and concern about the merchandising, in particular, the pricing of the product; in this study this consumer behavior notion is held to translate into an economic effect, measured by the one-way cross-elasticity of a product.

Shadow Price   The opportunity cost for one unit of the fixed resource, which for this study is one square foot of shelf space.

Total Contribution   Contribution times the number of units sold.

Total Effect The total effect of advertising on retail brand gross margins; the sum of the direct and indirect effects; also referred to as the total margin elasticity (of advertising).

Total Margin Elasticity (of advertising) The total responsiveness of the retail brand gross margin to advertising, measured in percentage terms (percentage of product category levels); the sum of the partial and sales margin elasticities (of advertising); also the technical counterpart for the total effect.

Traffic Builder A product similar to a loss leader, but not necessarily sold at a loss.

Turnover Equivalent to rate of movement.

Unit Sales Ratio A brand's unit sales divided by the average brand unit sales in the product category, multiplied by 100.

Unit Sales Share A brand's unit sales divided by the level of category unit sales, multiplied by 100.

Upside Elasticity The price elasticity of a demand curve above a certain point on that demand curve; in this study, it is the retail price elasticity of a brand's market demand curve above (approximately) the average market price of the brand; to be distinguished from downside elasticity.

Variable Costs (Expenses) Other retail variable costs (retail handling expenses) plus merchandise costs.

Wholesale Price In this study, equivalent to factory price, since it is assumed that the retailers buy directly from the manufacturers.

Zero Profit Equilibrium The outcome of a competitive equilibrium, since "zero profit" includes a return on capital equal to the opportunity cost of capital (roughly the interest rate).

BIBLIOGRAPHY

AAKER, DAVID A., and GARY T. FORD. "Unit Pricing Ten Years Later," unpublished manuscript, University of California at Berkeley, October 1980.

AAKER, DAVID A., and JOHN G. MYERS. *Advertising Management*. Englewood Cliffs, N.J.: Prentice-Hall, 1975.

ALBION, MARK S. "The Structure of Retail Chain Incidence," unpublished manuscript, Harvard University, December 1979.

ALBION, MARK S. "The Effect of Manufacturer's Advertising on Retail Gross Margins in Supermarket Retailing," unpublished Ph.D. dissertation, Harvard University, May 1981.

ALBION, MARK S., and PAUL W. FARRIS. *The Advertising Controversy*. Boston, Mass.: Auburn House Publishing Co., 1981.

ALBION, MARK S., and PAUL W. FARRIS. "The Effect of Manufacturer Advertising on Retail Pricing," Report No. 81–105. Cambridge, Mass.: Marketing Science Institute, December 1981.

BAIN, JOE S. *Barriers to New Competition*. Cambridge, Mass.: Harvard University Press, 1956.

BELLENGER, DANNY N., THOMAS J. STANLEY, and JOHN W. ALLEN. "Food Retailing in the 1980s: Problems and Prospects," *Journal of Retailing*, 53 (Fall 1977), pp. 59–84.

BENHAM, LEE. "The Effect of Advertising on the Price of Eyeglasses," *Journal of Law and Economics*, 15 (October 1972), pp. 337–352.

BLOOM, GORDON F. "The Future of the Retail Food Industry: Another View," *Journal of Retailing*, 54 (Winter 1978), pp. 3–14.

BLOOM, PAUL N., and WARREN GREENBERG. "Packaging to Price: An Exploration of the Issues," in Kenneth L. Bernhardt (ed.), *1976 Educators' Conference Proceedings*. Memphis, Tenn.: American Marketing Association, 1976, pp. 560–563.

BORDEN, NEIL H. *The Economic Effects of Advertising*. Chicago, Ill.: Richard D. Irwin, 1942.

BROZEN, YALE. "Entry Barriers: Advertising and Product Differentiation," in Harvey J. Goldschmid and associates (eds.), *Industrial Concentration: The New Learning*. Boston, Mass.: Little, Brown and Co., 1974, pp. 115–137.

BURNETT, LEO. "What Makes a Top Brand?" London: Leo Burnett, Ltd., September 1979.

Business Week. March 23, 1981, pp. 70–73, 76, 80; August 17, 1981, p. 122.

BUZZELL, ROBERT D., and PAUL W. FARRIS. "Marketing Costs in Consumer Goods Industries," Report No. 76–111. Cambridge, Mass.: Marketing Science Institute, August 1976.

BUZZELL, ROBERT D., WALTER J. SALMON, and RICHARD F. VANCIL. *Product Profitability Measurement and Merchandising Decisions*. Boston, Mass.: Division of Research, Graduate School of Business Administration, Harvard University, 1965.

CABLE, JOHN. "Market Structure, Advertising Policy, and Intermarket Differences in Advertising Intensity," in Keith Cowling (ed.), *Marketing Structure and Corporate Behavior*. London: The Macmillan Press, Ltd., 1972, pp. 107–124.

CADY, JOHN. "Advertising Restrictions and Retail Prices," *Journal of Advertising Research, 16* (October 1976), pp. 27–30.

CADY, JOHN (ed.). "Marketing and the Public Interest," Report No. 78–105. Cambridge, Mass.: Marketing Science Institute, July 1978.

CARMAN, JAMES M. "A Summary of Empirical Research on Unit Pricing in Supermarkets," *Journal of Retailing, 48* (Winter 1972–1973), pp. 63–71.

CAVES, RICHARD E., and MICHAEL E. PORTER. "From Entry Barriers to Mobility Barriers," *Quarterly Journal of Economics, 91* (May 1977), pp. 421–441.

CAVES, RICHARD E., MICHAEL E. PORTER, and A. MICHAEL SPENCE, with JOHN T. SCOTT. *Competition in the Open Economy*. Cambridge, Mass.: Harvard University Press, 1980.

CHAIN STORE AGE SUPERMARKETS SALES MANUAL. New York: Lebhar-Friedman, Inc., July 1978 and July 1979.

CHAMBERLIN, EDWIN H. *The Theory of Monopolistic Competition*. Cambridge, Mass.: Harvard University Press, 1933.

CHAMBERLIN, EDWIN H. *The Theory of Monopolistic Competition*, 8th ed. Cambridge, Mass.: Harvard University Press, 1962.

CLARKE, DARRAL G. "Econometric Measurement of the Duration of Advertising Effect on Sales," *Journal of Marketing Research, 13* (November 1976), pp. 345–357.

COLE, ROBERT H., L. M. DeBOER, R. D. MILLICAN, and N. WEDDING. *Manufacturer and Distributor Brands*. Urbana, Ill.: University of Illinois Press, 1955.

COMANOR, WILLIAM S., and THOMAS A. WILSON, *Advertising and Market Power*. Cambridge, Mass.: Harvard University Press, 1974.

Cornell University, *Operating Results of Food Chains, 1978–79*. Ithaca, N.Y., July 1979.

COWLING, KEITH (ed.). *Marketing Structure and Corporate Behavior*. London: The MacMillan Press, Ltd., 1972.

CURHAN, RONALD C. "A Study of the Relationship Between Shelf Space and Sales for Selected Products in Self-Service Food Supermarkets," unpublished doctoral dissertation, Harvard University, 1971.

CURHAN, RONALD C. "The Relationship Between Shelf Space and Unit Sales in Supermarkets," *Journal of Marketing Research*, 9 (November 1972), pp. 406–412.

CURHAN, RONALD C. "Shelf Space Allocation and Profit Maximization in Mass Retailing," *Journal of Marketing*, 37 (July 1973), pp. 54–60.

DEMSETZ, HAROLD. "Advertising in the Affluent Society," in Yale Brozen (ed.), *Advertising and Society*. New York: New York University Press, 1974, pp. 67–77.

DORFMAN, ROBERT, and PETER O. STEINER. "Optimal Advertising and Optimal Quality," *American Economic Review*, 44 (December 1954), pp. 826–836.

ESKIN, GERALD J. "A Case for Test Marketing Experiments," *Journal of Advertising Research*, 15 (April 1975), pp. 27–33.

ESKIN, GERALD J., and PENNY H. BARON. "Effect of Price and Advertising in Test-Market Experiments," *Journal of Marketing Research*, 14 (November 1977), pp. 499–508.

FARRIS, PAUL W. "Advertising's Link with Retail Price Competition," *Harvard Business Review*, 59 (January/February 1981), pp. 40, 42, 44.

FARRIS, PAUL W., and MARK S. ALBION. "The Impact of Advertising on the Price of Consumer Products," *Journal of Marketing*, 44 (Summer 1980), pp. 17–35.

FARRIS, PAUL W., and MARK S. ALBION. "Determinants of the Advertising-to-Sales Ratio," *Journal of Advertising Research*, 21 (February 1981), pp. 19–27.

FARRIS, PAUL W., and ROBERT D. BUZZELL. "A Comment on 'Modelling the Marketing Mix Decision for Industrial Products,'" *Management Science*, 26 (January 1980), pp. 97–100.

FARRIS, PAUL W., and DAVID J. REIBSTEIN. "How Prices, Ad Expenditures, and Profits Are Linked," *Harvard Business Review*, 57 (November/December 1979), pp. 173–184.

Federal Trade Commission. *Chain Stores: Quality of Canned Fruits and Vegetables*. Washington, D.C.: U.S. Government Printing Office, 1933.

FERGUSON, JAMES M. "Comments on Farris and Albion, 'The Impact of Advertising on the Price of Consumer Products,'" *Journal of Marketing*, 46 (Winter 1982), pp. 102–105.

FOGG-MEADE, EMILY. "The Place of Advertising in Modern Business," *Journal of Political Economy*, 9 (March 1901), pp. 218–242.

GOLDSCHMID, HARVEY J., H. MICHAEL MANN, and J. FRED WESTON (eds.). *Industrial Concentration: The New Learning*. Boston, Mass.: Little, Brown and Co., 1974.

GRETHER, EWALD T. *Resale Price Maintenance in Great Britain*. Berkeley, Calif.: University of California Press, 1935.

GRETHER, EWALD T. *Price Control Under Fair Trade Legislation*. New York: Oxford Press, 1939.

GRILICHES, ZVI, and VIDAR RINGSTAD. *Economies of Scale and the Form of the Production Function*. Amsterdam: North-Holland Publishing Co., 1971.

HALL, MARGARET. *Distributive Trading*. London: William Brendon & Son, Ltd., 1949.

HARRIS, BRIAN F. "Shared Monopoly and the Cereal Industry: An Empirical Investigation of the Effects of the FTC's Antitrust Proposals," MSU Business Study. East Lansing, Mich.: Division of Research, Graduate School of Business Administration, Michigan State University, 1979a.

HARRIS, BRIAN F. "The Cereal 'Shared Monopoly' Case: Some Possible Effects of the FTC's Restructuring Proposals on Cereal Retail Prices," in Neil Beckwith and associates (eds.), *1979 Educators' Conference Proceedings*. Chicago: American Marketing Association, 1979b, pp. 631–635.

HAVENGA, J. J. D. *Retailing: Competition and Trade Practices*. Leiden: A. W. Sijthoff, 1973.

HOLDREN, ROBERT R. *The Structure of a Retail Market and the Market Behavior of Retail Units*. Englewood Cliffs, N.J.: Prentice-Hall, 1960.

HOLTON, RICHARD H. "The Role of Competition and Monopoly in Distribution: The Experience in the United States," in J. Perry Miller (ed.), *Competition, Cartels, and Their Regulation*. Amsterdam: North-Holland Publishing Co., 1962.

HOOD, JULIA, and B. S. YAMEY. "Imperfect Competition in Retail Trades," *Economica*, 18 (May 1951), pp. 120–137.

KALDOR, NICHOLAS. "The Economics of Advertising," *Review of Economic Studies*, 18 (December/January 1949–1950), pp. 1–27.

KOLLINER, SIM A. "How Advertising Affects the Cost of Selling," presentation to the Association of Industrial Advertisers, 41st Conference. New York: McGraw-Hill Research Report, June 24, 1963.

KRIESBERG, MARTIN, and MARTIN LIEMAN. "More Efficient Inventory Control and Space Management for Grocery Departments of Retail Foods Stores," presentation to the Food Retailers' Short Course, Newark, Del., April 4, 1961.

LAMBIN, JEAN J. *Advertising, Competition, and Market Conduct in Oligopoly Over Time*. Amsterdam: North-Holland Publishing Co., 1976.

LANCASTER, KELVIN J. "A New Approach to Consumer Theory," *Journal of Political Economy*, 74 (April 1966), pp. 132–157.

LANCASTER, KELVIN J. *Consumer Demand: A New Approach*. New York: Columbia University Press, 1971.

LEADING NATIONAL ADVERTISERS, INC., *Class/Brand YTD*. New York, 1974–78.

MANAGEMENT HORIZONS, INC., *Retail Performance Update*. Columbus, Ohio, 1979.

MARQUARDT, RAYMOND A., and ANTHONY F. McGANN. "Does Advertising Communicate Product Quality to Consumers? Some Evidence from Consumer Reports," *Journal of Advertising, 4* (Fall 1975), pp. 27–31.

MARSHALL, ALFRED. *Industry and Trade*. London: The Macmillan Press, Ltd., 1919.

MAURIZI, ALEX R. "The Effect of Laws Against Price Advertising: The Case of Retail Gasoline," *Western Economic Journal, 19* (September 1972), pp. 321–329.

McCONNELL, J. DOUGLAS. "The Price-Quality Relationship in an Experimental Setting," *Journal of Marketing Research, 5* (August 1968), pp. 300–303.

McELROY, BRUCE F., and DAVID A. AAKER. "Unit Pricing Six Years After Introduction," *Journal of Retailing, 55* (Fall 1979), pp. 44–57.

McKinsey–National Association of Food Chains Report. *An Identification of Problems in Food Industry Management*. Washington, D.C.: National Association of Food Chains, 1962.

McKinsey–General Foods Study. *The Economics of Food Distributors*. New York: McKinsey and Company, 1963.

MORAN, WILLIAM T. "The Advertising-Promotion Balance." Presentation to the Association of National Advertisers' Advertising Workshop, New York, 1978.

MURPHY, PATRICK E., and GENE R. LACZNIAK. "Generic Supermarket Items: A Product and Consumer Analysis," *Journal of Retailing, 55* (Summer 1979), pp. 3–14.

NELSON, PHILIP. "Information and Consumer Behavior," *Journal of Political Economy, 78* (March/April 1970), pp. 311–329.

NELSON, PHILIP. "The Economic Value of Advertising," in Yale Brozen (ed.), *Advertising and Society*. New York: New York University Press, 1974a, pp. 43–65.

NELSON, PHILIP. "Advertising as Information," *Journal of Political Economy, 81* (July/August 1974b), pp. 729–745.

NELSON, PHILIP. "The Economic Consequences of Advertising," *Journal of Business, 48* (April 1975), pp. 213–241.

NELSON, PHILIP. "Advertising as Information Once More," in David G. Tuerck (ed.), *Issues in Advertising: The Economics of Persuasion*. New York: New York University Press, 1978, pp. 133–161.

NERLOVE, MARC, and KENNETH J. ARROW. "Optimal Advertising Policy Under Dynamic Conditions," *Economica, 29* (May 1962), pp. 129–142.

ORNSTEIN, STANLEY I. *Industrial Concentration and Advertising Intensity*. Washington, D.C.: American Enterprise Institute, 1977.

PALDA, KRISTIAN S. *The Measurement of Cumulative Advertising Effects*. Englewood Cliffs, N.J.: Prentice-Hall, 1964.

POLANY, GEORGE. "Detergents: A Question of Monopoly," Institute of Economic Affairs Research Monograph No. 24, Transatlantic, 1972.

POPAI/DuPont Consumer Buying Habits Study, 1977, in *Chain Store Age Supermarkets*, 1978 Sales Manual. New York: Lebhar-Friedman, Inc., July 1978.

PORTER, MICHAEL E. *Interbrand Choice, Strategy, and Bilateral Market Power*. Cambridge, Mass.: Harvard University Press, 1976.

PORTER, MICHAEL E. *Competitive Strategy*. New York: The Free Press, 1980.

PRASAD, V. KANTI, and L. WINSTON RING. "Measuring Sales Effects of Some Marketing Mix Variables and Their Interactions," *Journal of Marketing Research*, *13* (November 1976), pp. 391–396.

PRESTON, LEE E. *Profits, Competition, and Rules of Thumb in Retail Food Pricing*. Berkeley, Calif.: Institute of Business and Economic Research, University of California, 1963.

REEKIE, W. DUNCAN. *Advertising and Price*. London: The Advertising Association, 1979.

ROTFELD, HERBERT J., and KIM B. ROTZOLL. "Advertising and Product Quality: Are Heavily Advertised Products Better?" *Journal of Consumer Affairs*, *10* (Summer 1976), pp. 33–47.

SAMI. *National Private Label Share Trends, Twelve-Week Period Ending September 26, 1975*. New York: Selling Areas Marketing, Inc., 1975.

SCHMALENSEE, RICHARD. *On the Economics of Advertising*. Amsterdam: North-Holland Publishing Co., 1972.

SCHMALENSEE, RICHARD. "A Model of Advertising and Product Quality," *Journal of Political Economy*, *86* (June 1978), pp. 485–503.

SCHULTZ, RANDALL L., and WILFRIED R. VANHONACKER. "A Study of Promotion and Price Elasticity," Paper No. 657, Krannert Graduate School of Management, Purdue University, May 1978.

STEINER, ROBERT L. "Does Advertising Lower Consumer Prices?" *Journal of Marketing*, *37* (October 1973), pp. 19–26.

STEINER, ROBERT L. "Learning from the Past—Brand Advertising and the Great Bicycle Craze of the 1890s," in Steven E. Permut (ed.), *1978 Proceedings of the Annual Conference of the American Academy of Advertising*. Columbia, S.C.: American Academy of Advertising, 1978a, pp. 35–40.

STEINER, ROBERT L. "Marketing Productivity in Consumer Goods Industries—A Vertical Perspective," *Journal of Marketing*, *42* (January 1978b), pp. 60–70.

STEINER, ROBERT L. "A Dual Stage Approach to the Effects of Brand Advertising on Competition and Price," in John F. Cady (ed.), "Marketing and the Public Interest," Report No. 78–105. Cambridge, Mass.: Marketing Science Institute, July 1978c, pp. 127–150.

STEINER, ROBERT L. "Brand Advertising and the Consumer Goods Economy," unpublished manuscript, 1979.

STERN, LOUIS W. "The New World of Private Brands," *California Management Review,* 8 (Spring 1966), pp. 43–50.

STIGLER, GEORGE J. "The Economics of Information," *Journal of Political Economy,* 69 (June 1961), pp. 213–225.

Target Group Index. New York: Axiom Market Research Bureau, 1977.

TEEL, SANDRA J., JESSE E. TEEL, and WILLIAM O. BEARDEN. "Lessons Learned from the Broadcast Cigarette Advertising Ban," *Journal of Marketing,* 43 (January 1979), pp. 45–50.

TELSER, LESTER G. "How Much Does It Pay Whom to Advertise?" *American Economic Review,* 51 (May 1961), pp. 194–205.

TELSER, LESTER G. "Advertising and Competition," *Journal of Political Economy,* 72 (December 1964), pp. 537–562.

TUERCK, DAVID G. (ed.). *Issues in Advertising: The Economics of Persuasion.* Washington, D.C.: American Enterprise Institute for Public Policy Research, 1978.

U.S. Department of Commerce, Bureau of Foreign and Domestic Commerce. "Louisville Grocery Survey: Part II—Costs, Markets, and Methods in Grocery Retailing, Distribution Cost Studies," Report No. 8. Washington, D.C.: Government Printing Office, 1931.

WIDRICK, STANLEY M. "Quantity Surcharge: A Pricing Practice among Grocery Store Items," *Journal of Retailing,* 55 (Summer 1979), pp. 47–58.

WITTINK, DICK R. "Advertising Increases Sensitivity to Price," *Journal of Advertising Research,* 17 (April 1977), pp. 39–42.

INDEX

Aaker, David A., 29, 105, 241
Absolute market price, and advertis-
    ing, 7–8, 24, 27, 33–37, 38, 253
Advertising
    as creating vs. fulfilling needs, 21
    in economic theory, 16, 16t
    as information vs. persuasion, 14–
        15, 16–17, 37, 234–235
    market competition model of, 16–
        17, 18t, 19, 21, 35
    market power model of, 16, 17–19,
        35
Advertising, manufacturers' (see also
    Advertising–gross margin rela-
    tionship; Category advertising;
    Margin elasticity of advertising)
    and absolute market price, 7–8,
        24, 27, 33–37, 38, 253
    as barrier to entry, 8, 242, 260–
        262
    brand vs. category effects of, 99–
        100
    and competition, 79, 125–126
    cost savings from, 8–9, 27–33, 38,
        254–260
    criticism of, 227, 234
    decay rate of, 147–148
    and distributors' gross margin, 41,
        56–64
    four stages of, 51–54
    heavy vs. light impact of, 50t
    hidden effects of, 3–4, 9, 119, 120,
        235, 256, 265
    and investment, 28, 35
    measurement of, 8, 146–148, 182–
        183, 196–197, 209–210

    multiplier effect of, 242
    Porter's model of, 10, 42–48, 55,
        65–66 (see also Porter's model)
    and price sensitivity, 16–17, 20t,
        21–23, 37–38, 117
    and private label penetration, 106
    and relative prices, 24–27, 38
    retail-level significance of, 241–242
    and retail price, 1–2, 3–4, 7, 122
    Steiner's dual-stage model of, 10,
        48–55, 65–66 (see also Steiner's
        model)
    unrecognized revenues from, 49,
        51
Advertising, marginal elasticity of (see
    Margin elasticity of advertising)
Advertising-gross margin relationship,
    3, 99, 112, 136, 141–142 (see
    also Margin elasticity of
    advertising)
    brand factors in, 131–132, 133–136
    casual generalizations on, 6
    direct, 132, 134, 138, 177, 188,
        239 (see also Sales margin
        elasticity)
    factory price in, 116–119
    feedback effect in, 187–188
    in high-gross-margin categories,
        214, 221
    for high- vs. low-unit sales shares,
        185–186
    indirect, 132, 134, 138, 177, 188,
        239 (see also Partial margin
        elasticity)
    and manufacturers' budgeting, 4,
        242–246

299